LINUX eTudes

David Tancig

A|B|F Content
8536 SW St. Helens Drive, Suite D
Wilsonville, OR 97070
www.abfcontent.com

President and Publisher	Jim Leisy (jimleisy@fbeedle.com)
Production	Stephanie Welch
	Tom Sumner
Cover Design	Ian Shadburne
Marketing	Christine Collier
Order Processing	Krista Brown

Library of Congress Cataloging-in-Publication Data

Tancig, David.
Linux eTudes / by David Tancig.
p. cm.
ISBN 1-887902-62-7
1. Linux. 2. Operating systems (Computers) I. Title.

QA76.76.O63 T353 2001
005.4'32--dc21

2001035181

A|B|F Content is an imprint of Franklin, Beedle & Associates, Incorporated

DEDICATION

For my mother and father, who set the example by their own accomplishments.

For Allison and Justin, my children, who inspire me by their courage and accomplishments. And especially for Justin, captain and leading scorer of his bantam ice hockey team, elected to the student council, and winner of the VFW writing contest. So often during the past year he patiently entertained himself waiting for me as I snatched time from my life as a single parent to struggle with researching and writing this book.

For Janice, who has always worked to make sure our children still had a sense of family even though we were all separated. The Sun, the Moon, and all the jewels in the universe aren't as valuable as this unselfish effort she has made on their behalf.

For all the wolves that helped raise me to survive.

And, as Nelson Eddie said in *Canadian Sunset,* "They don't thank only one god, they thank all the gods."

PREFACE

An étude is a musical composition designed to build skill through practice. That is the concept behind this book. *Linux eTudes* teaches you how to use many peripheral pieces of software that will help you customize your computer desktop to best fit your business and the way you work. Linux programs that are real business solutions are presented, with many step-by-step examples included. With this foundation, you can expand the use of the utility programs to your own unique needs. You can pick and choose the études that interest you, or you can work your way through each étude in the book. Combine what you learn in this book with StarOffice5.2 or WordPerfect 8 for Linux, and you'll have a very potent and adaptable office-computer capability.

This book does not teach you how to install Linux. It is assumed you have a modern-type computer and either have installed or will install Linux.

All of the described programs, with the exception of one, come with the Red Hat 7.1 Deluxe Workstation distribution. That lone exception, Yabasic, must be downloaded from the Internet. But it is free and well worth the small effort. You are walked step by step through the details. The Red Hat 7.1 Deluxe Workstation distribution also contains a CD with the productivity suite StarOffice5.2. It's easy to install.

Linux offers the business community unparalleled adaptability. You can use office productivity suites, graphical user interface utility programs, and the command line. You can write your own scripts to automate processing and even write your own programs for those unique factors that constantly need recalculation. To be useful, this adaptability must be categorized or the situation becomes chaotic.

To bring some order to the wide range of topics in this book, the following scheme has been designed:

- Études 1 through 5 are considered core études. If you're unfamiliar with Linux, you really should work through Études 1, 2 or 3, 4, and 5.

Even if you jump to the click-and-run programs, it's inevitable you'll need to find a file, save a file, or read from and write to a floppy disk. All those topics are covered in these core études. Étude 6 explains how to share files between Linux and Microsoft in a dual-boot environment, and it discusses the pitfalls of this practice.

- Études 7 through 13 cover purely click-and-run, graphical user interface programs. These programs offer a lot of utility and are a good way to gain familiarity with Linux and build your confidence in your Linux-based system.
- Études 14 through 16 cover programs that must be installed. Étude 15, "GnuCash," and Étude 16, "Jpilot," cover programs that, once installed, are click-and-run graphical user interface programs. In Étude 14, Yabasic must be downloaded and then installed. Both the downloading and installing are very simple. None of this is difficult and you're walked through the steps. However, there is room for things to go wrong and experience with earlier études will give you some insights for troubleshooting.
- Étude 17 through 27 make use of the command line. They begin at the beginning and gradually increase your skill until you're able to write some impressive scripts to aid you in your work.
- The afterword discusses software that was considered and why it wasn't considered office ready. Appendix A discusses the office productivity software available in Linux. Appendix B discusses using the chmod command.

Linux gives you tool-making flexibility. Commercial software companies take it away. Linux is created in such a way that it is open for peer-review and improvement—flexible, modular, and convenient to modify to your business needs. You can work in a graphical user interface office suite one moment, switch to the command line the next moment to speedily execute commands, then switch over and write a script to automate a process, and, if you need to, write a computer program with your choice of either a graphical user interface or command line input.

Linux's cultural advantages are also important. There is no commercial pressure on you to change or upgrade software applications. Large software companies discontinue software maintenance on productive software (often referred to as "legacy" software) to churn the market to force you to buy what is not really needed. However, Linux software maintenance is continued, online, by groups devoted to each piece of software. It is passed to a project leader at a central Internet location. Bugs are reported and teams of programmers fix them—sometimes within hours. You can then download improved versions of the software free of charge. Most important to you, Linux software has greater consistency and endurance, resulting in lower learning costs.

I hope you find this book a great aid in your pursuit to expand the usefulness of your Linux-based computing system.

ACKNOWLEDGMENTS

Thanks must begin with the Linux community for the monumental sustained effort to make available without cost a world-class network operating system and world-class application software. This brings the entire world community into the computer revolution—the revolution of using machines to apply nearly unlimited amounts of energy to giving utility to information.

Jim Leisy, the publisher, originated the idea of using an étude as a metaphor for what each chapter should aim to do. It's a first-class idea that has come at the right moment, as the softening economy forces businesses to take another look at what Linux has to offer. It's time for an easily-used guide to help everyone, especially those using the computer in offices, to shuck the anxiety and unnecessary expense of endless software upgrades.

Special thanks is also due to Stephanie Welch, Tom Sumner, Ian Shadburne, Christine Collier, and Krista Brown, all at Franklin, Beedle & Associates.

Thanks also to my students, who asked me to give them draft copies of the études and then gave me enthusiastic and useful feedback. My belief that this type of writing filled a real market need began with them.

Special thanks is also due to my son Justin, who often sacrificed time he'd hoped to spend with me to allow me the writing and researching time I could find nowhere else in my routine as a single parent.

TABLE OF CONTENTS

THE KEDIT TEXT EDITOR

ÉTUDE 1

A text editor with easy-to-use commands is often all you need to accomplish your day-to-day tasks. With it you can record information and create quick memoranda. You can write simple scripts to automate work. A simple text editor is also the best tool for creating notes to upload to a PalmPilot or other Palm device.

An editor creates, saves, and retrieves ASCII text files. You'll learn each of these file operations in this étude. ASCII text files consist of basic alphanumeric characters without codes for stylizing or formatting the text. In Linux, ASCII text editors are used to write shell scripts, which help automate repetitive tasks. Later études will guide you through writing shell scripts.

KEdit is the text editor used in this book. If you are familiar with Windows Notepad, you will feel at home with KEdit. In addition to the features you probably know from Notepad, KEdit lets you check spelling, change font size and style, and use word wrap and automatic indentation. These features are important to most business users. Spelling checkers have become indispensable. With control over font size and style, users can optimize the readability of their communications. This improves their chances of communicating successfully. Word wrap and automatic indentation are also desirable. KEdit can set and insert the date with a single mouse click (a useful feature for memos). It can insert or paste another file within a document (which is useful when you're piecing together several memos).

TOPICS COVERED IN THIS ÉTUDE

- Starting KEdit
- KEdit components
- Configuring fonts, colors, and word wrap
- Copying, cutting, pasting, and undoing
- Checking spelling
- Saving and retrieving files
- Creating a memo template
- Using the memo template
- Printing your memo

STARTING KEDIT

Log on to your Linux system as a user if you have not done so.

If you are using the Gnome desktop environment:

1. CLICK on the Gnome footprint in the lower-left of the screen.
2. MOVE the mouse up to **KDE menus**.
3. MOVE the mouse over to **Editors**.
4. CLICK on **Text Editor**.
   The KEdit text editor opens. It should look like Figure 1.1.

If you are using the KDE desktop environment:

1. CLICK on the large K in the lower-left of the screen.
2. MOVE the mouse to **Editors**.
3. CLICK on **Text Editor**.
   The KEdit text editor opens. It should look like Figure 1.1.

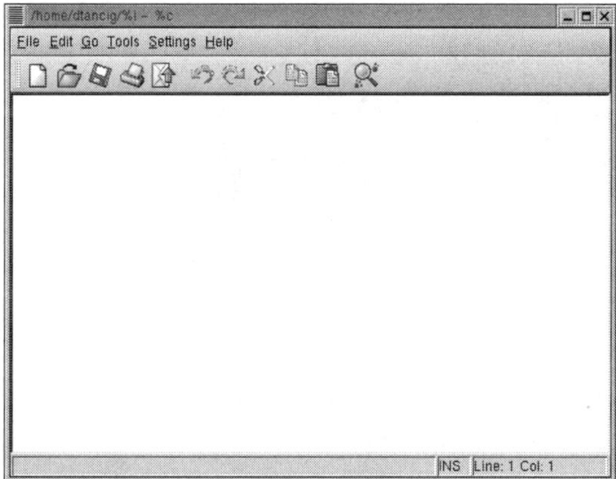

FIGURE 1.1: The KEdit window

THE KEDIT COMPONENTS

The top of the KEdit window has three bars. The top bar—the title bar—displays the path and name of the file KEdit is working with. The middle bar—the menu bar—displays menus of operations that can be performed. The bottom bar—the toolbar—displays icons for common file operations. These icons include New, Open, Save, Print, Mail, Undo, Redo, Cut, Copy, Paste, and Find.

The large white area in the KEdit window is where you type text.

CONFIGURING KEDIT

CHANGING THE FONT

The font style and size should be easily readable. The following instructions will change the font to fangsong ti and 14 points. There are sound reasons for these choices. People who wear reading glasses (perhaps one third of our population) will not have to put the memo aside until they have their glasses. The clean, block-style font will not aggravate problems for those with reading disabilities, as fancier fonts can.

1. CLICK the mouse on **Settings**.
   A menu drops down.
2. CLICK **Configure KEdit**.
   A dialog box opens. It looks similar to Figure 1.2.

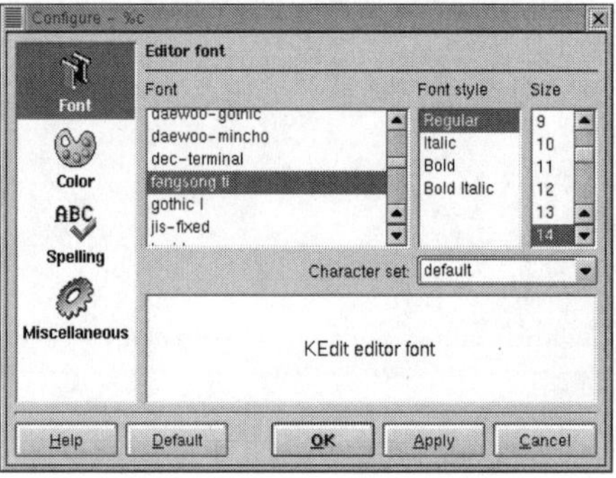

FIGURE 1.2: Configuring fonts

On the left side are four categories of configuration options.

3. CLICK the **Font** icon in the left side of the dialog box.
   A menu of fonts is displayed, as shown in Figure 1.2.
4. SCROLL down in the box labeled "Font" until "fangsong ti" comes into view.
5. CLICK **fansong ti**.
   The selected font is highlighted. Sample text in this font is displayed in the preview box.
6. SCROLL down in the box labeled "Size" until "14" comes into view.
7. CLICK **14**.
   "14" is highlighted. The sample text in the preview box displays the new font size.
8. CLICK **Regular** in the box labeled "Font style."
   You should have the same choices highlighted as are highlighted in Figure 1.2.
9. CLICK **Apply**.
10. CLICK **OK**.
    The window closes and you are returned to the editor.
11. TYPE **test**.
    KEdit is now using your font selections.

CHANGING THE BACKGROUND COLOR

Research done with focus groups by WordPerfect about 10 years ago uncovered that most people find a bright white background too bright, causing squinting and headaches. What most people preferred was a light blue background. In KEdit, you can set any background color.

1. CLICK the mouse on **Settings**.
   A menu drops down.
2. CLICK **Configure KEdit**.
   A dialog box opens.
3. CLICK the **Color** icon in the left side of the dialog box.
   Another window opens. It should look similar to Figure 1.3.

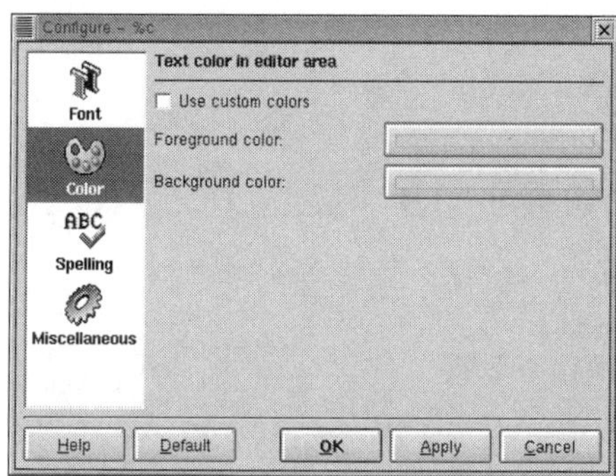

FIGURE 1.3: Configuring colors

4. CLICK in the box to the left of **Use custom colors** to set that option.
5. CLICK on the bar to the right of the label “Background color.”
   A window opens. It should look similar to Figure 1.4.

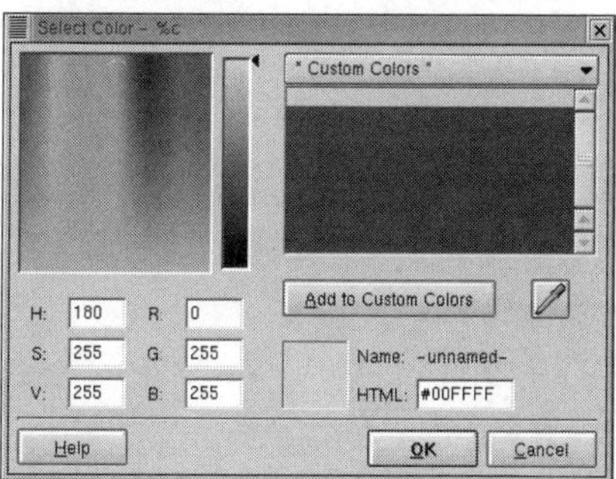

FIGURE 1.4: Selecting a color

6. CLICK anywhere inside the box with the multiple colors.
   The color you clicked appears in the color preview box. You can fine-tune a color using this display.

   There is a button with a drop-down arrow in the top-right part of the window. In Figure 1.4 it is labeled “Custom Colors.”

7. CLICK that drop-down arrow.
   A menu appears.
8. CLICK **40 Colors.**
   A window with squares of individual colors appears
9. CLICK the light aqua box near the right.
   The color preview box is filled with the color you've selected.
10. CLICK **OK.**
    The color selection window closes.
11. CLICK **Apply**.
    The background of your KEdit window changes to the new color.
12. CLICK **OK.**

CONFIGURING WORD WRAP

KEdit is distributed with word wrap disabled. Word wrap allows variable line length depending on the width and resolution of the screen. In an office situation, it is preferable to have word warp turned on and set to wrap at column 79. Regardless of screen size, the document created will be aligned on a standard 8½-inch-wide sheet of paper used by most printers.

1. CLICK **Settings**.
   The menu drops down.
2. CLICK **Configure KEdit**.
3. CLICK the **Miscellaneous** icon.
   Near the top of the box is the label "Word Wrap." To the right of that label is a button labeled "Disable wrapping."
4. CLICK the drop-down arrow to the right of the Word Wrap button.
5. CLICK **At specified column.**
   "At specified column" now appears on the Word Wrap button. A text box appears that displays "79" as the column where wrapping will occur.
6. CLICK **Apply**.
7. CLICK **OK.**
8. CLICK **Settings**.
   A menu drops down.
9. CLICK **Save Settings.**

COMMON KEDIT OPERATIONS

COPY, CUT, AND UNDO

The three basic editor actions are drag-and-drop operations. First we need some text to work with. This text will be used in later exercises.

1. CLICK the New icon on the toolbar (the first icon on the toolbar). A new document window opens.
2. TYPE the following into the new document, pressing Tab between the columns:

Ford	**Tempo**	91 Enter
Chevy	**Nova**	92 Enter
Ford	**Ranger**	98 Enter
Toyota	**Camry**	96 Enter

Copy and Paste

1. CLICK at the beginning of the word "Ranger" and DRAG the cursor across the word.
2. RIGHT-CLICK the mouse.
   A menu pops up.
3. CLICK **Copy**.
4. MOVE the cursor to the right of the number "96."
5. RIGHT-CLICK the mouse.
6. CLICK on **Paste**.
   The text is inserted at the cursor's position.

Cut and Paste

1. CLICK and DRAG the cursor across the word "Ranger" you just pasted to the right of "96."
2. RIGHT-CLICK the mouse.
   A menu pops up.
3. CLICK **Cut**.
4. MOVE the cursor to the position immediately below the last line.
5. RIGHT-CLICK the mouse.
6. CLICK on **Paste**.
   The word "Ranger" is inserted at the cursor's position.
   Note: When you click on Copy or Cut, the highlighted text is stored in a special memory area called a "buffer." When you click

on Paste, the text in the buffer is copied from the buffer. It is not actually removed from the buffer. You can paste the text to several points in the document by repeatedly clicking on Paste. The text in the buffer will not change until you copy or cut a different set of text.

Undo

Undo is capable of undoing multiple operations, as the following demonstrates.

In the following instructions, it is assumed you haven't changed anything from the the cut and paste exercise you just completed.

1. LOOK at the toolbar.
   Notice the green-colored arrow curving to the left. This is the Undo button.
2. CLICK the Undo button.
   The word "Ranger" you pasted on the last line is removed.
3. CLICK the Undo button again.
   The word "Ranger" is now placed next to "96."
4. CLICK the Undo button again.
   The word "Ranger" next to "96" is removed.

CHECKING SPELLING

1. DELETE the letter "e" in the word "Ranger."
2. CLICK **Tools**.
   A pull-down menu is displayed.
3. CLICK **Spelling**.
   The Spellcheck dialog box opens. The top text box shows you what the program thinks is misspelled. The middle text box offers a likely replacement. The bottom text box lists alternative replacements.
4. In the bottom text box, CLICK **Ranger**.
   "Ranger" is highlighted.
5. CLICK **Replace** in the list of options on the right side of the dialog box.
   "Rangr" is replaced with "Ranger."

SAVING

1. CLICK **File**.
   A menu drops down.
2. CLICK **Save As**.

A dialog box opens.

3. CLICK the Home directory icon (it looks like a house).
   We'd like to save this in the Desktop folder.

4. CLICK the **Desktop** folder.
   The text box at the top now displays the path to your Desktop folder. Your file will be saved in the right-most folder displayed in the path.
   You could click on the drop-down arrow to view other paths you have used and may want to choose.

5. CLICK in the box labeled "Location" at the bottom of the dialog box.
   We'd like to save this file with the name **cars**.

6. TYPE **cars**.

7. CLICK **OK**.
   You are returned to the KEdit window. The title bar displays the new path and file name of this file.

RETRIEVING

The following instructions assume you just completed the preceding saving exercise.

1. CLICK **File**.

2. CLICK **Close**.
   The contents of your **cars** file is cleared from the KEdit text area. The title bar now displays "New Document."

3. CLICK the Open icon on the toolbar. (It is the second icon from the left. It looks like an open folder.)
   A window displaying folders and files appears.

4. CLICK the Home directory icon.
   We'd like to retrieve the **cars** file. It is stored in the Desktop folder.

5. CLICK the **Desktop** folder.

6. CLICK the **cars** file.
   The bottom box labeled "Location" is filled with the file name "cars." The text box at the top of this window contains the path to the file we want to open.

7. CLICK **OK**.
   The contents of the **cars** file is copied from your file on disk into the text area of the KEdit window.

DISCARDING WITHOUT SAVING

It is assumed you just finished the previous file-retrieving exercise. In this exercise, any contents you have in the KEdit text area will be erased without being saved. (Of course, you can always click Undo if you lose text you didn't intend to discard.)

1. RIGHT-CLICK anywhere in the KEdit text area.
   A menu pops up.
2. CLICK **Clear**.
   The text area becomes blank. The title bar still has the path and file name for **cars.** This isn't a new document! If you saved, you'd overwrite **cars**.
3. CLICK **File**.
4. CLICK **Close**.
   A dialog box opens asking if you want to save this file.
5. CLICK **No**.
   The title bar says "New Document."

CREATING A MEMO TEMPLATE

Memoranda usually follow the same form and include the following:

- The word "Memorandum"
- The date
- A "To" line
- A "From" line
- A "Subject" line
- The body of the memorandum

1. START the KEdit text editor if it is not open.
   In the upper-right corner of the KEdit window are three boxes. You are probably familiar with these boxes if you use Windows programs.
   - A horizontal solid line or a small square—clicking this minimizes the window.
   - An empty square—clicking this makes the window fill the screen.
   - An X—clicking this closes the program.
2. CLICK the square to fill the screen with KEdit.
   Now we'll create the template.
3. PRESS **Tab** three times.

4. PRESS the Caps Lock key.
5. TYPE **MEMORANDUM**.
6. PRESS Enter
7. PRESS Tab three times.
8. TYPE the letter **X**.
9. PRESS Enter
10. PRESS Tab twice.
11. TYPE **CLICK AT X, CLICK EDIT, CLICK INSERT DATE**.
12. PRESS Enter three times.
13. TYPE **TO:**.
14. PRESS the Tab key twice.
15. PRESS Enter twice.
16. TYPE **FROM:**.
17. PRESS the Tab key twice.
18. PRESS Enter twice.
19. TYPE **SUBJECT:**.
20. PRESS the Tab key once.
21. PRESS the Enter key twice.
22. PRESS Caps Lock to turn it off.
23. TYPE **Click File. Click Save As. Type file name of this memo. Click OK. Delete this line.**
    What you have on screen should look similar to Figure 1.5.

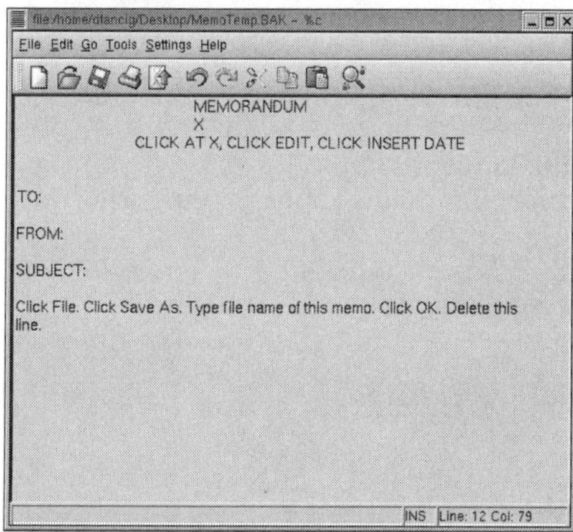

FIGURE 1.5: The memo template

SAVING YOUR MEMO TEMPLATE

These steps apply to any save operation. (It's assumed that you are logged in as a user and not as the root.)

1. CLICK **File**.
2. CLICK **Save As**.
   The "Save File As" dialog box opens.
3. CLICK the Home directory icon.
   A list of your folders and files in the home directory is displayed. We want to save our memo template in the Desktop folder.
4. CLICK **Desktop**.
5. TYPE **MemoTemp** in the "Location" box.
6. CLICK **OK**.
   The dialog box closes and the file is saved.

MAKING A BACKUP COPY

You likely will accidentally overwrite this template with an actual memo someday. If that happens, you can restore your template by opening your backup copy and saving it as MemoTemp.

Follow the steps under "Saving Your Memo Template" with the following exception:

5. TYPE **MemoTemp.BAK** in the "Location" box.

USING THE MEMO TEMPLATE

We're going to use the template to create a memo.

1. CLICK **File** on the menu bar.
2. Click **Open**.
3. CLICK the Home directory icon in the dialog box that opens.
4. CLICK **Desktop**.
   A list of your folders and files appears in the window.
5. CLICK **MemoTemp**.
   MemoTemp is highlighted.
6. CLICK **OK**.
   Your memo template should now appear.

INSERTING THE DATE

We are just following the instructions in all uppercase letters in the template.

1. PLACE the cursor immediately to the left of the X in the second line.
2. CLICK **Edit.**
   A menu drops down.
3. CLICK **Insert Date.**
   Notice that the date is inserted ahead of the cursor. The cursor is still next to the X.
   Now we will remove the "insert date" instructions.
4. CLICK the mouse in front of the X.
5. DRAG down and right to highlight the X and "CLICK AT X, CLICK EDIT, CLICK INSERT DATE."
6. RIGHT-CLICK.
   A menu pops up.
7. CLICK **Cut.**
   The process is quick once you've practiced it.

COMPLETING THE MEMO

Now we're going to follow the instructions in the last line of the template.

1. CLICK **File.**
2. CLICK **Save As.**
3. TYPE **Memo1** in the box labeled "Location."
4. CLICK **OK.**
   Notice the title bar of the KEdit window. It now shows "Memo1."
5. CLICK at the beginning of the line at the bottom of the document that instructs you to click, save, and delete and DRAG until the entire instructions are highlighted.
6. RIGHT-CLICK.
7. CLICK **Cut.**
   Remember that this is a template, not a new memo. Do not press the **Enter** key as you fill in the TO, FROM, and SUBJECT lines. Instead, press the down-arrow key (↓). When you constructed the template, you recorded the tab spaces. With a couple of presses of the down-arrow key, the cursor jumps to those positions. All you have to do is fill in the new information. Then move to the body of the memo and begin typing your information. Figure 1.6 shows a completed memo.

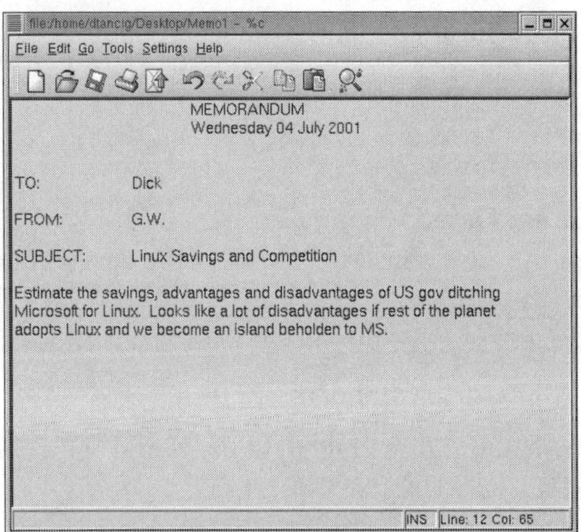

FIGURE 1.6: The completed memo

8. USE the arrow keys to move to the different lines and fill in the blanks. Fill in the blanks with your own information or copy Figure 1.6.

SAVING THE MEMO

1. CLICK on **File**.
2. CLICK on **Save**.
   Now we'll print the memo.
3. OPEN **Memo1** if it isn't already open.
4. CLICK the Print icon (it looks like a printer).
5. CLICK **OK** in the Print Document dialog box.
   Your memo is sent to the printer if you have one installed.

SUMMARY

KEdit is easy to use. We have seen how it can be used to create memoranda. It is useful for many of our daily tasks. Text editors basically create, save, and retrieve ASCII text files. In addition to the features seen in most text editors, KEdit lets you check spelling, change font size and style, and use word wrap and automatic indentation.You have learned each of these file operations in this étude.

In addition to creating memoranda, KEdit can be used to write simple scripts and to create notes to upload to a PalmPilot or other Palm device. Later études will guide you through these activities.

THE GNOME FILE MANAGER

ÉTUDE 2

Note: *If you have KDE (the K Desktop Environment) installed and have access to Konqueror (the KDE file manager), skip to Étude 3 and use Konqueror for your file manager in both the Gnome and KDE desktop environments. Konqueror is a generation ahead of even the best commercial products.*

When you're trying to use Linux productively, proficiency with a graphical file manager is essential. If you are unfamiliar with the Linux file managers, you should work through this étude.

In this étude, we will work with a graphical tool called a file manager. A file manager is used for carrying out file organization tasks. You can easily create folders and copy, move, delete, and rename folders and files.

The Gnome file manager is Gnome Midnight Commander. It is a graphical implementation of a command-line file manager named Midnight Commander.

TOPICS COVERED IN THIS ÉTUDE

- Getting started
- The parts of the file manager window

- Navigating the directory tree
- Common icons found in folders

GETTING STARTED

You should have Linux started on your computer and should be logged in.

OPENING GNOME MIDNIGHT COMMANDER

1. LOOK for the open file folder icon in the upper-left corner of the screen. It has the label "Home directory."
2. DOUBLE-CLICK on the **Home directory** icon.
   Midnight Commander opens. It looks similar to Figure 2.1.

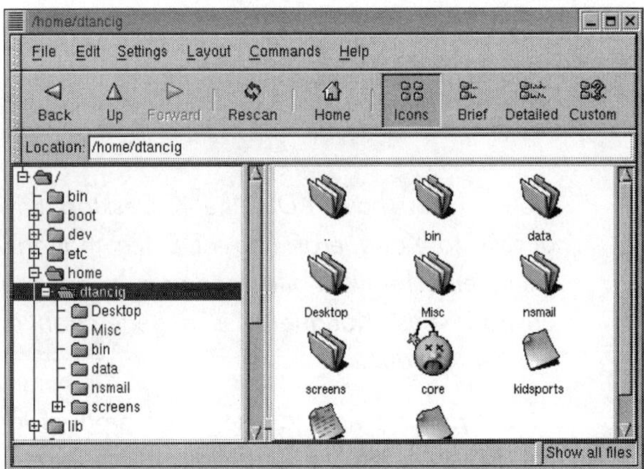

FIGURE 2.1: The Gnome file manager

THE PARTS OF THE FILE MANAGER WINDOW

As you look at the screen, you see a window divided into three general parts:

- A top portion with toolbars
- A left window pane with a directory tree that shows the relationships of the folders
- A right window pane that displays folder contents

The top portion includes the title bar, the menu bar, the toolbar, and the location box. At the very top is the title bar. This contains the name of the folder you are currently using, along with what is called the path to that folder. Below the title bar is the menu bar; each item displays a menu. The toolbar, immediately below the menu bar, allows you to change what is displayed or how it is displayed. Below the toolbar is a text box labeled "Location." You can type in a path to a folder and be immediately transported to that folder.

The directory tree pane shows you the tree-like, hierarchical relationship of folders to each other. Files are not displayed in this window.

The contents pane shows you the contents of a folder selected (opened) in the directory tree pane. If a folder contains files, the files are displayed in this window.

THE MENU BAR

The first bar below the title bar is the menu bar. In general, we won't use this bar for folder- and file-organizing tasks. Instead, we'll drag and drop to organize our files. On the menu bar, you will find several items, including File, Edit, and Layout.

File

1. CLICK on **File**.
   The important choices are Create New Window and New. The other choices aren't as important because we will generally use the mouse to move, copy, and delete folders and files instead of using this menu.
2. CLICK on **Create New Window**.
   Another file manager window opens. A second file manager window is used to drag and drop folders and files.
3. CLICK on **File**.
4. MOVE your mouse over **New**.
   A submenu appears. One choice is Directory. This creates a new folder.
5. CLICK on **Directory**.
   A dialog box appears, waiting for you to enter the name of the new folder.
6. CLICK **Cancel**.
   We don't need to create a new directory right now.

   There are other choices under New. "Terminal" opens a terminal emulator window so you can issue commands on the command line. This option would be valuable to a system administrator doing file management tasks.

   "The GIMP" starts the GNU Image Manipulation Program, a powerful, full-featured image processing program. It might be used if an image file had to be viewed. "Gnumeric" starts the Gnumeric spreadsheet program. You'd use this if you wanted to start it from here to view a spreadsheet file. "File" starts the emacs editor. You would use this if you wanted to create or modify a text file or script. This option is located here to assist system administrators.

Edit

1. CLICK **Edit.**
2. VIEW your choices.
   The important choices are Select All, Select Files, and Invert Selection.
   - Select Files allows you to select all the files with a particular extension.
   - Invert Selection, used after setting up Select Files, reverses the selection of files. This could be used to highlight a few unique files amid a swarm of files of the same type. You would first highlight the files with the extension you want to filter out and then choose Invert Selection to highlight the unique files.

Settings

1. CLICK **Settings.**
   A menu opens with one choice, Preferences.
2. CLICK **Preferences.**
   A window with several tabs opens. It opens to the "File display" tab. There is a check box you can click to display hidden files. These are not secret files but system files that would only create visual clutter during daily work.
3. CLICK the **Confirmation** tab.
   Check boxes related to types of confirmations are displayed, such as "confirm when deleting file" and "confirm when overwriting a file." These are turned on by default (the box looks indented).
   You might want to turn the delete confirmation off occasionally when you have a large number of files to delete.
4. CLICK **Close.**

Layout

Layout determines how the files in the contents pane are displayed: icons with names; a detailed view with all file names, sizes, and creation times; and a custom view with file and folder permissions.

1. CLICK **Layout.**
   A menu drops down.
2. CLICK **Detailed View.**

3. CLICK **Layout**.
4. CLICK **Custom View**.
5. CLICK **Layout**.
6. CLICK **Icon View** to return to the default view.
   The Sort By option lets you determine if upper and lower case are to be ignored and if the sort is to be in descending order rather than ascending order. The Sort files by button in the Sort By dialog box opens a box of items you can click to determine what is to be sorted, name, file type, size, and so on.
7. CLICK **Layout**.
8. CLICK **Sort By**.
   The dialog box opens.
9. CLICK the **Sort files by** box.
   A selection of options to sort by drops down.
10. CLICK **Size**.
11. CLICK **Cancel**.

THE TOOLBAR

Many buttons on this bar are self-explanatory to modern computer users. Rescan updates the tree and contents panes in the event that changes didn't appear when they were made. Four buttons on the far right side of the bar determine the appearance of the display in the contents pane. These are the same options you can access from the Layout menu.

- Icons—icons and file names (this is the default display)
- Brief—file names only
- Detailed—file names, file sizes, and creation times
- Custom—file names, file sizes, and file permissions (you can customize which file characteristics are shown)

1. CLICK on each button: **Icons**, **Brief**, **Detailed**, and **Custom**.
2. NOTICE the format change of the information displayed in the contents pane.

THE LOCATION BOX

This is similar to the URL location bar on a Web browser. You type in the path to a directory and press the **Enter** key. You are taken to that directory.

1. CLICK in the location box at the right end of the directory path.

2. PRESS the **Backspace** key until you've deleted the current directory path.
3. TYPE **/usr/games** **Enter**
4. NOTICE that in the directory tree pane the usr folder is now opened and highlighted. In the contents pane, the contents of the games folder is displayed.
5. CLICK the **Home** icon on the toolbar.
   You are returned to your home directory.

NAVIGATING THE DIRECTORY TREE

Although you can use the location box to specify the path to a folder, what if you don't know the path? Use the directory tree instead to find and select the folder you want to open.

The directory tree only displays folders (subdirectories). It does not display files. The contents pane displays files if files are contained in the selected folder.

EXPANDING AND CONTRACTING THE DIRECTORY TREE

Look at Figure 2.1 again, and you will see that the directory tree under home has been expanded to show its subordinate parts. Notice the small boxes with + and - signs in them. The plus sign means that the folder contains other folders and it can be expanded. The minus sign means that the folder has been expanded.

The boxes with the signs in them act like toggle switches. Click on a plus sign and it expands and changes to a minus sign. Click on a minus sign and it contracts and changes to a plus sign.

1. SCROLL to the folder labeled "home."
2. CLICK on the small box to the left of the home folder. Most likely that box contains a minus sign (-).
3. NOTICE, if it was a minus sign, that the directory tree is collapsed. NOTICE the minus sign changed to a plus sign.
4. CLICK the plus sign on the home folder.
   The directory tree expands beneath the home folder.
5. LOOK at the contents pane to the right of the directory tree. What you see is that the contents did not change. The contents are still the same that were displayed for the home folder.
6. CLICK on the folder with your login name. This folder is your personal home folder.
7. NOTICE the contents pane.

Now it displays the contents of the your personal home folder.
What happens if you don't click the box with the plus sign?

8. NOTICE the small box to the left of the your personal folder.
It may have a plus sign; the directory did not expand. (The + means that this folder contains at least one additional folder.) Clicking the folder displays the contents but does not change the directory tree.
9. CLICK on the + for the folder with your login name if the tree is not already expanded.
The directory tree expands and reveals Desktop.

A SUMMARY OF NAVIGATING THE DIRECTORY TREE

If you click on a small box with a plus sign, you expand the directory tree but you do not change the contents window. When you click on a folder, a folder name, or to the right of a folder name, you highlight the folder and display its contents in the contents window pane.

COMMON ICONS FOUND IN FOLDERS

File icons indicate file type. The following are a few of the icon types important to business users:

- a folder (subdirectory)
- a data file (a letter or stored text of some sort)
- an executable program

1. SCROLL to the top of the directory tree to the folder labeled "boot."
2. CLICK on the **boot** folder.
3. NOTICE the icons in the contents pane.
A folder is a container for other files or folders.
4. CLICK on the **Icons** button on the toolbar.
An automotive piston represents a program than can be run. A plain sheet of paper represents a file storing information of some sort.

SUMMARY

Proficiency with a graphical file manager is essential in Linux. In this étude, we worked with the Gnome file manager. A file manager is used for carrying out file organization tasks. You can easily create folders and copy, move, delete, and rename folders and files. A file manager allows you to work with your files and folders quickly and easily.

THE KONQUEROR FILE MANAGER

ÉTUDE 3

Proficiency with a file manager is essential to productive use of any information-processing system. A file manager is a tool for organizing your folders and files. With it you can create folders and delete, copy, move, rename, and delete folders and files.

The KDE (K Desktop Environment) Project recently introduced Konqueror. Konqueror is a one-stop viewing portal for a wide range of media. Using it alone, you can view Web sites, FTP sites, pictures, video, disk contents, and text. Konqueror can be used as a Web browser, a file manager, and a file viewer—separately or simultaneously.

Although this sounds complex, it works well because it is built on the Linux architecture model of separate components with well-defined tasks being individually accessible. As a result of Konqueror's careful design, Konqueror and the user interact as if Konqueror were a single-task utility program. The user is not bewildered with controls, but all the viewing capabilities a user might want are readily available, including multiple-window options.

This étude discusses Konqueror only as a file manager. The Web browser controls are similar to those found in most other popular Web browsers.

TOPICS COVERED IN THIS ÉTUDE

- Getting started
- Components of the file manager window
- Navigating the directory tree
- Common file icons
- Using multiple views

GETTING STARTED

You should have Linux started on your computer. You should be logged in.

OPENING KONQUEROR

In KDE:

1. CLICK the large K. This icon is located on the left side of the panel (the bar across the bottom of the desktop with icons on it).
   A menu opens.
2. CLICK **System**.
3. CLICK **Konqueror** (if Konqueror doesn't appear as an option, CLICK **File Manager**).
4. If a dialog box opens asking for the root password, CLICK **Ignore** to continue as a user.
   After several moments, the Konqueror screen is displayed.

In Gnome:

1. CLICK the Gnome footprint. This icon is located on the left side of the panel (the bar across the bottom with icons on it).
   A menu opens.
2. MOVE the mouse up to **KDE menus**.
3. MOVE the mouse over to **System**.
   The System menu opens.
4. CLICK **Konqueror**.
   After several moments, the Konqueror screen is displayed. The Konqueror display looks similar to Figure 3.1.

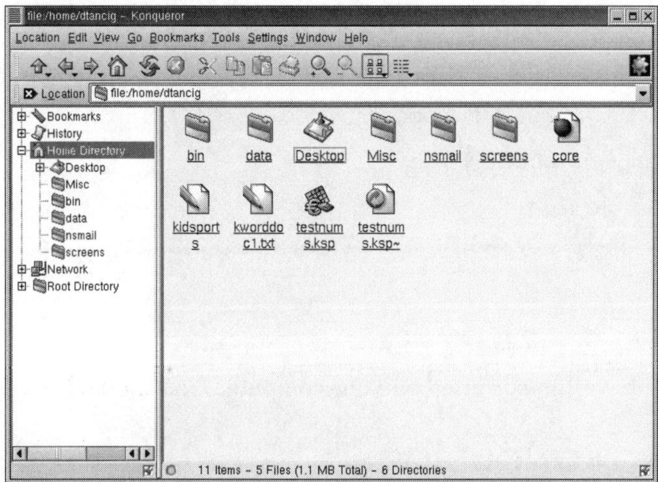

FIGURE 3.1: The Konquerer program

COMPONENTS OF THE FILE MANAGER WINDOW

The window is divided into three general areas:

- an area across the top with toolbars
- a left window pane with a file tree showing the relationships between folders
- a right window pane that displays the contents of the folder that has been selected and highlighted in the directory tree

1. If your window doesn't show a directory tree, CLICK **Window** on the menu bar.
2. CLICK **Show Sidebar**.

The top area includes the title bar, the menu bar, the toolbar, and the location toolbar. At the very top of the window is the title bar. The title bar contains the name of the folder you are currently using along with what is called the "path" to that folder. Below the title bar, the menu bar has buttons that activates menus for actions that can be performed on files. The toolbar, which is below the menu bar, allows you to change what is displayed or how it is displayed. Below the toolbar is the location toolbar, which allows you to type in a path to a folder or URL to a Web site and be immediately taken to that folder or Web site.

The directory tree is in the left pane. It uses a hierarchical, tree-like display to illustrate the relationships between folders. The contents pane is on the right side of the window. It displays the contents of a folder selected (opened) in the directory tree pane.

USING THE TOOLS

Again, the first bar below the title bar is the menu bar. In general, we won't use this bar for file activities. We'll drag and drop to organize our files instead.

Location

1. CLICK **Location** on the menu bar.
   The important options here are New Window and Duplicate Window. You also may have a Print option available.
2. MOVE your mouse to the directory tree.
3. CLICK the + next to Home Directory (the directory or folder labeled with the name you use when you log in).
   The directory tree expands for Home Directory.
4. CLICK **Desktop**.
   The folders and files stored in your desktop folder are displayed in the contents pane.
5. CLICK **Location** on the menu bar.
   A menu drops down.
6. CLICK **New Window**.
   Another file manager window opens. It is based on your personal home directory and does not look like the other Konqueror window you have open.
7. CLICK on the ☒ in the upper-right corner of the Konqueror window that you just opened.
   The window closes.
8. CLICK **Location** on the menu bar.
9. CLICK **Duplicate Window**.
   A duplicate of your current window appears.
10. CLICK on the ☒ in the upper-right corner of the Konqueror window that you just opened.
    The window closes.

Edit

1. CLICK on **Edit**.
   Here you see several options for file operations. Most of them are likely grayed out.
2. CLICK on **Create New**.
   A submenu opens. We'll use this menu later to create new folders. Other new items can be created, as indicated by the menu.

The four options at the bottom of the Edit menu are selection options. These allow you to select only certain types of files, such as all those files ending in .txt. A particularly useful option is Invert Selection. If you have selected all files with .txt and then select Invert Selection, all files not ending in .txt will be shown. This saves time if you have many files with one extension and you want to find the few that do not have the common extension.

View

1. Click on **View**.
   The menu is divided into areas. The top area is headed by View Mode, the most important item in the top portion. In the next portion of the menu you can reload the item being viewed and change the icon size. In the next portion you can change what information you want to use to content window pane display and set the option to show hidden files.
   Hidden files are files that are seldom worked with during daily production and are not displayed when you request a normal listing of files. This cuts down on some of the visual clutter. Hidden files all have file names that start with a period, for example, .tcshrc.
   The last part of the menu has options that allow you to change the background color and the background image.
2. CLICK on **Home Directory** in the directory tree pane.
3. CLICK **View**.
4. MOVE the mouse to **View Mode**.
   A menu opens. Icon View is already checked. This is the standard view.
5. CLICK **MultiColumn View**.
   The files listed in your contents pane are now displayed in vertical columns.
6. CLICK **View** and move the mouse to **View Mode**.
7. CLICK **Tree View**.
   You should see a display similar to what is shown in Figure 3.2.

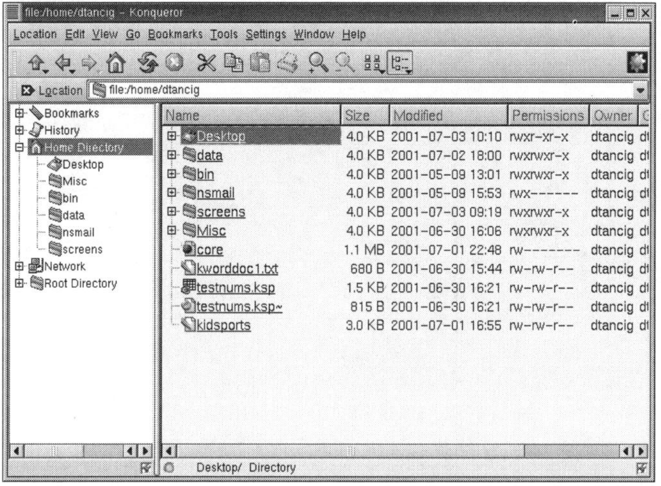

FIGURE 3.2: Konqueror in tree view mode

This is a tree view of the contents of the directory selected in the directory tree pane.

8. CLICK **Desktop** in the contents pane.
   Your display changes to show the contents of the Desktop folder.
9. CLICK **View** and move the mouse to **View Mode**.
10. CLICK **Detailed List View**.
    The view looks similar to tree view only without the connecting vertical lines. But there is a difference.
11. CLICK **Desktop** in the contents pane.
    The contents pane is cleared and only the contents of the Desktop folder are displayed.
12. Click **Home Directory** in the directory tree pane.
13. CLICK **View** and move the mouse to **View Mode**.
14. CLICK **Text View**.
    You should see a display similar to what is shown in Figure 3.3.

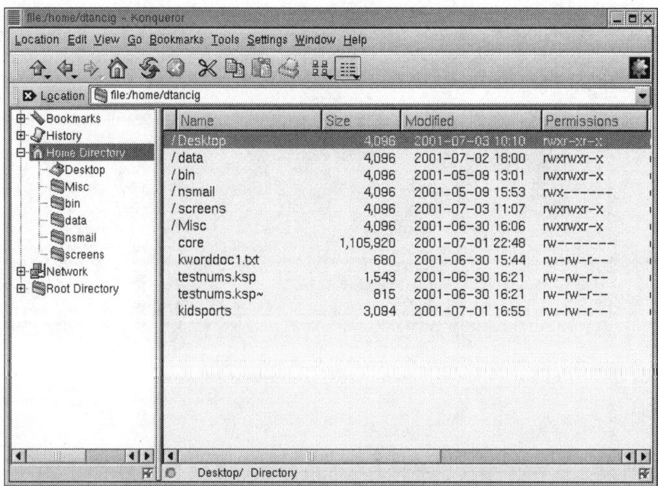

FIGURE 3.3: Konqueror in text view mode

This is a text-only (no icons) listing of the contents of the directory selected in the directory tree pane. Some people find this less confusing to look at than views containing icons. A nice feature of Text View is that you can still do drag-and-drop file operations even though the display is text only. Notice that folders all begin with a /.

15. CLICK **/Desktop** in the contents pane.
    The contents pane is cleared and the Desktop folder contents are displayed.
16. On the toolbar, CLICK the blue-colored arrow pointing to the left.
    You are taken back to the previous display in the contents pane.
17. CLICK **View**.
18. CLICK **View Mode**.
19. CLICK **Icon View**.

Go

1. CLICK **Go** on the menu bar.
   A menu drops down that allows you to move backward and forward through displays, go to various configuration files (also available in Settings), and go to URLs you've visited recently.

Bookmarks

This records the path or location of anything you might be viewing when you press the bookmark button. You can bookmark files you want to jump back to as well as Web sites.

1. CLICK on **Home Directory** in the directory tree pane or on the house icon on the toolbar.
2. CLICK on **Desktop** in the directory tree pane.
   The contents of the Desktop folder are displayed.
3. CLICK on **Bookmarks**.
   A menu drops down.
4. CLICK on **Add Bookmark**.
   The path to Desktop is added to the bookmark list.
5. CLICK on the house icon again.
   The contents of Home Directory are displayed.
6. CLICK on **Bookmarks**.
   A menu drops down.
7. CLICK the last item in the bookmark list, which should be the path to Desktop.
   The contents pane immediately changes to display the contents of Desktop.

Tools

This gives you quick access to useful options for file operations. You can open a terminal emulator window, which gives you access to the command line. The terminal emulator window is entirely separate from Konqueror.

Settings

The important option here is Configure Konqueror.

1. CLICK **Settings**.
2. CLICK **Configure Konqueror**.
   The display changes to what you see in Figure 3.4.

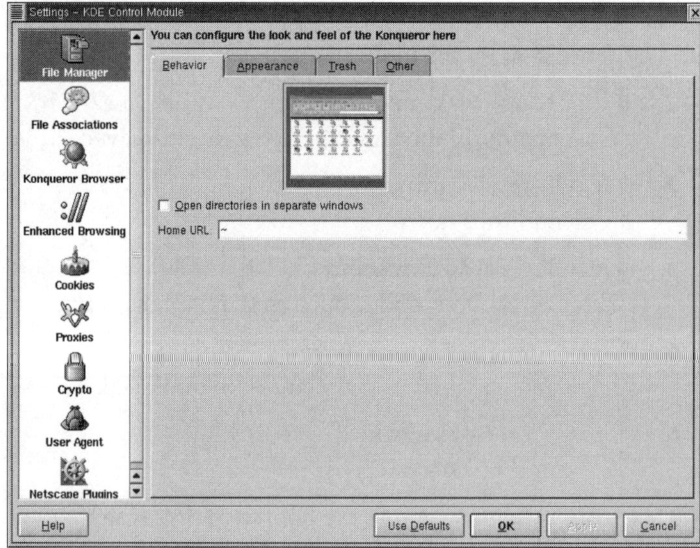

FIGURE 3.4: Configuring Konqueror

You are in the File Manager mode and have four configuration tabs: Behavior, Appearance, Trash, and Other.

3. CLICK the **Appearance** tab.
   You can change the font size, type, and color.

4. CLICK the **Trash** tab.
   You can specify if you want to be asked before Konqueror moves an item to trash, deletes it, or shreds it. Normally it is a good idea to leave those checked and turned on. On the occasions when you have a lot of file deletions and don't want to be asked before deleting every file, you now know where to turn those warnings off.

5. CLICK **Cancel** to exit the configuration window.

Window

This button allows you to display views with multiple windows. Two options are very useful when doing file management operations: Show Sidebar and Show Terminal Emulator.

1. CLICK **Window**.

2. CLICK **Show Sidebar**.
   Since this option was set, when you click it now, it is unset. The directory tree pane closes. This gives you a larger working area.

3. CLICK **Window** and then **Show Sidebar**.

The way Konqueror literature describes it, when the sidebar is open, it makes all the system resources visible. Now the sidebar is visible again.

4. CLICK **Window**.

5. CLICK **Show Terminal Emulator.**
The display changes to one similar to Figure 3.5.

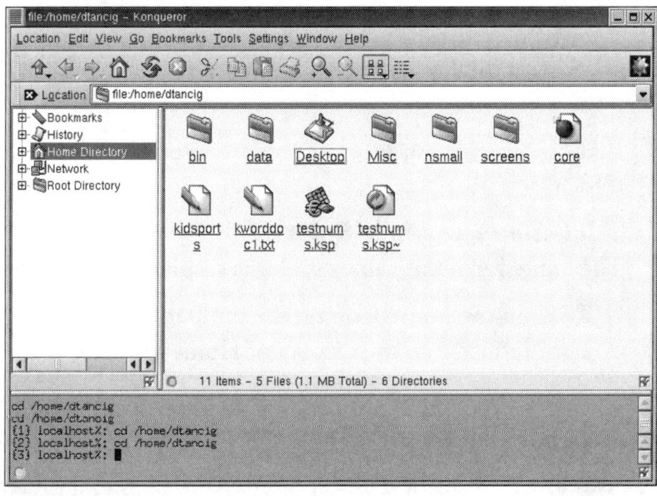

FIGURE 3.5: Konqueror with a terminal emulator window

There is a dot in the lower-left corner of the contents pane. There is another one in the lower-left corner of the terminal emulator window.

6. CLICK the dot in the lower-left corner of the contents pane.
The dot turns green (if it wasn't already).

7. CLICK the dot in the terminal emulator window.
The dot turns green and a white bar appears across the bottom of the emulator window. These dots are used to indicate which window you want to work in.

8. TYPE **ls** (the letters "l" and "s"; not the number "1" and the letter "s") Enter
You just used the command line to obtain a listing of your files.

9. CLICK the dot in the contents pane.
You have now made the contents pane active.
As you become more familiar with command line commands, you'll find this is an arrangement that will speed file operations considerably because you can essentially combine the best features of the command line and of windows for file operations.

10. CLICK **Window**.
11. CLICK **Show Terminal Emulator**.
    The terminal emulator window closes.

The Location Toolbar

This works the same as the location bar in a Web browser, only in this situation we're going to use it to take us to files. If you type in the path to a directory and press the Enter key, you are immediately taken to that directory.

1. CLICK in the Location box to the right of the current directory path.
2. PRESS the Backspace button until you've deleted the current directory path.
3. TYPE **file:/usr/games** Enter
   The contents of the games folder is displayed in the contents pane.
4. CLICK on the house icon on the toolbar.
   You are returned to the display of Home Directory.

NAVIGATING THE DIRECTORY TREE

Although you can use the Location box to specify the path to a folder, what if you don't know the path? Use the directory tree instead to find and select the folder you want to open.

The directory tree contains only the names of folders. The directory tree does not contain the names of files. The contents pane displays the names of files if the selected folder contains files.

EXPANDING AND CONTRACTING THE DIRECTORY TREE

Look at Figure 3.1 again. The directory tree under Home Directory has been expanded to show its subordinate parts. Notice the small boxes with + and - signs in them. The plus sign means that the folder contains other folders and it can be expanded. The minus sign means that the folder has been expanded.

The boxes with the signs in them act like toggle switches. Click on a plus sign and it expands and changes to a minus sign. Click on a minus sign and it contracts and changes to a plus sign.

1. CLICK on the plus sign to the left of the Home Directory folder in the directory tree pane. If there is a minus sign by the folder, skip this step.

2. NOTICE that the directory in the directory tree pane expanded to the next level. Also notice that the + changed to a -. The display looks similar to Figure 3.1.
   An important point is that clicking on the + will expand the directory tree, but it does not change the display in the contents pane.
3. CLICK the + next to your Desktop folder.
   The Desktop folder now expands to reveal the folders it contains.
4. LOOK at the contents pane. The contents did not change. The contents are still those of the Home Directory folder.
5. CLICK on the word **Desktop** in the directory tree pane.
6. NOTICE the contents pane. Now it displays the contents of the Desktop folder.
   What happens if you click the folder name but not the box with the plus sign?
7. CLICK the minus sign in the box next to Home Directory.
   The contents pane does not change, but the directory tree for Home Directory is now collapsed.
8. CLICK on the words **Home Directory** in the directory tree pane.
   The contents pane now displays the contents of Home Directory. Also, the directory tree did not expand. The only change occurred in the contents pane.
9. CLICK on the + next to Home Directory.
   The directory tree opens and your Desktop directory, which had been expanded before you closed the Home Directory tree, is still expanded.

A Summary of Navigating the Directory Tree

If you click on a small box with a plus sign, you expand the directory tree but you do not change the contents pane. When you click on a folder, a folder name, or to the right of a folder name, you highlight the folder and display its contents in the contents pane.

COMMON FILE ICONS

File icons indicate file type. A few icons important to business users are

- a folder (subdirectory)
- a data file (a letter, or stored text of some sort)
- an executable program

  Look at Figure 3.6.

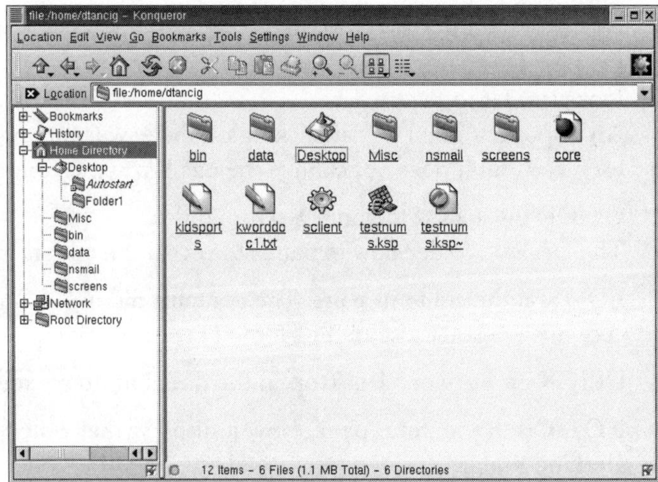

FIGURE 3.6: File icons in Konqueror

This shows a copy of my Home Directory. The folders obviously indicate folders or subdirectories. A sheet of paper with a pencil indicates a text file. A gear represents a program than can be run. The gear is the symbol for a program that can be "launched," to use Linux terminology.

SUMMARY

A file manager is a tool for organizing your folders and files. With it you can create folders and delete, copy, move, rename, and delete folders and files. Konqueror is the very useful file manager included with KDE.

GNOME AND KDE FILE OPERATIONS

ÉTUDE 4

Études 2 and 3 teach you how to use the Gnome and KDE file managers. This étude teaches you how to move, copy, delete, and rename folders and files.

Before you read this étude, you should have worked through Étude 2 (if you are using the Gnome file manager) or Étude 3 (if you have installed the KDE desktop environment). This étude does not cover the basics of using your file manager.

The fundamentals of dragging and dropping are the same to organize folders as to organize files. This étude does not cover file operations with floppy disk drives. File operations with floppy disk drives are covered in Étude 5.

TOPICS COVERED IN THIS ÉTUDE

- Working with folders in Gnome
- Working with folders in KDE
- Working with files in Gnome
- Working with files in KDE

WORKING WITH FOLDERS IN MIDNIGHT COMMANDER

ADDING A FOLDER

In this section, you are going to create a temporary folder with the name Folder1 that will be immediately subordinate to your personal Desktop folder.

1. OPEN Midnight Commander, using the steps described in Étude 2.
2. CLICK the **Home** icon on the toolbar to make sure you are in your home directory.
3. CLICK **Desktop** under your home directory in the directory tree window.
   This makes the Desktop folder the working or current folder. New directories are always created off of the working folder (directory).
4. RIGHT-CLICK in the contents pane.
5. CLICK **New Directory**.
6. TYPE **Folder1** into the dialog box that opens.
7. CLICK **OK**.
8. NOTICE that Folder1 is added to the contents pane and that the Desktop folder icon has a + to its immediate left.
9. CLICK the + next to Desktop in the directory tree pane.
   The directory tree below Desktop expands.
10. NOTICE that Folder1 is subordinate to (contained within) the Desktop folder.

MOVING A FOLDER

Periodically, files need to be reorganized to reflect new relationships and responsibilities. On a computer, part of this reorganizing involves moving folders from one location to another.

The most reliable way to make file system changes using Gnome Midnight Commander is to open two file manager windows. The first file manager window is the source window. In the first window you open the folder holding the folder you want to move. The second file manager window is the destination window. In the second window you open the folder that is to receive the folder from the source file manager. Drag the folder from the contents window of the source file manager and drop it into the destination file manager contents window.

There are other methods. This étude reinforces the method that is clearest and most reliable. "Move" means to remove from one location and place in another location. It does not make a duplicate.

We are going to move Folder1, which we just created, from the Desktop folder to your personal home folder. It is assumed you already have one file manager window open with Desktop folder's contents displayed in the contents pane.

1. CLICK **File**.
2. CLICK **Create New Window**.
   Now you have a second file manager window open.
3. GRAB the title bar of the second file manager window and MOVE it to the lower-right part of the screen to make sure you can see both windows.
4. CLICK the **Home** icon on the toolbar of the second file manager.
   We are opening the destination folder in the destination file manager.
5. CLICK the **Folder1** icon in the contents pane of the source (first) file manager.
6. DRAG **Folder1** to any blank spot in the contents pane of the destination (second) file manager.
7. RELEASE the mouse button.
   Folder1 disappears from the source file manager's contents pane. It appears in the destination file manager's contents pane. Folder1 appears as part of your home directory tree in the destination file manager.

A Summary of Moving a Folder

- Open a source file manager window.
- In the directory tree pane, select and open the parent folder of the folder to be moved.
- Open a second (destination) file manager window.
- In the directory tree pane, select and open the parent folder that is to receive the folder that is being moved.
- In the contents pane of the source file manager, drag the icon of the folder to be moved to the contents pane of the destination file manager.
- Drop the folder being moved into the contents pane of the destination. It is automatically sorted into place in the window.

COPYING A FOLDER

1. In the second file manager window, CLICK **Folder1** in the contents pane.
2. CLICK **File** on the menu bar.

3. CLICK **Copy**.
4. TYPE the path to your Desktop folder in the text box, for example, **/home/dtancig/Desktop**.
5. CLICK **OK**.
   Folder1 is still shown in the contents pane. Folder1 is also listed in the directory tree under the Desktop folder.
6. CLICK **Desktop** in the directory tree pane to display its contents.
   A copy of Folder1 is in the Desktop folder.

A Summary of Copying a Folder

- Display in the contents window the folder you desire to copy.
- Click File and then Copy.
- Type in where you want the folder copied to.
- Click OK.

RENAMING A FOLDER

In the Linux world, the move command is also used to rename. When you rename a folder, open only one file manager window.

Caution: Do not have a second file manager window open. If you do, the computer will assume that the selected, or open, folder in the second file manager window is the destination. After renaming the folder as you instruct, the computer will move the folder to the open folder in the second file-manager window.

We will rename Folder1 in your home directory Folder2.

1. CLOSE all open file managers.
2. DOUBLE-CLICK the **Home directory** icon on the desktop (in the upper-left corner of your monitor screen).
3. CLICK the **Home** icon on the toolbar of the file manager that just opened.
   This opens your home directory folder where Folder1 is located.
4. RIGHT-CLICK **Folder1** in the contents pane.
   A menu pops up.
5. CLICK **Move**.
   A dialog box opens. The dialog box states "Move directory 'Folder1' to:". Do not erase the contents. This is the path to the file. It doesn't change in a renaming.
6. CLICK in the text box at the end of its contents.
7. TYPE **/Folder2**.

8. CLICK **OK**.
   The folder name is changed both in the contents pane and in the directory tree pane.

A Summary of Renaming a Folder

- Open only one file manager window.
- In the directory tree pane, open the parent folder of the folder to be renamed.
- In the contents pane, right-click on the folder to rename it.
- Click on the Move menu item.
- Delete the contents of the dialog box and type in the new folder name.
- Click on Yes to accept the new name.

DELETING A FOLDER

In this section, you will delete the temporary folders you just created.

1. CLICK the **Home** icon on file manager toolbar.
2. RIGHT-CLICK **Folder2** in the contents pane.
3. CLICK **Delete**.
   A dialog box opens asking if you really want to delete the folder.
4. CLICK **Yes**.
   The folder is deleted. Its icon disappears from the contents pane and from the directory tree pane.
5. CLICK **Desktop** in the directory tree pane.
   The contents of the Desktop folder appear in the contents pane.
6. RIGHT-CLICK **Folder1** in the contents pane.
7. CLICK **Delete**.
   A dialog box opens asking if you really want to delete the folder.
8. CLICK **Yes**.
   The folder is deleted. Its icon disappears from the contents pane and from the directory tree pane.

Note: The rule in Linux is that a folder (a directory) must be empty before it can be deleted. If it is not empty, a dialog box will open asking you if you want to delete it recursively. If you want to delete all the contents and the folder, click Yes. Everything will be removed.

WORKING WITH FOLDERS IN KONQUEROR

ADDING A FOLDER

In this section, we will create a temporary folder with the name Folder1, which will be immediately subordinate to your Desktop folder.

1. OPEN Konqueror, using the steps described in Étude 3.
2. CLICK **Window** and **Show Sidebar** if you don't already have the directory tree pane displayed.
3. CLICK the + next to Home Directory to expand its directory (if it's not already expanded).
4. CLICK the + next to Desktop to expand its directory (if it's not already expanded).
5. CLICK the word **Desktop** in the directory tree pane to display its contents.
6. Click **Edit**.
7. CLICK **Create New**.
   A submenu opens.
8. CLICK **Directory**.
   This will create a new folder. A dialog box opens asking for the name of the new folder (directory).
9. TYPE **Folder1**.
   Notice that you didn't have to erase the previous contents. They were erased as soon as you began typing.
10. CLICK **OK**.
    The dialog box closes. A folder icon appears in the contents pane with the name Folder1.
11. CLICK on **Folder1** in the contents pane.
    The contents window pane is empty (your new folder has no contents). The directory tree pane displays Folder1 as subordinate to Desktop.

A Faster Way to Add a Folder

1. RIGHT-CLICK in the contents pane.
   A menu pops up.
2. CLICK **Create New**.
   A submenu opens that offers a list of items you can create. Now you could create a folder as you did before.

3. CLICK somewhere in the window to make the pop-up menu disappear.
   You don't need to create a new folder right now. But you can see how this is a faster way to create a folder.

MOVING A FOLDER

Periodically, files need to be reorganized to reflect new relationships and responsibilities. On a computer, part of this reorganizing involves moving folders from one location to another.

1. CLICK **Desktop** in the directory tree pane.
   You want to have your Desktop folder contents displayed in the contents pane.
2. DRAG **Folder1** from the contents pane to Home Directory in the directory tree pane.
   When you are correctly positioned over Home Directory, it becomes highlighted.
3. RELEASE the mouse button.
   When you release the left mouse button, a pop-up menu appears. You can copy, move, or link. You want to move.
4. CLICK **Move Here**.
   Folder1 disappears from the contents pane.
5. CLICK **Home Directory** to display its contents.
   Folder1 is now located in Home Directory.

A Summary of Moving a Folder

- Display in the contents window the folder you desire to move.
- In the directory tree window, expand the tree to show the destination folder for the folder you are moving.
- Starting in the contents window, drag the icon of the folder to be moved to the destination folder in the directory tree window. The destination folder will highlight when you are correctly positioned.
- Release the left mouse button to drop the folder being moved into the destination folder.
- Click on Move Here in the pop-up menu that appears.

COPYING A FOLDER

Copying a folder is nearly identical to moving a folder. The difference is clicking on Copy Here instead of Move Here in the pop-up menu that appears.

1. DRAG **Folder1** from the contents pane to the Desktop folder in the directory tree pane.
2. CLICK **Copy Here.**
   The contents of Desktop appear in the contents pane. Folder1 is there.
3. CLICK **Home Directory** to display its contents.
   Folder1 remains in Home Directory. As we saw before, a copy is in the Desktop folder too.

A Summary of Copying a Folder

- Display in the contents window the folder you desire to copy.
- In the directory tree window, expand the tree to show the destination folder for the folder you are copying.
- Starting in the contents window, drag the icon of the folder to be copied to the destination folder in the directory tree window. The destination folder will highlight when you are correctly positioned.
- Release the left mouse button to drop the folder being copied into the destination folder.
- Click on Copy Here in the pop-up menu that appears.

RENAMING A FOLDER

1. CLICK **Home Directory** to display its contents.
2. RIGHT-CLICK **Folder1.**
   A menu pops up.
3. CLICK **Rename.**
   A text box opens around "Folder1."
4. REPLACE "Folder1" with **Spare.**
5. CLICK anywhere in the contents pane.
   Spare is accepted as the new name in the contents pane.

A Summary of Renaming a Folder

- In the directory tree pane, open the parent folder of the folder to be renamed.
- In the contents pane, right-click on the folder to rename it.
- Delete the contents of the dialog box and type in the new folder name.
- Click on OK to apply the new name.

DELETING A FOLDER

In this section, we will delete the folders Spare and Folder1.

1. RIGHT-CLICK **Spare** in the contents pane.
   A menu pops up.
2. CLICK **Delete**.
   A dialog box opens asking if you really want to delete this folder.
3. CLICK **Yes**.
   Caution: This deletion removes the folder and its contents without warning you! The rule in Linux is that a folder (a directory) must be empty before it can be deleted.
4. CLICK **Desktop** in the directory tree pane.
5. RIGHT-CLICK **Folder1** in the contents pane.
6. CLICK **Delete**.
7. CLICK **Yes**.

A Summary of Deleting a Folder

- In the directory tree pane, open the parent folder of the folder to be deleted.
- In the contents pane, right-click on the folder to delete.
- Click Delete.
- Click Yes in the dialog box that asks if you really want to delete. Remember that all the contents of the folder will be deleted!

WORKING WITH FILES IN MIDNIGHT COMMANDER

CREATING A FILE

First we need a file to use. Perform the following steps:

1. START KEdit, using the steps given in Étude 1.
2. TYPE **This is a test file.** in the text area.
3. CLICK **File**.
4. CLICK **Save As**.
   A dialog box appears.
5. CLICK the Home directory icon (the house) on the toolbar of the dialog box.
   This makes your home directory the working directory, the directory where the file will be saved.

6. TYPE **File1** in the Location box, deleting any prior contents.
7. CLICK **OK**.
8. CLICK the ☒ in the upper-right corner of the KEdit window.
   This closes KEdit.

If you haven't worked through Étude 1 but you can use one of the editors available in Linux, instead of following the above steps, just create a text file named File1 in your home directory. It doesn't matter if you use KEdit or another editor.

COPYING A FILE FROM ONE FOLDER TO ANOTHER

When you make a copy, you make a duplicate. This is a simple clicking operation. We are going to copy File1 from your home directory to the Desktop folder.

1. OPEN Midnight Commander.
2. CLICK your personal folder in the directory tree pane.
   The contents of your personal folder appear in the contents pane. You should see File1.
3. RIGHT-CLICK **File1**.
   A menu pops up.
4. CLICK **Copy**.
   A dialog box opens with the name of your working directory.
5. TYPE the path to your Desktop folder in the text box, for example, **/home/dtancig/Desktop**.
   This is where the file will be copied.
6. CLICK **OK**.
   You just completed the process of selecting the directory where you want the file saved.
7. NOTICE the contents pane.
   File1 is still present.
8. CLICK **Desktop** in the directory tree pane.
   You should see File1. You have made a duplicate of File1 in your Desktop folder.

MAKING A COPY OF A FILE IN THE SAME FOLDER

You may have two or more copies of a file in the same folder, but they may not have the same file name. The difference between copying to the same folder and copying to a different folder is that when copying to the same folder you must also rename the file.

1. RIGHT-CLICK **File1**.
   The file name is highlighted.
2. CLICK on **Copy**.
   A dialog box opens.
3. CLICK at the end of the path in the text box.
4. TYPE /**File2**.
5. CLICK **OK**.
   A second file is created in the same folder with the name File2.

MOVING A FILE TO ANOTHER FOLDER

When you move a file, it is removed from one location and placed at another location. You are not making a duplicate. This is a simple drag-and-drop operation.

We will move File2 from your Desktop folder to your personal folder.

1. CLICK on **Desktop** in the directory tree pane.
   Its contents are displayed in the contents pane.
2. CLICK **File2**.
3. DRAG **File2** to your personal folder in the directory tree window.
   Your personal folder is highlighted when your cursor targets it.
4. RELEASE the mouse button.
   The file is moved to your personal folder and removed from your Desktop folder.
5. CLICK your personal folder.
   Now File2 is shown in the contents pane of your personal folder.

RENAMING A FILE IN THE SAME FOLDER

We are going to rename the File1 file in your Desktop folder with the name of File2.

1. CLICK **Desktop** in the directory tree pane.
   File1 is shown in the contents pane.
2. RIGHT-CLICK **File1**.
   A menu pops up.
3. CLICK **Move**.
   A dialog box opens. The dialog box states "Move file 'File1' to:". Do not erase the contents. This is the path to the file. It doesn't change in a renaming.
4. CLICK in the text box to the right of its contents.

5. TYPE /**File2**.
6. CLICK **OK**.
   File1 changes to File2 in the contents pane.

DELETING A FILE FROM A FOLDER

We will delete the files we created.

1. CLICK the **Home** icon on the toolbar.
2. RIGHT-CLICK **File1** in the contents pane.
3. CLICK **Delete**.
   A dialog box opens, asking "Delete file 'File1'?"
4. CLICK **Yes**.
   The file is deleted. Its icon disappears from the contents pane.
5. RIGHT-CLICK **File2** in the contents pane.
6. CLICK **Delete**.
7. CLICK **Yes**.
8. CLICK **Desktop** in the directory tree pane.
9. RIGHT-CLICK **File2** in the contents pane.
10. CLICK **Delete**.
11. CLICK **Yes**.
    All of the files we created are deleted.

WORKING WITH FILES IN KONQUEROR

CREATING A FILE

First we need a file to use. Perform the following steps:

1. START KEdit, using the steps given in Étude 1.
2. TYPE **This is a test file.** in the text area.
3. CLICK **File**.
4. CLICK **Save As**.
   A dialog box appears.
5. CLICK the Home directory icon (the house) on the toolbar of the dialog box.
   This makes your home directory the working directory, the directory where the file will be saved.
6. TYPE **File1** in the Location box, deleting any prior contents.

7. CLICK **OK**.
8. CLICK the ☒ in the upper-right corner of the KEdit window.
   This closes KEdit.

If you haven't worked through Étude 1 but you can use one of the editors available in Linux, instead of following the above steps, just create a text file named File1 in your home directory. It doesn't matter if you use KEdit or another editor.

COPYING A FILE FROM ONE FOLDER TO ANOTHER

1. OPEN Konqueror.
2. CLICK **Home Directory** in the directory tree pane.
   The contents pane displays the contents of Home Directory. You should see File1.
3. CLICK the + in front of Home Directory to expand the directory tree.
4. CLICK and DRAG **File1** from the contents pane to Desktop in the directory tree pane.
   Desktop is highlighted when your cursor targets it as the destination.
5. RELEASE the mouse button.
   A menu opens.
6. CLICK **Copy Here**.
   After the file is copied, you can see File1 in the contents pane.
7. CLICK **Home Directory**.
   File1 is still in the contents pane of Home Directory. It has been successfully copied.

MAKING A COPY OF A FILE IN THE SAME FOLDER

You may have two or more copies of a file in the same folder, but they may not have the same file name. The difference between copying to the same folder and copying to a different folder is that when copying to the same folder you must also rename the file.

It is assumed that you have Konqueror open and the contents of Home Directory displayed in the contents pane.

1. RIGHT-CLICK **File1**.
   A menu pops up.
2. CLICK **Copy**.
   It appears that nothing happened.

3. MOVE the cursor to a blank spot in the contents pane.
4. RIGHT-CLICK.
   A menu pops up.
5. CLICK **Paste**.
   A dialog box opens.
6. CLICK in the text box at the bottom of the dialog box.
7. REPLACE "File1" with **File2**.
   The Rename button appears as soon as you begin deleting.
8. CLICK the **Rename** button.
   File2 appears in the contents pane.

MOVING A FILE TO ANOTHER FOLDER

When you move a file, it is removed from one location and placed at another location. You are not making a duplicate. This is a simple drag-and-drop operation.

We will move File2 from your personal folder to the Desktop folder.

1. CLICK the + next to Home Directory in the directory tree pane if the directory tree is not already expanded.
   Your home directory expands.
2. CLICK and DRAG **File2** in the contents pane to the Desktop folder in the directory tree pane.
   The Desktop folder is highlighted when your cursor targets it.
3. RELEASE the mouse button.
   A menu opens.
4. CLICK **Move Here**.
   File2 disappears from the Home Directory contents pane.
5. CLICK your **Desktop** folder in the directory tree pane.
   File2 is now in the contents pane of the Desktop folder.

RENAMING A FILE IN THE SAME FOLDER

We are going to rename the File1 in the home directory with the name of File2.

1. CLICK **Home Directory** in the directory tree pane.
2. RIGHT-CLICK **File1**.
   A menu pops up.
3. CLICK on **Rename**.

A text box opens around the name of "File1."

4. REPLACE "File1" with **File2**.
5. CLICK anywhere in the contents window.
   The new name is accepted.

DELETING A FILE FROM A FOLDER

We will delete the files we created.

1. CLICK **Home Directory**.
2. RIGHT-CLICK **File2**.
   A menu pops up.
3. CLICK **Delete**.
   A dialog box opens, asking if you really want to delete this file.
4. CLICK **Yes**.
5. CLICK **Desktop** in the directory tree pane.
6. RIGHT-CLICK **File1**.
7. CLICK **Delete**.
8. CLICK **Yes**.
9. RIGHT-CLICK **File2**.
10. CLICK **Delete**.
11. CLICK **Yes**.

SUMMARY

This étude taught you how to move, copy, delete, and rename folders and files. The fundamentals of dragging and dropping are the same to organize folders as to organize files. You saw that a file manager is a tool for organizing your folders and files.

USING FLOPPY DISKS WITH LINUX

ÉTUDE 5

One of the first facts you learn about computers is that the floppy disk drive is the A: drive. Linux does not use letters to designate disk drives. Linux treats devices connected to it as though they were files. Information is saved to the floppy disk as though it were saving to a file in a subdirectory. That subdirectory is often named "floppy." In Linux, what we consider the A: disk drive is accessed by the path and name of /dev/fd0.

In Linux, a floppy disk must be mounted before it is used and unmounted after it is used. A floppy disk is a device with a file system. That file system must be integrated into the file system that Linux sets up when it is started. To integrate the floppy disk, which Linux will see as simply another file address, Linux must be told the address of "the file" (the disk). Mounting also activates the device driver so the operating system has instructions for the physical communication with the disk drive. Mounting and unmounting a floppy disk may seem awkward at first, but it is easily done. This must also be done with CD-ROMs.

Traditionally, access to the floppy disk is limited to the person logged in as root, typically the system administrator. Some distributions of Linux continue that limitation, but Red Hat allows a person without root access to use the floppy disk.

Using the collection of command line utility programs called Mtools, you can do floppy disk file operations even if you do not have root access, if you are working with a Windows-formatted floppy disk. Mtools requires the floppy disk be unmounted when a command is issued. Mtools mounts and unmounts the floppy disk for you.

There is also the issue of formatting your floppy disk. When you format a disk, you code onto it an information storage scheme. This information storage scheme is called a "file system." The floppy disk is a round piece of durable plastic with an iron oxide coating applied with a high degree of uniformity across the bottom and top surface. You can code any sort of file system you desire onto it.

In Linux, you can use MS-DOS formatting or the Linux floppy disk format ext2fs. If you'll be working between Windows and Linux systems, you should continue with an MS-DOS format. KFloppy, the KDE floppy-disk formatting utility, makes formatting floppy disks very simple. Formatting a disk can also be done from the command line by using an option string instead of KFloppy, but that is not discussed in this étude.

We assume you learned to use a graphical file manager by completing Étude 2 or 3. If you want more information about issuing commands on the command line, you might read through Étude 17.

TOPICS COVERED IN THIS ÉTUDE

- Getting started
- Formatting floppy disks
- Mounting and unmounting floppy disks
- Copying or moving files
- Mtools

GETTING STARTED

Take a look at the desktop environment on your computer monitor. Most likely, you will see a small picture that looks like a floppy disk in the lower-left corner. It might be labeled "Floppy 0" or "Floppy Disk." That is your floppy-disk icon.

If you do not have the icon installed on your desktop, read through your installation manual. You may just need to right-click the desktop and launch /mnt/floppy. Most likely, though, you will have to go through a configuration process to link the file named floppy with fd0, the name that Linux associates with the first floppy-disk drive. That's beyond the technical scope of these études.

Even if you do not have a floppy disk icon, you will still be able to use Mtools to complete file operations.

FORMATTING FLOPPY DISKS

There are two methods for formatting a floppy disk. One involves the command line. The other involves using the KFloppy utility program, which is part of KDE. Since KFloppy covers the all the situations the business desktop user is likely to encounter, this étude guides you through the use of KFloppy.

DISK FORMATTING ISSUES

When you format a floppy disk using KFloppy, you must make three choices:

- DOS or Linux format
- High density or double density
- 3½-inch or 5¼-inch disk size

The disk size and type choices are forced on you by the floppy disk drive installed on your computer and the type of floppy disks you are using. The choice to use a disk size of 5¼ inches may seem superfluous in North America, but these disks are still commonly encountered throughout the world outside of North America.

Of the three choices you need to make using KFloppy, only one decision needs discussion: whether to use a DOS or Linux format. The Linux file system used for floppy disks is named ext2fs.

- Choose ext2fs if you are using your disks in a Linux-only environment.
- Choose the DOS file system if you are using your disks in both Linux- and Windows-based computers.

FILE CONVERSION CONCERNS

It is possible to save an ASCII text file that has been created using a Linux text editor and then open it using a Windows text editor. The characters will be correctly interpreted. There is a catch. A DOS system stores each press of the Enter key, such as at the end of a line, with two nonprinting characters: the carriage the line feed character and the carriage return character (0A and 0D in hexadecimal representation). Linux saves a press of the Enter key with only the line feed character (the 0A hexadecimal character).

This means that when a Linux-based editor reads an ASCII file created using a Windows-based editor, the Linux editor will see an extra character at the end of each line. It also means that when a Windows-based editor reads an ASCII file created using a Linux-based editor, the Windows editor will not find characters it can interpret as the press of an Enter key. You can end up with a screen filled with a continuous stair-stepped line of words snaking down the screen.

There are conversion programs available. Some Linux editors are beginning to correctly interpret Windows-created ASCII files. Also, if StarOffice 5.1/5.2, or ApplixWare or Correl WordPerfect for Linux word processor is used, the file conversion is done when you specify what file format to use when importing or exporting the file.

STEP-BY-STEP FLOPPY DISK FORMATTING

We could use the main menu to access KFloppy. It is listed as Floppy Formatter under Utilities. Unfortunately, even with a custom installation specifying the installation of the KDE and the Gnome desktop environments, when using the Gnome desktop, which I prefer, many of the utility programs listed in the KDE utility menu are not linked to their executable files. Those executable files are, indeed, loaded correctly into /usr/bin, where they belong. These utility programs do launch correctly when clicked from the KDE desktop.

The easiest and a most convenient long-term solution if you are in the Gnome desktop environment is to install a desktop icon on the Gnome desktop that is linked to the KFloppy executable file. If you generally prefer to use the Gnome environment, follow the following steps. We assume you are in the Gnome environment.

Installing a KFloppy Icon on the Gnome Desktop

Again, we assume you are in the Gnome environment.

1. RIGHT-CLICK on the desktop.
2. CLICK **Launcher** in the submenu of **New**.
3. TYPE in the following information in the dialog box that appears:
   Name: **Floppy Formatter**
   Comment: **KDE Floppy Disk Formatter**
   Command: **/usr/bin/kfloppy**
4. CLICK the drop down arrow next to the Type box.
5. CLICK **Application**.
6. CLICK the **No Icon** button.
7. SELECT an apple icon.
   When choosing an icon, you should choose one that seems appropriate or that you will remember. An apple is distinctive and we won't confuse this with other programs.
8. CLICK **OK**.
9. CLICK **Apply**.
10. CLICK **OK**.

Starting KFloppy

1. If you are in Gnome, DOUBLE-CLICK your KFloppy icon. If you are in KDE, CLICK the large K, then **Utilities**, then **Floppy Formatter**.
   The formatter opens. It looks similar to Figure 5.1.

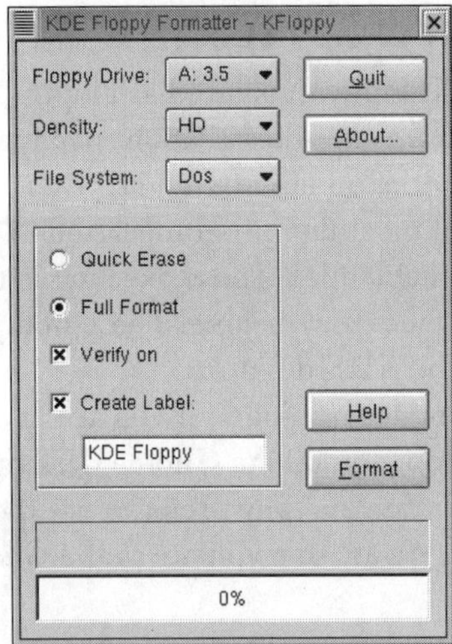

FIGURE 5.1: KFloppy

Formatting Choices

1. PLACE a floppy disk that either is blank or has contents that can be erased in your floppy disk drive.
2. CLICK the down arrow next to the box labeled "Floppy Drive."
3. CLICK the proper disk size and drive letter.
4. CLICK the down arrow next to the box labeled "Density."
5. CLICK **HD** (high density) or **DD** (double density), according to your disk.
6. CLICK the down arrow next to the box labeled "File System."
7. CLICK **Dos** or **ext2fs**.
   Choose ext2fs if you are using your disks in a Linux-only environment. Choose the DOS file system if you are using your disks in both Linux- and Windows-based computers.
   Note: None of the down arrows have to be clicked if the choice already in the box is what you want to use.
8. CLICK **Full Format**.
   Quick Erase just erases a disk.

If you wanted a label on your disk, you would make sure there was a check in the box by Create Label. We won't create a label for this disk.

9. CLICK **Format**.
   Formatting begins. The completion bar moves across the screen. After the formatting is completed, the disk is verified. The progress bar moves across the screen again. Any bad blocks are reported to you and marked.
   When verification is completed, an information box opens. It reports the formatting completion, the number of bad blocks marked, and the number of raw bytes.
10. CLICK **OK**.
    This closes the box telling you about the formatting.
11. CLICK **Quit** to close KFloppy.
    The formatting is complete.

MOUNTING AND UNMOUNTING FLOPPY DISKS

DETERMINING IF ROOT PERMISSION IS REQUIRED TO USE THE FLOPPY DISK ICON

Someone logged in as root will always be able to use the floppy disk icon to copy and transfer files. Users without root access are sometimes not allowed to use the floppy disk icon, but must use Mtools instead.

We don't have to test if you have permission to use the floppy disk icon if you're logged in as root. You do. If you are logged in as a user, follow these instructions to determine if you have floppy access as a user.

1. RIGHT-CLICK the floppy disk icon.
   One of two things happens. One is that a menu pops up. In this case, take the following step:
2. CLICK **Mount**. (If Unmount is showing, CLICK **Unmount**, then CLICK **Mount**.)
   Watch the floppy disk drive light. It should light up when you click Mount.
   The other thing that could happen after you take Step 1 is that a message appears, asking for the root password. This means that you don't have access to the floppy as a user.
   If you don't have access to the root password, skip the following sections and move to the sections with the Mtools instructions. If

not being able to use the floppy disk icon is a major inconvenience, you can ask the system administrator either to grant everyone floppy disk access permission or to at least add your login to the file that lists who has floppy disk access.

MOUNTING AND UNMOUNTING USING THE FLOPPY DISK ICON

1. INSERT a formatted floppy disk into your floppy disk drive.
2. RIGHT-CLICK the floppy disk icon on the desktop.
   A menu pops up.
   Either a Mount option or an Unmount option is displayed in the menu.
3. CLICK on whichever item is displayed, **Mount** or **Unmount**.
   If you click on Unmount, the drive light is not lit. If you click on Mount, the drive light is lit as Linux links to and reads the disk directory.
4. If you clicked on Unmount, RIGHT-CLICK the floppy disk icon again and click on **Mount**.
   Now the disk is mounted.
5. If you are in Gnome, DOUBLE-CLICK the floppy disk icon. If you are in KDE, CLICK the floppy disk icon.
   A file manager window opens. Which file manager opens depends on whether you are using KDE or Gnome.
6. NOTE the contents pane. If your directory tree pane does not display the floppy folder, EXPAND the tree under the root directory until it is displayed.
   If your floppy disk has any files on it, they are displayed as icons in this window. If the disk is empty, then only the symbol for a file folder is displayed.
7. CLOSE the file manager window.

COPYING OR MOVING FILES INVOLVING A FLOPPY DISK

These instructions assume you have access to the root password. If you don't, skip to the Mtools instructions. First we're going to create a file to work with.

1. OPEN the KEdit text editor.
2. TYPE **This is a test file.** in the text area.

3. CLICK **File**.
4. CLICK **Save As**.
5. TYPE **/mnt/floppy/** in the text box near the top of the dialog box, replacing the current path.
6. TYPE **tfile.txt** in the Location text box.
   We are saving the file on the floppy with the name of **tfile.txt**.
7. CLICK **OK**.
8. EXIT the editor.

COPYING OR MOVING A FILE FROM THE HARD DISK TO THE FLOPPY DISK

We will use the same process that you learned in Étude 2 or 3 to copy a file.

Using Gnome Midnight Commander:

1. OPEN Midnight Commander.
2. DISPLAY the file you just created (/mnt/floppy/tfile.txt) in the contents pane. The /mnt folder should be off the root directory. Since we want to move the file to the Desktop folder, we need to make sure the Desktop folder is displayed in the directory tree.
3. If the Desktop folder is not displayed in the directory tree pane, click the + sign by Home Directory to expand the tree.
4. CLICK **tfile.txt** and DRAG it from the contents pane to the Desktop folder in the directory tree pane.
5. RELEASE the mouse button to drop the file in the folder.
   You have moved the file to the Desktop folder. We will copy the file back to its original location to illustrate the difference between moving and copying.
6. CLICK the **Desktop** folder in the directory tree pane to display its contents.
7. CLICK the **tfile.txt** file.
8. PRESS and HOLD the **Ctrl** key while you DRAG **tfile.txt** from the Desktop folder back to the floppy folder.
9. RELEASE the mouse button.
   The file is still in the Desktop folder.
10. CLICK the **floppy** folder in the directory tree pane.
    The file was copied.
11. CLOSE the file manager window.

Using Konqueror:

1. OPEN Konqueror.
2. DISPLAY the file you just created (/mnt/floppy/tfile.txt) in the contents pane. The /mnt folder should be off the root directory. Since we want to move the file to the Desktop folder, we need to make sure the Desktop folder is displayed in the directory tree.
3. If the Desktop folder is not displayed in the directory tree pane, click the + sign by Home Directory to expand the tree.
4. CLICK and DRAG **tfile.txt** from the contents pane to the Desktop folder in the directory tree pane.
5. RELEASE the mouse button to drop the file.
   A menu pops up.
6. CLICK **Move Here** to move the file.
   You have moved the file. Now we will copy the file back to its original location to illustrate the difference between moving and copying.
7. CLICK **Desktop** in the directory tree pane to display its contents in the contents pane.
8. CLICK and DRAG **tfile.txt** from the contents pane to the floppy folder in the directory tree pane.
9. RELEASE the mouse button.
10. CLICK **Copy Here**.
    The file is still in the Desktop folder.
11. CLICK the **floppy** folder in the directory tree pane.
    The file was copied.
12. CLOSE the file manager window.
    Copying and moving files with a floppy disk is just like copying and moving files between folders.

MTOOLS

In the event that the floppy disk icon is reserved to the root user, you can still use the command line to copy files to and from a formatted floppy disk using the Mtools utility programs.

Rule 1: Do not mount your disk before using Mtools. Mtools assumes the disk is unmounted. Mtools mounts and unmounts the disk. You do not.

Rule 2: Mtools assumes that the floppy drive is the A: drive. There are exceptions to this, such as when using the copy command. The safest way is to type A: any time you mean to reference the A: drive. This will always work and will eliminate any margin for error.

Rule 3: Mtools will only work if the disk is DOS-formatted.

The following Mtools commands are most useful to business users:

Command	**Action**
mcd	Changes the directory
mcopy	Copies a file
mdel	Deletes a file
mdir	Displays a listing of files in the current directory
mlabel	Changes the label on a disk
mmd	Makes a new directory
mrd	Removes a directory
mren	Renames a file
mtype	Writes the contents of a file to the screen

STEP-BY-STEP MTOOLS USE

Making a Directory Listing of the Floppy Disk

Using terminal emulators is covered in Étude 17. If you need help in working with a terminal emulator, look at the instructions in that étude before proceeding with this exercise.

We're assuming that the floppy drive is not mounted. Mtools will mount the drive itself.

1. CLICK the icon on the panel that looks like a computer monitor. The terminal emulator opens.
2. TYPE **mdir a:** Enter on the command line.
   If you get output that looks similar to Figure 5.2, the command worked and you can move on to the next section. The files in your display will be different. But the display should include "Directory for A:/."

```
{1} localhost%: mdir a:
 Volume in drive A is ECU MAIN
 Volume Serial Number is 2C34-0ED9
Directory for A:/

ECUREG   EXE    944209 05-24-1995   7:16
ECUSHARE EXE    440086 05-09-1995   6:58
INSTALL  EXE     12544 04-13-1995  10:21
CON1520  EXE      8192 04-13-1995   9:18
        4 files           1 405 031 bytes
                             51 712 bytes free
```

FIGURE 5.2: Mdir output

If the floppy disk were mounted before you issued the mdir command, you would get a message telling you that the device is busy and cannot be accessed.

3. If you got this message, RIGHT-CLICK the floppy disk icon on the desktop and CLICK **Unmount** to unmount the floppy disk.
4. If you need to unmount your floppy disk and cannot use the floppy disk icon, TYPE **umount /dev/fd0** [Enter] at the command line. That is not a misspelling. The command is "umount." And the last character in that command is a zero, not a letter "O."
5. If you needed to unmount your disk, check to see if you have successfully unmounted it by typing **mdir a:** [Enter] again.

Creating a Subdirectory

1. On the command line, TYPE **mmd a:\testdir** [Enter]
2. TYPE **mdir a:** [Enter]
   Your directory listing includes testdir.

Changing to Another Subdirectory

1. TYPE **mcd a:\testdir** [Enter]
   The terminal emulator does not indicate a change in path.
2. TYPE **mdir a:** [Enter]
   You get a directory listing for testdir—you really did change to the testdir directory.

Changing to a Parent Directory

1. TYPE **mcd ..** (two periods) [Enter]
2. TYPE **mdir a:** [Enter]
   You are back in the root directory of the floppy disk.

Making a Copy of a File in the Same Directory on a Floppy Disk

1. TYPE **mcopy -t a:\tfile.txt a:\moretext.txt** Enter
2. TYPE **mdir a:** Enter
   You see that **moretext.txt** is now a file.
3. TYPE **mtype a:\moretext.txt** Enter
   The contents of the file are displayed in the terminal emulator.

Copying a File from a Floppy Disk to a Hard Drive

1. TYPE **mcopy -t a:\moretext.txt /tmp/moretext.txt** Enter
   This copies **moretext.txt** from the floppy in the A: drive to the /tmp directory on your hard drive.
2. TYPE **ls /tmp** Enter
   You see **moretext.txt** listed.
3. TYPE **cat /tmp/moretext.txt** Enter
   The contents of the file are displayed on the screen.

Copying a File from a Hard Drive to a Floppy Disk

1. TYPE **mcopy -t /tmp/moretext.txt a:\more2.txt** Enter
   We renamed it while we copied it so we didn't overwrite the copy of moretext.txt already on the floppy disk.

   Caution: You cannot use simply a:\ as the destination as you can in DOS. You must specify a file name. If you don't do this, the system will stop and wait for you to make an entry. If that happens, press Control + c to end the process, retype the command, and make sure that you include a file name.

Renaming a File

1. TYPE **mren a:\more2.txt a:\more3.txt** Enter
   The file is renamed.
2. TYPE **mdir a:** Enter
   The directory listing now shows more3.txt and not more2.txt.

Deleting a File

1. TYPE **mdel a:\more3.txt** Enter
2. TYPE **mdir a:** Enter
   The file more3.txt is no longer in the directory listing.

Deleting a Subdirectory

We will delete testdir. You will have to make sure the directory is empty. Mtools won't delete a directory with contents. What won't work is the command **mdel a:\ testdir*.***—even though this kind of use of wildcards would work in DOS.

First, make the directory you want to delete the working directory.

1. TYPE **mcd testdir** Enter
   If there were files in this directory, you would delete them now, using a command like **mdel tfile.txt**. You couldn't use **mdel *.***. The ***.*** would be misinterpreted by the shell as it was passed to the mdel command.
2. TYPE **mdir a:** Enter
   The directory is empty.
3. TYPE **mcd ..** Enter
   You made the parent directory the working directory. The directory to be deleted cannot be the working directory. The operating system wouldn't know where to transfer control to when the directory address was removed.
4. TYPE **mrd a:\testdir** Enter
   You told the operating system to remove the directory.
5. TYPE **mdir a:** Enter
   Testdir is no longer in the listing.

SUMMARY

In this étude you have learned that formatting a disk is a matter of placing on the disk a data storage scheme. Different schemes are used for MS-DOS and Linux. Linux can read MS-DOS-formatted disks; this is the format to use if you have to transfer files between Linux and Windows-based machines. KFloppy is a useful and reliable disk formatting tool. Gnome also has gfloppy.

A floppy disk (and CD-ROM drive) must be mounted before it can be used. Before it is removed, it should be unmounted. Mounting integrates the address of the device into the pre-existing Linux file system. Mounting and unmounting can be done by right-clicking the floppy disk icon and then clicking on mount or unmount.

Files can be dragged and dropped if the user has permission to use the floppy disk file manager. If not, the user can use Mtools to perform file management tasks. Mtools requires the floppy disk to start out unmounted. Mtools also always assumes that it is working with the A: drive. Do not use *.* with Mtools because the *.* is interpreted by the Linux shell interpreter and yields incorrect results.

APART NO MORE: SHARING FILES BETWEEN THE LINUX AND WINDOWS PARTITIONS

ÉTUDE 6

Once most Linux users experience the feature-rich StarOffice 5.1/5.2 and Anyware Desktop (formerly Applixware 5.0), they realize that the only reason they have a dual-boot installation (where they can restart the computer and select either Windows or Linux) is so that they can have access to their Windows-based files.

This étude will show you how, while using Linux, you can read from and write to your Windows files in the Windows partition. This isn't a tricky, unstable stunt. It is stable and takes advantage of the well-designed ability to mount another partition as part of the Linux file system. (A few recent distributions of Linux have automatically detected if a Windows partition was present, and, if so, automatically mounted the Windows partition in the /mnt subdirectory.)

Can you reverse the process? Can you create a file in Linux and save it for use by a Windows program in the Windows partition? Yes. The technique is simple and relies on the fact that StarOffice, Anyware Desktop, AbiWord, and WordPerfect 8 for Linux allow files to be saved with a Windows or DOS text format. Similarly, these office programs can be instructed to read files created with various Windows and DOS text formats.

We assume you have a dual-boot installation and need to access files created and saved in the Windows partition.

TOPICS COVERED IN THIS ÉTUDE

- The mount command
- Mounting the Windows partition
- Reading and writing files in the Windows partition

THE MOUNT COMMAND

The Linux kernel is designed so that additional file systems can be connected to it and be removed as the situation warrants. The file system is the storage scheme that is applied to each disk, CD-ROM, or partition that Linux is asked to fetch data from.

The Linux kernel must be configured to accept DOS file systems. In early distributions of Linux, this feature may not have been enabled. In all of the recent distributions tested, this feature has been enabled.

Before the arrival of Linux, Windows was the dominant operating system on PCs. Windows came automatically installed. Most computer users never installed an operating system, let alone even knew about disk partitions. Given that they believed that they were the only game in town, Windows developers designed Windows to always take over the first position in the master boot record (MBR).

Consequently, when someone tries to create a dual-boot system, one of two situations arises.

- If Windows currently exists on disk and the user doesn't want to lose the files, the user makes partitions with a utility such as Partition Magic. Windows keeps its position as the first partition on the hard drive and consequently, in Linux parlance, has the first hard drive partition designation of "hda1."
- If the user wants to create a dual-boot system from scratch, the user first uses fdisk to repartition the disk (which reformats and wipes out all the files on the disk). Then, if the user is savvy as to how Windows works, the user installs the Windows operating system and lets it take over the first position in the MBR. Again, Windows ends up in the partition that Linux calls "hda1."

The designation "hda1" is used in the mount command discussed below. If, for some reason, your Windows partition is located on a different partition, then use that particular designation. In the overwhelming majority of cases, the Windows partition will be designated as "hda1."

Linux is made aware of file systems through the mount command. The entry to the file system is actually an address. The mount command lets Linux know that this address is actually the entry point to a file system and associates it with a device-driver file that contains instructions about how to access that file system. The main file system, in its own partition on a hard drive, is mounted automatically by the script of operating system commands that controls system startup. The user can instruct Linux to mount other file systems, such as the floppy disk drive and CD-ROM drive, after the system has started.

Without getting too far into detail, hda1 is seldom put into the file system table (fstab) as an MS-DOS file system. This means that the complete command must be issued on the command line. This isn't much of chore after you do it once or twice. If you prefer, you can put the command in a script file that has a simple file name to type when you need access to your Windows files. Writing script files is covered in Étude 23. A third option is to embed the script command in your .profile file. This file contains files that are executed every time you log in. You could also enter it into your /etc/fstab file, but that would be a little risky for a new Linux user.

MOUNTING THE WINDOWS PARTITION

PREPARATION

This is two-step process. First, you need a directory, off the /mnt subdirectory, where the address to the Windows partition can be stored. Second, you must actually mount the Windows partition into your Linux file system. You must either log in as root or issue the su command and type in the root password when asked. I'll assume the su case in the following instructions.

1. CLICK the terminal emulator icon (it is an icon on the panel that looks like a computer monitor).
   A terminal emulator opens.
2. TYPE **su** [Enter]
   "Password:" appears.
3. TYPE the root password and PRESS [Enter]
4. TYPE **cd /mnt** [Enter]
5. TYPE **mkdir WinRoot** [Enter]
6. TYPE **ls** [Enter]
   Observe your newly created directory. Your terminal emulator window should look similar to Figure 6.1.

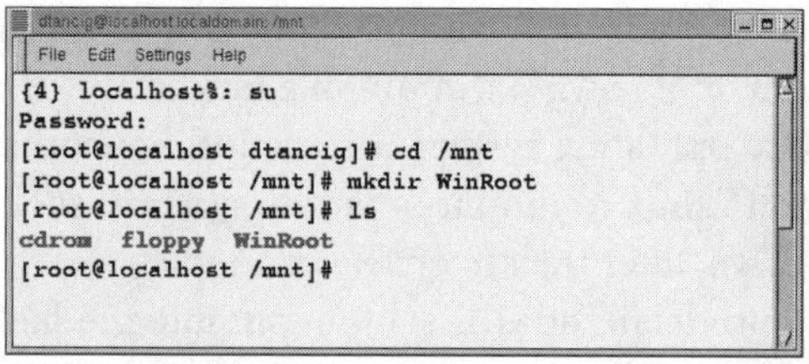

```
{4} localhost%: su
Password:
[root@localhost dtancig]# cd /mnt
[root@localhost /mnt]# mkdir WinRoot
[root@localhost /mnt]# ls
cdrom  floppy  WinRoot
[root@localhost /mnt]#
```

FIGURE 6.1: Creating WinRoot

Notice the three directories: your cdrom drive, your floppy disk drive, and now WinRoot. It is standard to place mounted file systems in the /mnt subdirectory.

Note: The name WinRoot was chosen to remind you that, although you are saving files to what appears to be a subdirectory of Linux, that subdirectory actually represents the root directory of the Windows system.

MOUNTING THE WINDOWS PARTITION

It is assumed you are still have root permission either because you logged in as root or because you still have permission through the su command.

1. TYPE **mount -t msdos /dev/hda1 /mnt/WinRoot** Enter
2. TYPE **ls /mnt/WinRoot** Enter
   You should see all of the Windows system root directory files and subdirectories.

That's it. It's that simple. Now you have complete access to your Windows files.

You are still in Linux. Don't use DOS commands in the WinRoot directory. Use Linux commands. To change directories use the cd command. To display a directory listing you use the ls command, not the dir command. If you want to perform file operations such as copying, moving, or deleting in this directory, read through Étude 2 or 3 and use a graphical file manager to do your file operations.

UNMOUNTING THE WINDOWS PARTITION

You cannot unmount this partition while it is the working directory. You will get a message that it is busy and cannot be unmounted. You must first change directories and make another directory the working (also called current) directory.

You must be logged in as root or have root permission through the su command to perform these operations.

1. TYPE **cd /mnt** Enter if you are not already in the mnt directory.
2. TYPE **pwd** Enter to check where you are.
   The computer should display /mnt.

3. TYPE **umount WinRoot** Enter
   This is not a misspelling. The command is umount.

4. TYPE **ls WinRoot** Enter
   Nothing appears. The file has been unmounted.
   Note that if you type ls, you will still see a listing for WinRoot. That is correct. WinRoot is a directory. We didn't remove the directory when we unmounted WinRoot. We merely took away its contents—which is why it appears empty when you type ls WinRoot. If WinRoot had been removed, an error message would have told us the file or directory was not found.

READING AND WRITING FILES IN THE WINDOWS PARTITION

FILE CONVERSION PROBLEMS

Although Linux and Windows both use ASCII text characters, Linux and Windows files are not identical because Windows and Linux handle end-of-line markers differently. Linux uses the nonprinting ASCII character called a line feed. Windows uses two nonprinting ASCII characters—a line feed and a carriage return.

There are other file-conversion issues related to special characters. This conversion business can get out of hand very quickly. We need a simple, works-every-time solution.

A business user will always have an office suite installed. There is no reason not to. StarOffice 5.1/5.2 is free and is easily installed. Anyware Desktop and AbiWord are useful if you need to convert Office 2000 files. The works-every-time solution is below.

Note: All your conversions will be done in Linux.

CONVERTING A LINUX FILE TO USE IN A WINDOWS ENVIRONMENT

In preparation for the following activity, create a word-processing document in Linux. This document is what we will use. You may need to be logged in as root to write to WinRoot. If this is the case, log in as root or contact your system administrator to change permissions.

1. OPEN your office suite.
2. From within the word processor of your office suite, OPEN the file you want to export to a Windows environment.
3. SAVE the file with the correct type for the Windows environment.

- If it will be used in Microsoft Word, save it as a Word97 file or as a Rich Text Format (RTF) file.
- If it is to be used with an ASCII text editor (such as would be the case for a source code file), save it as Text.

4. SAVE the file to your WinRoot subdirectory.
   Now your file is accessible from Windows.

CONVERTING A WINDOWS FILE TO USE IN A LINUX ENVIRONMENT

In preparation for the following activity, create a word-processing document in Windows. This document is what we will use. You may need to be logged in as root to write to WinRoot. If this is the case, log in as root or contact your system administrator to change permissions.

1. OPEN your office suite in Linux.
2. From within the word processor of your office suite, OPEN the file you want to import from the WinRoot subdirectory.
3. OPEN the file with the correct type for the Windows environment.
   - There may be an option for the word processor to automatically detect what kind of file it is. This option sometimes is the best.
   - Otherwise, if it was a Win97 file, you can open as a Word97 file, etc. If was an ASCII text editor file (such as would be the case for a source code file), you can open it as Text.

   The document opens in your word processor. Now you could work with it, making changes, and save it to work with later in Linux or save it back to the WinRoot directory, where it could be worked on later in Windows.
4. SAVE the file.
   Make sure you select the correct data type if you are saving it in a Linux partition. If you are saving it back to the WinRoot subdirectory, then just select Save from the File menu. You will be saving it with the same data type it had in Windows.

Several experiments were conducted concerning these transfers. The above instructions should work every time. But here are some scenarios to walk you through more concrete examples.

Scenario 1

If you create an ASCII text file in Linux using a standard editor such as KEdit and do not save it as Text:

- If you open it in Windows using Notepad, the lack of carriage returns will cause the file to be one long continuous line. The line feeds will show up as black squares in the text.
- WordPad will correctly format the file created in Linux without any conversion. This can be important if you are transferring source code that you want to recompile and try in a Windows environment.
- Both Notepad and WordPad correctly recognize word wrap.

Remember, when you save a file to the WinRoot directory, you are saving it to the root directory of Windows. That is why we named our directory "WinRoot"; so we would remember that it is the root directory.

Scenario 2

If you create a file in Windows using a text editor:

- KEdit will not recognize word wrap, regardless of whether you save it as ASCII or as MS-DOS text using WordPad or Notepad.
- KEdit will correctly format lines, even though Windows includes a carriage return at the end of every line. This means source code can easily be imported from the Windows partition.
- StarOffice 5.1 will read word wrap in the Windows file. Once you've opened the file in Linux, go through and at the end of each line where StarOffice 5.1 forced the text to word wrap, press the **Enter** key to insert a carriage return. Save the file. Then when you open the file in KEdit, it will be properly formatted.
- To our knowledge, there is no format you can save the file in that will automatically apply word wrap correctly.

SUMMARY

The design of the Linux operating system allows external partitions to be mounted in the Linux partition. This allows us to mount the Windows partition, in a multiple-boot configuration, in the Linux file system. The Windows partition appears as merely another subdirectory.

Gaining access to the Windows partition is a two-step process. First, a subdirectory must be created in the /mnt subdirectory. Then the command is issued to mount the Windows partition in the subdirectory created for it. It can be removed using the umount command. Both mounting and umounting require root permission.

When working with a file in both Linux and Windows, there are some conversion issues you'll have to deal with. For example, Windows inserts two characters, a carriage return and a linefeed, each time the **Enter** key is pressed, such as at the end of a line or a paragraph. Linux inserts only one character, a linefeed character, each time the **Enter** key is pressed. This can create conversion problems. The easiest way to avoid the problem is to use your office software's import and export features to convert to a file type that is compatible between the Windows program and the Linux program—such as the Office 97 format between Win2000 and StarOffice. Some Linux editors and Microsoft editors correctly read each other's files. Also, conversion utility programs exist that can convert between the two types of files.

PERSONAL ORGANIZERS AND A SPECIAL CALENDAR TOOL

ÉTUDE 7

Linux has two categories of personal organizers. One category links to PalmPilot-type devices and one category does not. Linux software and organizers that do link with PalmPilot-type devices are discussed in Études 16 and 26. This étude works with the category of devices that do not link with the Palm devices. Also, these organizers do not maintain an address book, as PalmPilot devices do.

There are two organizers in this desktop-only group. One is the KDE KOrganizer and the other is Gnome Calendar. Another useful tool is the cal program available on the command line in Linux. A few examples are given showing how this can be useful in business and for students.

If you need an address book, you could use Gnome Address, a seasoned, stable contact manager. Which organizer you choose will depend on your personal style and your work requirements. Gnome calendar is shown in Figure 7.1.

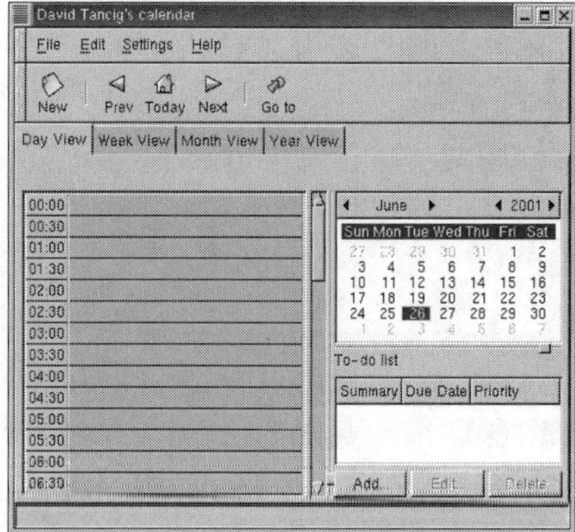

FIGURE 7.1: Gnome Calendar

It opens in what is called the "agenda view." You are shown your calendar on an hourly basis, your to-do list, and a calendar for the month. The help manual is complete and illustrated. All the controls are nearly intuitive and easily accessed. It has a lot of the feel of using a Palm-type device. On the down side, Gnome Calendar does not have print capability and no means for editing task categories. But for someone who needs to casually keep a schedule on their computer, this is a good choice because the controls are so intuitive.

KOrganizer, shown in Figure 7.2, can print the calendar and the to-do list. KOrganizer does allow category editing. It, like Gnome Calendar, starts up in the agenda view. It has an extensive and complete help manual. The controls are nearly intuitive, but because this organzier has more features, you occasionally have to try to remember which menu has the submenu with the feature you need. This an excellent organizer for those who want to organize the entire range of their activities. Before leaving the computer, all they have to do is print out their schedule or to-do list, or both. Then the organizer can be updated the next day when they're at the computer again. This scheme also works well if you carry an agenda binder when you're away from your computer.

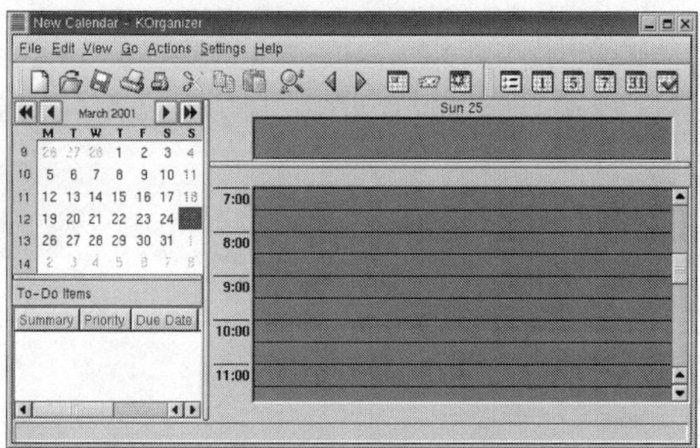

FIGURE 7.2: KOrganizer

Electronically-based organizers are an extension of your personal organization. They won't organize you if you aren't organized. Organization is a state of mind and results from planning, carefully thought-through decisions, and self-discipline. If your life is a scattering of reminders in many places, the electronic organizer will become just one more place to squirrel away and lose information. If you are looking at organizers because you want to become organized, first read *The Organized Executive* by Stephanie Winston. It has been updated to include using electronics aids. This is where you discover that the ability to edit information categories down to a bare minimum is crucial and how to make an organizer work.

TOPICS COVERED IN THIS ÉTUDE

- Using Gnome Calendar
- Using KOrganizer
- Using cal

GETTING STARTED WITH GNOME CALENDAR

In Gnome:

1. CLICK on the Gnome footprint.
   A menu opens.
2. MOVE the cursor to **Programs**.
   A menu opens.
3. MOVE the cursor to **Applications**.
   A menu opens.
4. CLICK **Calendar**.
   Gnome Calendar opens. It should look similar to Figure 7.1.

In KDE:

1. CLICK on the stylized K.
   A menu opens.
2. MOVE the mouse up to **GNOME Programs**.
   A menu opens.
3. MOVE the cursor to **Applications**.
   A menu opens.
4. CLICK **Calendar**.
   Gnome Calendar opens. It should look similar to Figure 7.1.

THE ELEMENTS OF GNOME CALENDAR

Gnome Calendar has four general areas:

- a top area for controls
- a left area for your daily appointment calendar
- an upper-right area showing the calendar for the current month
- a lower-right area displaying your to-do list

The title bar is the top-most bar. It may display your name followed by "Calendar." The title bar can be used to drag the window to a different location on the screen. The menu bar is immediately below the title bar. It contains several items, each of which drops down a menu when clicked. The third bar from the top is the toolbar. Icons on this bar control movement through your schedule, used when creating a new appointment or jumping to a far-removed date. The tabs bar is the fourth bar and is located immediately above the agenda view. You can easily select any view, from daily to annual.

The appointment calendar window displays each hour for 24 hours. In the settings, you can state normal working hours. Normal working hours are then displayed in a lighter shade of gray. Each entry in this calendar is called an appointment. You can right-click on a time, then click new appointment when it appears and schedule the appointment. The time covered by an appointment is shown by a white text box. You can click this box and directly edit the appointment summary. You can also right-click an appointment and then delete it, do a formal edit or create a new appointment. If two appointments overlap, their two boxes will be displayed side-by-side.

The to-do area displays your entire to-do list. You can right-click in this window to delete, edit, or add a to-do item.

THE MENU BAR

The menu bar has several important areas for issuing commands. We will highlight some of the most important commands on each menu.

On the File menu, two important items are "New calendar" and "Open." New calendar is useful if you are keeping a separate calendar for a certain project. Open retrieves a calendar saved to a file. You would only save a calendar to a file if it was special in some way. Gnome Calendar automatically saves all stored information when closed. You do not have to do a separate save.

The commands on the Edit menu allow you to create and manipulate appointments. On the Settings menu is the Preferences option. The Preferences menu has tabs for time display, colors, the to-do list, and alarms. The commands on the Help menu provide descriptions of Calendar's functions.

THE TOOLBAR

The first icon, New, allows you to create a new appointment. The last four icons allow you to move to different dates: backward, today, forward, and jump to a distant date.

WORKING IN GNOME CALENDAR

SETTING UP CHARACTERISTICS

We'll begin by setting up Gnome Calendar.

1. CLICK **Settings**.
2. CLICK **Preferences**.
   A dialog window similar to Figure 7.3 opens.

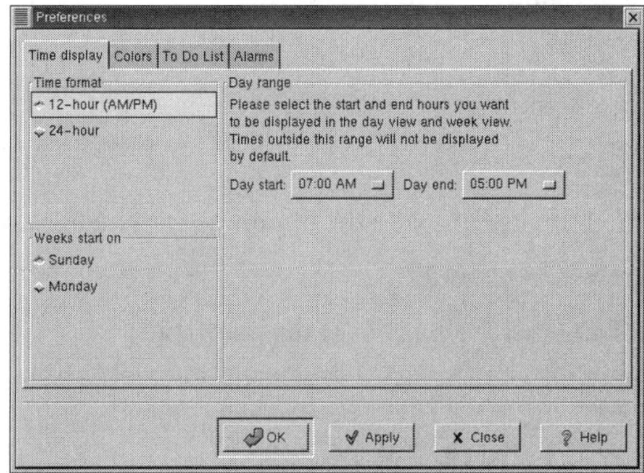

FIGURE 7.3: The Preferences window

3. CLICK **12-hour (AM/PM)**.
4. CLICK the **Day end** button.
   A menu of times opens.
5. CLICK **05:00 PM**.
6. CLICK **Apply**.
7. CLICK the **To Do List** tab.
8. CLICK **Highlight overdue items**.
9. CLICK **Apply**.
10. CLICK **OK**.
    You are returned to your calendar.

ADDING AN APPOINTMENT

1. RIGHT-CLICK in the Day View appointment area.
   A menu item appears.
2. CLICK **New appointment**.
   A dialog box opens.
3. CLICK the button that sets the start time.
   A selection box of times opens.
4. MOVE the cursor to **09:00 AM**.
   Another selection box of times in 15-minute increments opens.
5. CLICK **09:15 AM**.
6. CLICK the button that sets the end time.
   A selection box of times opens.
7. MOVE the cursor to **09:00 AM**.
8. CLICK **09:30 AM**.
9. CLICK **OK**.
10. CLICK in the text box by the appointment you just created.
11. TYPE **Create calendar**.
12. CLICK somewhere outside of the text box.
    Your appointment is shown in the appointment listing.

DELETING AN APPOINTMENT

1. RIGHT-CLICK the appointment you just created.
2. CLICK **Delete this appointment**.
   The appointment is removed and the calendar area by 9 a.m. returns to a gray color.

ADDING A TO-DO ITEM

1. CLICK the **Add** button below the "To-do list" area in the window.
   A dialog box opens.
2. CLICK in the Summary text box.
3. TYPE **Wash car**.
4. CLICK in the **Item Comments** text box.
5. TYPE **Wash and vacuum. Take quarters.**
6. CLICK the **Calendar** button.

7. DOUBLE-CLICK the date one week from today.
   The calendar closes and the date you chose appears in the text box to the left of the Calendar button.
8. CLICK the button by the time.
9. CLICK **12:00 PM**.
10. CLICK **12:00 PM** in the submenu that opens.
11. CLICK the down arrow by "Priority" twice.
    This changes the priority rating to 3.
12. CLICK **OK**.
    The item now appears in your to-do list.

DELETING A TO-DO ITEM

1. RIGHT-CLICK the to-do item you just created.
2. CLICK **Delete this item**.
   The item is removed.

GETTING STARTED WITH KORGANIZER

In Gnome:

1. CLICK on the Gnome footprint.
   A menu opens.
2. MOVE the cursor to **KDE menus**.
   A menu opens.
3. MOVE the cursor to **Applications**.
   A menu opens.
4. CLICK **Organizer**.
   KOrganizer opens. It should look similar to Figure 7.2.

In KDE:

1. CLICK on the stylized K.
   A menu opens.
2. MOVE the cursor to **Applications**.
   A menu opens.
3. CLICK **Organizer**.
   KOrganizer opens. It should look similar to Figure 7.2.

THE ELEMENTS OF KORGANIZER

KOrganizer has four general areas:

- a top area for controls
- an upper-left area for your monthly calendar
- a lower-left area displaying your to-do list
- a right area displaying your daily calendar

The title bar is is the top-most bar. It displays "KOrganizer." This bar can also be used to drag the window to a different location on screen. The menu bar is immediately below the title bar. It contains several items, each of which will drop down a menu when clicked. The toolbar is the third bar from the top. Icons on this bar control movement through your schedule, printing your calendar or do list, creating a new appointment, or jumping to a far-off date.

When the calendar is in daily view, the window displays each hour for 24 hours. In the settings, you can change this to normal working hours. Normal working hours are then displayed in a lighter shade of gray. Each entry in this calendar is called an appointment. You can double-click on a time and schedule a new appointment when the appointment dialog box appears. The time covered by an appointment is shown by a gray, raised box with the appointment summary as its label. You can right-click this box and click show to see the appointment details or edit to directly edit the appointment. You can also right-click an appointment and then delete it. If two appointments overlap, their two boxes will be displayed side-by-side.

The "To-Do Items" area displays your entire to-do list. You can right-click in this window to delete, edit, or add a to-do item.

THE MENU BAR

The menu bar has several important areas for issuing commands. We will highlight some important commands on these menus.

On the File menu, some important commands are New, Open, Print, and Print Preview. New is useful if you are keeping a separate calendar for a certain project. Open retrieves a calendar saved to a file. You would save to a file only a calendar that was special for some reason. KOrganizer automatically saves all stored information when closed. You do not have to do a separate save.

Important items on the Edit menu are Cut, Copy, and Paste. You can use these commands on any item you've clicked on in the calendar or the to-do list. On the View menu, you can select To-do list (to view your to-do list) or Day, Week, and so on (to view the calendar daily, weekly, and so on). The Go commands allow you to jump ahead one day, backward one day, or to today.

The commands on the Actions menu let you add a new event or a new to-do item and to show, edit, and mail appointments. On the Settings menu, you have several settings options. Particularly useful on this menu is the Configure KOrganizer option near the bottom. The items on the Help menu provide descriptions of the KOrganizer functions.

THE TOOLBAR

The first icon allows you to create a new appointment. The next few relate to file operations, including printing. On the far right side are icons that set the view in the KOrganizer window.

WORKING IN KORGANIZER

SETTING UP KORGANIZER

We'll begin by setting up KOrganizer.

1. CLICK **Settings**.
2. CLICK **Configure KOrganizer**.
   A dialog box similar to Figure 7.4 opens.

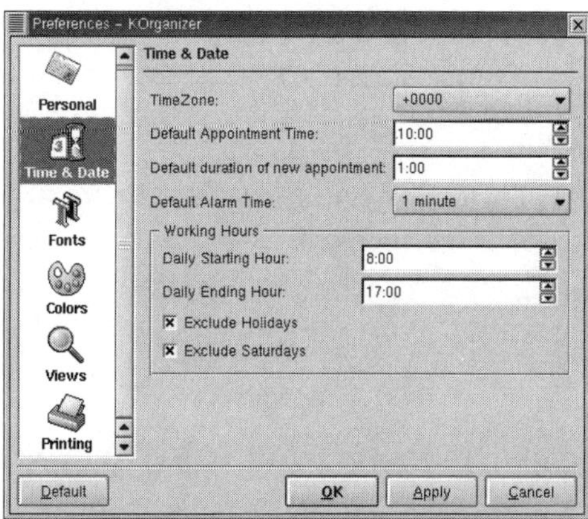

FIGURE 7.4: The Preferences window

3. Click **Time & Date** in the left area of the dialog box.
4. CLICK the arrows to the right of the "Default duration of new appointment" text box to set the duration to 2:00.
5. CLICK the arrows to the right of the "Default Appointment Time" text box to set the time to 10:00.
6. CLICK **Apply**.
7. CLICK **Colors** in the left area of the dialog box.
8. CLICK the **Default Event Color** bar.

9. CLICK a pale green or blue from the color boxes.
10. Once the color you want is displayed in the preview box, CLICK **OK**.
11. CLICK **Apply**.
12. CLICK **OK**.
    You are returned to the KOrganizer window.

ADDING AN APPOINTMENT

1. CLICK the icon above the calendar that has a "1" in it.
   This sets the appointment window to show appointments just for today.
2. DOUBLE-CLICK in the text area near 9am.
   A dialog box appears.
3. CLICK in the Summary text box.
4. TYPE **Phone appointment for directions**.
5. CLICK the down arrow by Start Time.
   A selection box of times opens.
6. CLICK **09:15 am**.
7. CLICK the down arrow by End Time.
   A selection box of times opens.
8. CLICK **09:30 am**.
9. CLICK **Apply**.
10. CLICK **OK**.
    You are returned to the KOrganizer window. Your new appointment is now listed in the daily calendar.

DELETING AN APPOINTMENT

1. RIGHT-CLICK the appointment you just created.
   A menu pops up.
2. CLICK **Delete**.
   A confirmation box opens.
3. CLICK **Delete**.
   The appointment is removed.

ADDING A TO-DO ITEM

1. RIGHT-CLICK in the To-Do Items text area.
   A menu opens.
2. CLICK **New To-Do**.
3. CLICK in the Summary text box.
4. TYPE **Wash car**.
5. CLICK in the large text box at the bottom of the dialog box.
   This is the comments area.
6. TYPE **Wash and vacuum. Take quarters.**.
7. CLICK the check box by "No due date" to empty the check box.
8. CLICK the calendar icon that appears.
9. CLICK the date one week from today.
10. CLICK the check box by "No time associated" to empty the check box.
11. CLICK the drop-down arrow by the time box that appears.
12. CLICK **12:00 pm**.
13. CLICK the down arrow by "Priority."
14. CLICK 3.
15. CLICK **Apply**.
16. CLICK **OK**.
    The item now appears in your To-Do Items list.
17. RIGHT-CLICK the to-do item you just created.
    A menu pops up.
18. CLICK **Show**.
    A full description of your task appears.
19. CLICK **OK** to close that box.
20. CLICK the check box to the left of "Wash car."
    Checking this box marks the item as done.

DELETING A TO-DO ITEM

1. RIGHT-CLICK the to-do item you just created.
2. CLICK **Delete**.
   A confirmation window opens.
3. CLICK **Delete**.

USING THE CAL PROGRAM

Most organizers guarantee accuracy only back to 1900. Linux has a useful calendar program that is accurate back to the year 1 and takes into account the Gregorian Reformation change that occurred September 3, 1752. It is not a graphical user interface program. You have to start it from the command line, but that's simple to do.

1. CLICK the terminal emulator icon.
   The window that opens should look similar to Figure 7.5.

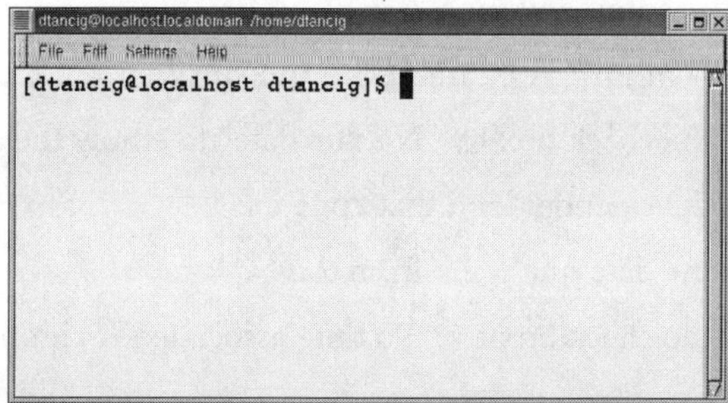

FIGURE 7.5: The terminal emulator screen

2. TYPE **cal** Enter
   The calendar for the current month appears. It should look similar to Figure 7.6.

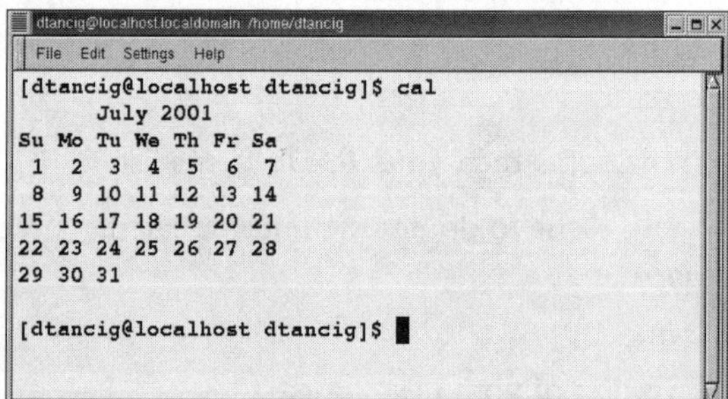

FIGURE 7.6: The current calendar

3. TYPE **clear** Enter
4. CLICK the full-screen icon (the box in the middle of the three icons at the upper-right corner of the window).
   You made the terminal emulator window fill the screen.
5. TYPE **cal** -3 Enter
   Calendars for three months appear, with the months before and after the current month displayed.

6. TYPE **cal -3j** Enter
Calendars for three months appear, with the months before and after the current month displayed. The dates have been replaced by numbers. Those are Julian days for the year. January 1 is day 1 and December 31 is day 365 or 366.

You can click your desktop calendar, subtract two from a date and find out how many days exist between two dates in the same year. The j can also be used without the 3. In that case you'd be finding the number of days between two dates within a month.

DISPLAYING OTHER MONTHS AND YEARS

You specify other months and years by using the month number and the entire year number. If you use only the year abbreviation, such as 86, instead of 1986, you will be given the calendar for A.D. (or C.E.) 86, not 1986. Also, this calendar does not go back before year 1 AD (C.E.)

For example, a colleague who is retiring was born on October 27, 1930, and came to work for the company on January 17, 1978. You're preparing remarks for the retirement dinner. What days of the week were those? Might be some nugget of insight you can use to add interest.

The format for the command is cal *month year.*

1. TYPE **cal 10 1930** Enter
We typed 10 because October is the tenth month. We now can see that he was born on a Monday.

2. TYPE **cal 1 1978** Enter
He came to work on a Tuesday. With a little thought you could even quickly compute how many days this person has been employed.

History students can use this cal command to shed some light on some dates. The day of the week can yield some surprising insights. Let's check July 4, 1776, the day, as the newspapers of the era stated, "In Congress, A Declaration."

3. TYPE **cal 7 1776** Enter
July 4, 1776, was a Thursday. Kind of a strange day for a major announcement. But not really, for the times. Finishing up business on Thursday meant the delegates had two days to travel to their homes or families they were staying with before Sunday.

It's recorded that Christopher Columbus encountered the outer reaches of the American landmass October 12, 1492. It's also stated that before doing so, he had a near-mutiny. He convinced his men to sail on for another three days. Perhaps some of his confidence was because Columbus had seen flotsam as Prince Henry the Navigator had described seeing before he, Prince Henry, discovered the Azores. It's said that Prince Henry also convinced his men to give him three more days. What day was October 12?

4. TYPE **cal 10 1492**.
   October 12 was a Friday. Maybe part of his persuasive argument was simply along the lines of, "Look, give me until Friday. If we haven't reached land by then, we'll go home."
   Here is a third example. In school we learn that World War II began when the Nazi Germans invaded Poland on September 1, 1939. September 1? Did they just want to be tidy and start a war on the first day of the month?

5. TYPE **cal 9 1939**.
   September 1 was a Friday. The Nazi government knew that their attack would likely begin a war with the other European powers. European ministers would have to meet before taking a course of action. Having to hold those meetings over the weekend without the usual ministerial support systems being active meant the response would be slowed. A Friday attack would give the attackers time to attack and consolidate their gains before facing the European response.

SUMMARY

This étude dealt with two organizers: KOrganizer and Gnome Calendar. Another useful tool is the cal program available on the command line. A few examples are given showing how this can be useful in business and for students. These programs can help you organize your time and your data.

REFERENCE

Winston, Stephanie. *The Organized Executive: The Classic Program for Productivity: New Ways to Manage Time, Paper, People, and the Digital Office*. New York: Warner Books, 2001.

GTIMETRACKER: THE TIME-TRACKING TOOL

ÉTUDE 8

There are several uses for a time-tracking tool in a modern office. Obviously, if you bill for your time, you want to keep track of the time you've devoted to a client and to the client's project. You can also use a time-tracking tool to optimize your work by keeping track of how much time you are spending on various tasks. By making use of the copy mechanism in GTimeTracker, you can not only continue keeping track of the total time you are devoting to a task but also keep a separate record of the time spent on that task each time you perform it. Then you can determine whether any time-saving devices or equipment you introduce really lower the amount of time you spend on each task.

In addition to recording elapsed time, GTimeTracker's logging capability allows you to log the absolute times (clock times) when tasks are started and completed. This is useful if you discover that you have an interruption that keeps happening. You'll be able to determine when in the day it occurs and determine how best to reduce that loss of time (perhaps the best solution will simply be to schedule time for whatever or whoever is causing the interruption). This is a quick and easy tool available on the Gnome desktop.

TOPICS COVERED IN THIS ÉTUDE

- The elements of GTimeTracker
- Working with projects
- Using a project timer
- Using the log file

GETTING STARTED

Figure 8.1 shows you how simple this tool is and how easily it can fit on your desktop.

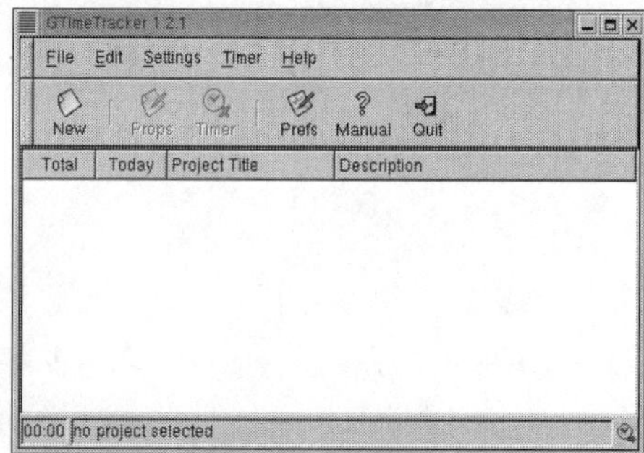

FIGURE 8.1: GTimeTracker

OPENING GTIMETRACKER

In Gnome:

1. CLICK on the Gnome footprint.
   A menu opens.
2. MOVE the cursor to **Programs**.
   A menu opens.
3. MOVE the cursor to **Applications**.
   A menu opens.
4. CLICK **Time tracking tool**.
   GTimeTracker opens. It should look similar to Figure 8.1.

In KDE:

1. CLICK on the stylized K.
   A menu opens.
2. MOVE the mouse up to **GNOME Programs**.
   A menu opens.

3. MOVE the cursor to **Applications**.
   A menu opens.
4. CLICK **Time tracking tool**.
   GTimeTracker opens. It should look similar to Figure 8.1.

THE ELEMENTS OF GTIMETRACKER

GTimeTracker has three general areas:

- a top area with controls for file and timing activities
- a large white area for listing projects
- an information bar across the bottom of the window

You will find several different activity bars. The title bar is the top-most bar. It has the name of GTimeTracker displayed. This bar can also be used to drag the window to a different location on screen.

The menu bar is immediately below the title bar. It contains several items, each of which will drop down a menu when clicked. The toolbar is the third bar from the top. Icons on this bar control timing activities such as turning the timer on or off.

The fourth bar is the project headings bar. It is located immediately above the white project window. The items on this bar are simply labels. They have no actions associated with them. The large white area in the center of the window is the project window. Projects to be timed are displayed in this window.

The information bar is at the bottom of the timer window. A counter in the lower-left corner shows total accumulated time for all activities since timing began that period (that day). The middle area on this bar displays the name of the project being timed.

THE MENU BAR

The menu bar has several important areas for issuing commands. We'll highlight some of the more important commands.

Important commands on the File menu are New Project and Exit. When you select New Project, a dialog box opens and asks for a name for the project. Exit closes GTimeTracker.

On the Edit menu are the Cut, Copy, Paste, Clear Daily Counter, and Properties options. You can cut, copy, and paste projects into different positions in the project window. This is useful if you need to time the same type of project repeatedly. Cut deletes a project from the project list. Clear Daily Counter is also useful. The project window has two counters, one that is cumulative and one that is daily and is reset to zero at the start of each new day. This command clears the daily counter. The Properties option has two purposes. The first purpose is to name and describe your files. Once a new project has been created and named, you click Properties to type in a brief description of the project. You can also edit a project name in the dialog box that opens. The second purpose is to allow you to reset the daily and cumulative counters for a project.

The Settings menu has the Preferences option. With Preferences, you can control display properties and the creation of a log file. The Timer menu is not often used. Instead, timing is done by clicking the Timer icon and by clicking on a project. The Help menu provides an extensive, illustrated description of the functions.

THE TOOLBAR

These icons duplicate actions on the menu bar. They are more convenient to use. The two important icons are New and Timer. You can click on New to add and name a new project. You can click on Timer to start and stop timing a project.

SETTING UP THE TIMER CHARACTERISTICS

1. CLICK on **Settings** on the menu bar.
2. CLICK on **Preferences.**
   A dialog window similar to Figure 8.2 opens.

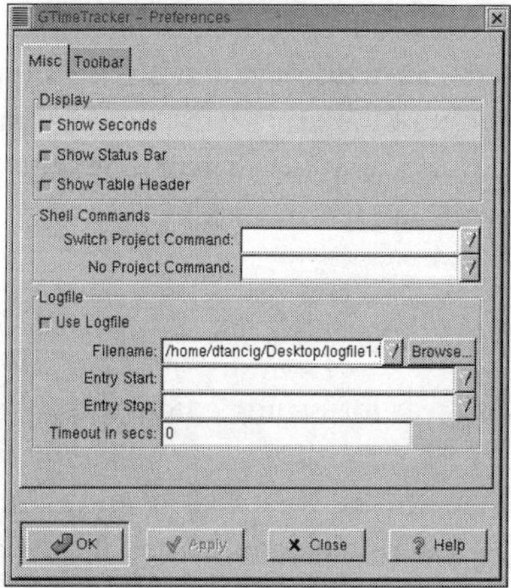

FIGURE 8.2: The Preferences dialog box

3. CLICK **Show Seconds**.
4. CLICK **Use Logfile**.
   When this is clicked, logging is turned on.
5. CLICK **Browse**.
   A directory selection window opens.

6. BROWSE the folders in the Directories window and SELECT **Desktop**. See Figure 8.3.

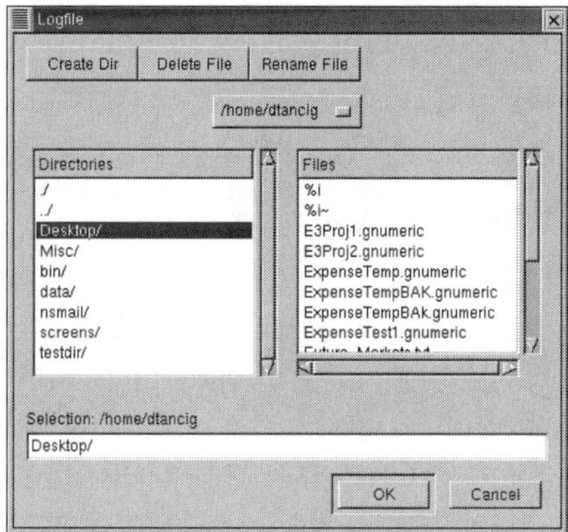

FIGURE 8.3: Directory selection

7. CLICK **OK**.
   The Preferences dialog box returns. The Filename text box contains a path that ends with Desktop/.
8. CLICK after Desktop/ in the Filename text box.
9. TYPE **logfile1.txt** (this will be the name of your log file).
10. CLICK **Apply**.
11. CLICK **OK**.
   You are returned to GTimeTracker.

ADDING A PROJECT

1. CLICK on the **New** icon to start a project.
   A dialog box for the new project name opens.
2. TYPE **Johnson Contract** in the Project Title text box.
3. TYPE **McLean County Grain Augers** in the Description text box.
4. CLICK **OK**.
   "Johnson Contract" appears in the project window. The total time and daily time counters are set to zero.
   Note: Creating a timer does not start it running.

CHANGING A PROJECT DESCRIPTION

1. CLICK **Johnson Contracts** in the projects window.
2. CLICK on the **Props** icon ("Props" is sort for "Properties"). A dialog box opens.
3. DELETE the contents of the Project Description text box.
4. TYPE **Sprinkler sales to Johnson Co.**.
5. CLICK **OK**.
   If you wanted to edit the project name, you would do it in the above dialog box. If you needed to edit or update the total project time, you would type in the values next to the boxes labeled "Project Time ever" in the above dialog box. If you needed to edit the daily time, you would type the new values in the boxes next to the label "Project Time today" in the above dialog box.

ADDING A SECOND PROJECT

1. CLICK on the **New** icon to start a project. A dialog box for the new project name opens.
2. TYPE **Friday File Backup** in the Project Title text box.
3. CLICK **OK**.
   "Friday File Backup" appears in the project window. Both the total time and daily time counters for this project are set to zero.
4. CLICK **Friday File Backup**.
5. CLICK **Props**.
6. TYPE **Weekly computer file backup** in the Project Description text box.
7. CLICK **OK**.

USING A PROJECT TIMER

1. CLICK **Johnson Contract**.
   The project is highlighted. The timer begins running.
2. CLICK **Johnson Contract**.
   It becomes unhighlighted and the timer stops.
3. CLICK **Johnson Contract** to restart timing it.
   Let's say a colleague just walked in and needs to talk with you about a coworker. The company is planning a retirement dinner for that

coworker at a local restaurant, and your advice is needed. You don't want to charge the time for that to Johnson.

4. CLICK the **Timer** icon.
   The timing stops. The project remains highlighted.
   Now let's say your colleague leaves and you start to work on the Johnson Contract again.
5. CLICK on **Timer** again.
   The timing restarts.

CUTTING AND PASTING A PROJECT

You can cut and paste projects into different positions within the project window. If you need to time the same project repeatedly or rearrange the order of your project list, these commands are useful. Also, you can delete a project from the project list by using Cut.

1. CLICK **Friday File Backup**.
2. CLICK the **Timer** icon to stop the timer.
3. RIGHT-CLICK in the project window.
4. CLICK **Cut**.
   The Friday File Backup project disappears from view.
5. CLICK **Johnson Contract**.
   This is the project above which you want to insert the Friday File Backup project.
6. CLICK the **Timer** icon.
7. RIGHT-CLICK in the project window.
8. CLICK **Paste**.
   The Friday File Backup project is now at the head of the list.

COPYING A PROJECT

You can use this command if you want to compare the time it takes you to perform an action. You time yourself the first time, copy the project, and then time yourself using the copy of the project. The difference between the times shows in the increase or decrease in execution time. You can also use this command to record the cumulative time on a project.

When you copy a project, the Project Description and the Project Timers are copied. You could accumulate time on these projects by changing the Daily Timer but not the Total Time in the Properties dialog box.

1. CLICK on **Friday File Backup**.
2. CLICK the **Timer** icon to stop timing.
3. RIGHT-CLICK in the project window.
   A menu opens.
4. CLICK **Copy**.
5. CLICK the last item in the list, **Johnson Contract**.
6. CLICK the **Timer** icon to stop timing.
7. RIGHT-CLICK in the project window.
8. CLICK **Paste**.
   A second copy of Friday File Backup appears above the item that had been highlighted.

USING THE LOG FILE

Log files record the time you spend on each project. We will click on three separate projects to see how the log file works.

1. CLICK on **Johnson Contract**.
2. If the timer doesn't start, CLICK on it again.
3. WAIT one full minute.
4. CLICK on a **Friday File Backup**. Wait one full minute.
   Every time you change to a different project, the clock time of when the new project is started is recorded. The clock time for the last project is recorded when you exit GTimeTracker.
   Now we'll exit GTimeTracker so we can view the log file.
5. CLICK **File**.
6. CLICK **Exit**.
   You have exited GTimeTracker, and you are now ready to observe the log file in a text editor.

VIEWING THE LOG FILE

The log file is an ASCII text file and can be read with any text editor or word-processing program.

1. OPEN KEdit.
2. CLICK **File**.
3. CLICK **Open**.
   Recall that we put the log file in our Desktop directory.

4. CLICK the **Desktop** folder.
5. CLICK **logfile1.txt**.
6. CLICK **OK**.
   The editor displays something similar to Figure 8.4.

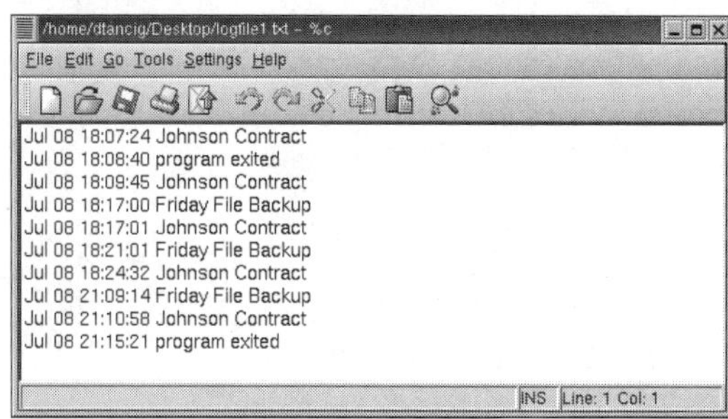

FIGURE 8.4: A log file

7. NOTE that absolute clock times, not elapsed times, are logged. These times are recorded only when you change projects or when you exit the program. A current project in a timer that is still running will not show its time in the log file.
   You can do a screen capture if you want a printout of elapsed times.

SUMMARY

GTimeTracker can be very useful in an office setting. If you bill for your time, you can use GTimeTracker to keep track of the time you've devoted to the client and to the client's project. You can also use a time-tracking tool to optimize your work by keeping track of how long you are spending on various tasks.

You use GTimeTracker by creating projects. When you select a project in GTimeTracker, a timer starts to record the time spent doing your tasks. You can start and stop this timer whenever you need to so you can keep an accurate count of minutes spent on each task. By using the Copy mechanism in GTimeTracker, you can continue to keep track of the total time you devote to a task but keep a separate record of the time spent on that task each time you perform it.

You use the Cut and Paste mechanisms if you need to time the same project repeatedly or rearrange the order of your project list. You can delete a project from the project list by using Cut.

In addition to recording elapsed time, GTimeTracker's logging capability allows you to log absolute times (clock times) when tasks are started and completed. You can observe the starting times of each task in the log file, which is an ASCII file and can be read in any text editor.

KJOTS: ORGANIZED NOTE-TAKING

ÉTUDE 9

Advances in almost every aspect of business begin with the same scenario: a blizzard of related scraps of information. This could be a set of notes from a brainstorming session about improving service or papers from personal research into a new market opportunity (which could include pages from sources such as community documents, periodicals, and other market research). Every project typically starts with the collection and development of information—usually someone jotting down notes.

Two problems impede success at this early stage. The first is keeping all of those scraps of information together and organized. The second is the problem of coordinating the information in all those loose notes into a coherent document or set of documents. A word-processing program has long been the software tool for creating finished documents. But the software tool that is ideal for this stage of information gathering and winnowing is KJots. KJots helps you channel information into appropriate categories and coordinate the collected information into a coherent document or set of documents.

KJots is organized around the concepts of books and pages. A book is a general topic. A page is a category—a mental concept—within the general topic. The typed-in information can be as long as necessary. Each page is given its own unique title—the "subject title." KJots has a mechanism so you can easily jump between pages (categories or subjects). Books, general topics, are kept in a menu. From this menu, you can quickly open any book, topic, you have created.

You can put up to eight books on a "hotlist." Each hotlist item is a button on the hotlist bar. Click on the button and you open the book. You aren't interrupted by having to stop and open another file. You can also remove books from the hotlist. The hotlist allows you to cluster together related groups of information. This can include assorted bits of gathered information that you need to jump around and access as you try to piece together a document. Or the hotlist can include multiple documents that are to be created from a central outline. For example, one book could list the basic points that have to be communicated; the second book could be the executive briefing; the third could be instructions for how employees are to implement the policies; and the fourth book could be a letter sent to external logistical or support providers.

A big advantage to this program is that each book can be saved as an ASCII text file. An ASCII file can be opened with any text editor or word-processing program and sent to a printer. KJots automatically includes the page headings (subject titles) in the ASCII text file. This means that the complete set of organized jotted notes can be printed and set beside you as you create the final document.

TOPICS COVERED IN THIS ÉTUDE

- Creating a KJots book
- Putting a KJots book on the hotlist
- Saving a KJots book
- Copying text between KJots books
- Examining your saved ASCII text file

GETTING STARTED

When you start KJots, it looks like Figure 9.1. It looks pretty tame. The excitement comes when you actually use it in an information-coordinating process.

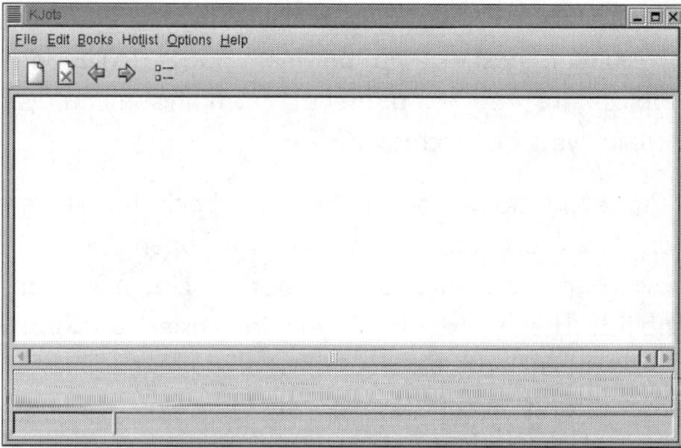

FIGURE 9.1: KJots

The KJots window is divided into a group of action bars at the top, a text window, a bar for hotlist buttons, and a bar at the bottom for page titles (Subject Titles).

OPENING KJOTS

In KDE:

1. CLICK on the stylized K.
2. MOVE the mouse to **Utilities**.
3. CLICK on **KJots**.
   KJots opens.

In Gnome, try the following:

1. CLICK on the Gnome footprint.
2. MOVE the mouse to **KDE menus**.
   A menu opens.
3. MOVE the mouse to the **Utilities** menu.
   A submenu opens.
4. CLICK the mouse on **KJots**.
   Sometimes, KJots and other KDE utilities are not linked to the KDE Utilities menu in Gnome. The following is an easy way to make KJots readily available.

   By long-standing Linux convention, most application-type programs that a person runs are located in the /usr/bin directory (folder). We are going to insert KJots on the panel. We'll have to tell the activation program (launcher) to look in the /usr/bin folder for the KJots program.

Adding KJots to the Gnome Panel

1. CLICK the Gnome footprint.
   The main menu opens.
2. CLICK **Panel**.
3. MOVE the cursor to **Add to panel**.
4. CLICK **Launcher**.
   A dialog box opens.
5. TYPE **KJots** in the Name text box.
6. TYPE **Note Taking Utility** in the Comment text box.
7. TYPE **/usr/bin/kjots** in the Command text box.
   Note that "kjots" is all lower case in the Command text box.
8. CLICK the **No Icon** button.
   A large list of icons you may use is displayed.
9. SCROLL down about 30 rows of icons until the "gnome-note" image comes into view. We'll use that.
10. CLICK **gnome-note.png**.
    Its name is highlighted.
11. CLICK **OK**.
    The image now appears on the Icon button. At this point, your dialog box should look similar to Figure 9.2.

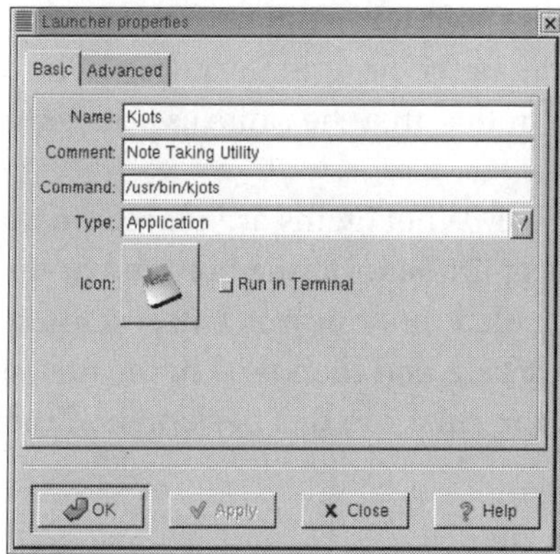

FIGURE 9.2: A completed launcher window

12. CLICK **OK**.
    The note icon appears on your panel.
13. CLICK the note icon on the panel.
    KJots opens.

THE KJOTS DISPLAY

Three bars are at the top of the display:

- Title bar
- Menu bar
- Toolbar

The title bar displays the name "KJots" and can be used to move the window to different locations on your screen.

The menu bar is immediately below the title bar. Each item can display a menu related to its label. On the File menu, you'll see menu items for creating, saving, and deleting a book (most of the options are grayed out until you have entered information for the first time). On the Edit menu, there are options to cut, copy, and paste text; find and replace text; create a new page; and delete a page.

The Books item is what you click on when you want to use a book you created but did not place on the hotlist. Books has a permanent list of the books you have created. They remain in existence until you use File > Delete current book. The Hotlist item allows you to add or remove a book from the hotlist. This button does not select books on the hotlist; buttons on the hotlist bar select books.

The Options menu let's you set various options for your book, using Config (to set fonts and font attributes). The Help menu provides some help options.

The toolbar contains icons for single-click access to some key commands. You can click the New Page icon to create a new page. The Delete Page icon deletes the current page. The Previous icon (the left arrow) moves you to the previous page. The Next icon (the right arrow) moves you to the next page. The Subject List icon opens the subject list (at this point it is empty).

The large white area in the middle of the program window is the text area. You can type in text here. You type in this area the same as you would using a simple text editor.

Below the text area is the hotlist bar. When items are placed on the hotlist, their buttons appear here. The subject list bar is at the bottom bar on the screen. The title of the current KJots page, called the "Subject Title," is listed here. When you create a new page, you can click here and then type in the new page name. Or you can press **Ctrl** + m to shift the cursor to this position and then type in the new page name.

CREATING A KJOTS BOOK

The following activity introduces most of the features of KJots. First, we will set the options for our book. Then we will create a book named FutureMarkets and fill in some pages in that book. Then we'll save the book, open a second book, do some cutting and pasting, and finish up by printing the book saved as an ASCII text file.

SETTING THE OPTIONS FOR YOUR BOOK

1. CLICK **Options**.
   A menu drops down.
2. CLICK **Configure KJots**.
   A dialog box with two tabs opens.
3. CLICK the **Editor Font** tab.
4. SCROLL through the contents of the Font box until "song ti" comes into view.
5. CLICK **song ti** to select it.
   Leave the other two boxes set at Regular and 12, unless you want to change them.
6. CLICK **Apply**.
7. CLICK **OK**.

OPENING A BOOK

1. CLICK **File**.
2. CLICK **New Book**.
   A dialog box opens, asking you for a book name.
3. TYPE **FutureMarkets** as the book name.
   A book name is a file name, so do not put / or blank spaces in it. Choose the name carefully. You cannot change a book name.
4. CLICK **OK**.
   The book title appears in the lower-left corner of the display.
5. CLICK **Books** on the menu bar.
   FutureMarkets is now a menu item.

CREATING A SUBJECT TITLE

Your first page (category) needs a page title.

1. CLICK in the subject list text box at the bottom of the display (or press Ctrl + **m**).
2. TYPE **Introduction**.
3. CLICK on the Subject List icon on the toolbar (it's the last icon on the bar).
   The subject title you created is now in the subject list.
4. CLICK **Close**.

CREATING AN ADDITIONAL PAGE AND GIVING IT A TITLE

1. CLICK the New Page icon (the first icon on the toolbar).
2. CLICK the cursor in the subject list text box.
3. TYPE **BioTech**.
4. CLICK the Subject List icon.
   The subject list now has two titles. "BioTech" is highlighted.
5. CLICK **Introduction**.
6. CLICK **Close**.
   You are transferred to the Introduction page.
7. TYPE some text into the Introduction page's text area. (A sample of text you could type is below. Enter any text that can be logically extended to a second page.)
   KJots does not have word wrap. Press the **Enter** key when you get to the edge of the window to move to the next line.

   Two major developments appear poised to radically shift funds placement in the national and international marketplace: biotechnology and the relentless convergence of personal communications and information technology.

   The convergence of personal communication and information technologies is the most unheralded change, but this change will have enormous impact on productivity and revenue streams.

COPYING TO A SECOND PAGE

You will now copy text to its related page (category) in your book.

1. HIGHLIGHT the second paragraph with the cursor.
2. CLICK **Edit**.
3. CLICK **Copy**.
4. CLICK on the Subject List icon on the toolbar.
5. CLICK **BioTech**.
6. CLICK **Close**.
   You are transferred to the BioTech page.
7. RIGHT-CLICK in the text area.
   A menu pops up.
8. CLICK **Paste**.
   The information is now copied to the second page.

PUTTING A KJOTS BOOK ON THE HOTLIST

1. CLICK **Hotlist** on the menu bar.
2. CLICK **Add current book to hotlist.**
3. LOOK at the hotlist bar in the lower-right part of the screen. You'll see a hotlist button for your book named FutureMarkets.

SAVING A KJOTS BOOK

1. CLICK **File.**
2. CLICK **Save current book.**

SAVING A KJOTS BOOK AS AN ASCII TEXT FILE

1. CLICK **File.**
2. CLICK **Save book to ascii file.**
3. TYPE **FutureMarkets.txt** in the Location text box.
4. CLICK OK.

OPENING A SECOND KJOTS BOOK

1. CLICK **File.**
2. CLICK **New Book.**
   A dialog box opens, asking you for a book name.
3. TYPE in **PerComm** as the book name.
   A book name is a file name, so do not put / or blank spaces in it. Choose the name carefully. You cannot change a book name.
4. CLICK **OK.**
   The book title appears in the lower-left corner. This is how you can tell what book you're in.

VIEWING THE RESULTS

Now you get to see how these actions have affected your menu bar.

1. CLICK on **Books.**
2. NOTICE that PerComm is now a menu item.
3. CLICK **Hotlist.**
4. CLICK **Add current book to hotlist.**

5. NOTICE that a button for the current book (PerComm) appears next the hotlist button for FutureMarkets.

COPYING TEXT BETWEEN KJOTS BOOKS

1. CLICK the hotlist button for **FutureMarkets**.
2. HIGHLIGHT the first paragraph of the text you entered.
3. CLICK **Edit**.
4. CLICK **Copy**.
5. CLICK the PerComm hotlist button.
   You are transferred to the PerComm book.
6. PLACE the cursor where you want the text inserted.
7. RIGHT-CLICK.
   A menu pops up.
8. CLICK **Paste**.
   The information is now copied to the second book.

SAVING YOUR SECOND BOOK

1. CLICK **File**.
2. CLICK **Save current book**.

EXAMINING YOUR SAVED ASCII TEXT FILE

To do this exercise, either close or minimize KJots.

1. OPEN KEdit.
2. CLICK **File**.
3. CLICK **Open**.
4. NAVIGATE to the folder where you saved FutureMarkets.txt.
5. CLICK on the **FutureMarkets.txt** file.
6. CLICK **OK**.
   The file opens. The subject titles (page or category titles) are set off with pound signs. The information contained in each page is printed beneath its subject title. This file could easily be printed and kept beside you as you created other documents from this information.

SUMMARY

KJots helps you organize separate pieces of information into one file. A word-processing program has long been the software tool for creating finished documents. But the software tool that is ideal at this stage of a project is KJots. KJots helps you channel information into appropriate categories and coordinate the collected information into a coherent document or set of documents.

KJots is organized around the concepts of books and pages. Think of a book as a general topic. Think of a page as a category within the general topic. Each page is given its own unique title. Books are kept in a menu. From this menu, you can quickly open any book you have created.

You can put up to eight books on a "hotlist." Each hotlist item is a button on the hotlist bar. Click on the button, and you open the book. You aren't interrupted by having to stop and open another file. The hotlist allows you to cluster together related groups, topics, of information. This can include assorted bits of gathered information that you need to jump around and access as you try to piece together a document. Or the hotlist can include multiple documents that are to be created from a central outline.

A big advantage to this program is that each book can be saved as an ASCII text file. An ASCII file can be opened with any text editor or word-processing program and sent to a printer. KJots automatically includes the page headings (subject titles) in the ASCII text file. This means that the complete set of organized jotted notes can be printed and set beside you as you create the final document.

MUSIC TO WORK BY ÉTUDE 10

Music CDs on the business desktop? Sure. Many of us grew up with music playing in the background as we did our homework and as we wrote our research papers in high school and college. What we know is that, at certain times, listening to music improves our focus by overwhelming distracting sounds. When my students start writing programming code from the planning documents they've developed, I encourage them to bring in their favorite music CD and headphones and listen as they code. The music blocks all the gossip and idle chatter in the work area that may distract their focus.

Both Gnome and KDE have their own CD player. The differences between CD players are minor. The KDE CD player has a button to loop the CD so it replays after it plays the last track. The Gnome CD player automatically closes the CD tray when the Play button is clicked. You will probably use the CD player program native to the desktop environment you are working in; for example, you would use the Gnome CD player in Gnome.

TOPICS COVERED IN THIS ÉTUDE

- The Kscd CD player
- The Gnome CD player

OPENING THE KDE CD PLAYER

1. CLICK on the stylized K.
2. MOVE the mouse to **Multimedia**.
   A menu opens.
3. CLICK **CD Player**.
   The KDE CD Player window opens. It should look similar to Figure 10.1.

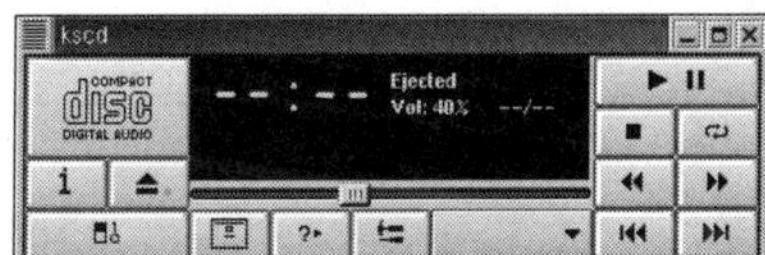

FIGURE 10.1: Kscd Player

USING THE KSCD CD PLAYER

Kscd is a CD player for the KDE desktop. Kscd roughly stands for "KDE small/simple CD player." The symbols on the CD-player panel are the same as the buttons on an actual CD player. You will find buttons for the play, pause, stop, and eject functions. Let the cursor hover over a button for moment, and the label for that button appears. There are also buttons for moving ahead or back 30 seconds. These buttons will move back to the previous track or ahead to the next track if they are double-clicked. The button in the middle on the far right side, which looks like looping arrows, will cause the CD to automatically replay after the last CD track has played.

In the middle of the CD-player display is a slide bar that controls volume. If it is pushed completely to the right and the volume is still too low, turn the volume control up on the speakers or the headphones.

Along the bottom of the CD-player display is a button that will display a menu of tracks that can be played. Click on the track you want played, and it will begin playing. The Quit button, at the bottom left, closes the CD-player program.

OPENING THE GNOME CD PLAYER

1. CLICK on the Gnome footprint.
2. CLICK **Programs**.
3. CLICK **Multimedia**.
4. CLICK **CD Player**.
   The Gnome CD-player window opens and looks similar to Figure 10.2.

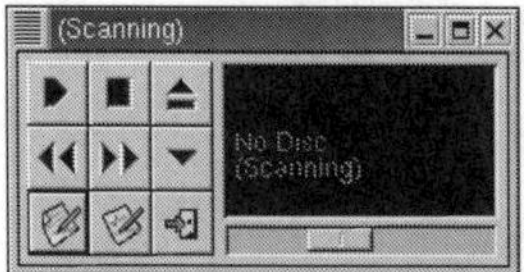

FIGURE 10.2: Gnome CD Player

USING THE GNOME CD PLAYER

The music controls are clustered on the left side of the CD-player panel. Move the mouse over each one and read the description. The CD-player image can be resized so that only the control buttons are visible. Move the mouse slowly over the right edge of the image. When double arrows appear, drag to the left until the CD-player display disappears and only the buttons are left.

The button symbols on the CD-player panel are the same as the buttons on an actual CD player. You will find buttons for the play, pause, stop, and eject functions. The Play/Pause button also closes the CD-player tray when it is clicked.

The buttons with double arrows on them help you navigate your CD. Clicking them will move you ahead or back one track. The Gnome CD player does not have automatic CD replay. At the bottom of the CD-player display is a slide bar that controls volume. If it is pushed completely to the right and the volume is still too low, turn the volume control up on the speakers or the headphones. The button with the down-facing arrow will display a play list. If you click one of the tracks, that track will be played. The Quit button, the button in the lower-right corner, removes the CD-player image, but the CD player continues playing the CD. Eject the CD if you have quit the player and want the music to stop.

WHAT IS GRACENOTE?

Each music CD has its own unique recording title code. The titles of all the tracks on a CD are associated with these codes. These codes are maintained in an enormous CD database on the Internet called Gracenote! If you connect to the Internet and start your CD player, the player will contact Gracenote! on the Internet and enter the play list for the CD you have installed.

SUMMARY

Both Gnome and KDE have their own CD player. The differences between CD players are minor. The KDE CD player has a button to loop the CD so that it replays after it plays the last track. The Gnome CD player automatically closes the CD tray when the Play button is clicked. You should probably use the CD player program native to the desktop environment you are working in. The controls are pretty intuitive if you've used a real CD player.

DESKTOP CALCULATORS

ÉTUDE 11

A calculator on the desktop is a time-saver as long as it does what you need and doesn't overwhelm you. Red Hat Linux has two, and both are well designed. The Gnome Calculator, GCalc, is a basic scientific calculator with log and trig functions. A handy feature is the EXC button which exchanges the contents of the display with what is stored in memory. KCalc is the KDE calculator. It has a layout reminiscent of the Hewlett Packard HP-10 series. It can operate as either a scientific calculator or, with a click of a button, as a statistical calculator. This reduces the keyboard clutter. It also has a results stack that keeps a list of previous results, the number of digits to the right of the decimal point can be specified, and the background colors of the keyboard can be configured. This may sound trivial, but the coloring is applied to logical groups of keys and speeds the use of the keys because the colors limit the area you search for a key.

Both have useful built-in help manuals. Since the calculators are both well-designed, you will probably want to use the calculator native to your desktop environment.

GCalc is shown in Figure 11.1.

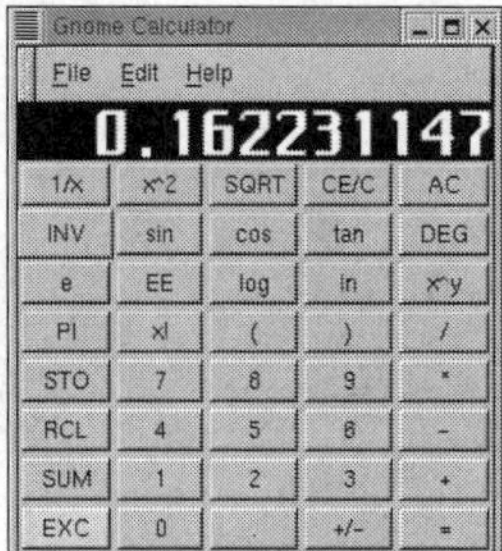

FIGURE 11.1: The Gnome calculator

KCalc is shown in Figure 11.2.

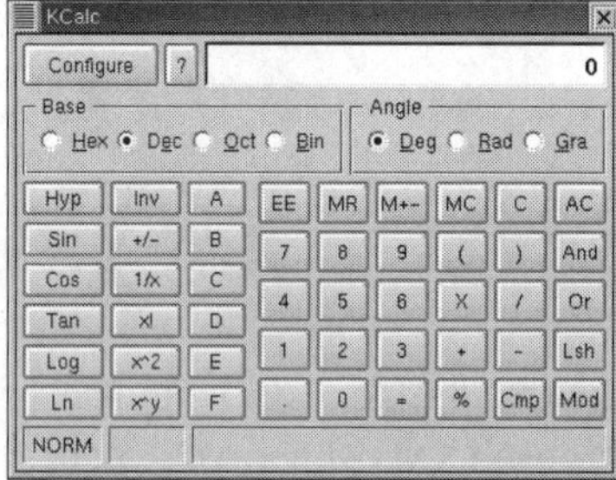

FIGURE 11.2: The KDE calculator

TOPICS COVERED IN THIS ÉTUDE

- A tour of the Gnome calculator
- A tour of the KDE calculator
- Installing a calculator on your desktop

THE GNOME CALCULATOR

OPENING THE GNOME CALCULATOR

1. CLICK the Gnome footprint.
2. MOVE the cursor to **Programs**.
   A menu opens.
3. MOVE the cursor to **Utilities**.
   A menu opens.
4. CLICK **Simple Calculator**.
   The Gnome Calculator window opens and looks similar to Figure 11.1.

USING THE GNOME CALCULATOR

The calculator has the standard title bar along with the minimize, full-screen, and close buttons. Below the title bar is a menu bar. The only option under File is to quit. Edit allows you to copy the contents of the calculator display to another document. Help opens a manual.

You can resize the calculator, but all that does is put more space between the buttons. It doesn't increase the size of the fonts or the keys. With only a few exceptions, Gnome Calculator works like any standard scientific calculator. The AC button clears all storage including memory. Memory can also be cleared by storing a zero.

The SUM button works the same as the M+ button on a calculator. SUM adds the contents of the display to memory.

1. CLICK **1**.
2. CLICK the **STO** button.
3. CLICK **2**.
4. CLICK the **SUM** button.
5. CLICK the **RCL** button.
   3, the sum of 1 and 2, is displayed.

The EXC button exchanges the display and memory contents.

1. CLICK the **AC** button.
2. CLICK **5**.
3. CLICK the **STO** button.
4. CLICK **7**.
5. CLICK **EXC**.
   5 is displayed.
6. CLICK **EXC** again.
   7 is redisplayed.

This calculator has no 10X button. This usually is needed to take the inverse of the base 10 log (the base 10 antilog). But this is not a problem. In Gnome Calculator, you can use the x^y (x raised to the y power) button.

1. CLICK the **AC** button.
2. CLICK **1** and **0** to enter a 10 into the display.
3. CLICK the **x^y** button.
4. CLICK **3**.
   We want to raise 10 to the third power, cubing it.

5. CLICK =.
   1000 appears in the display.

In most cases, the exponent would be a calculated value. You'd store it, enter 10, click x^y, click RCL to retrieve the exponent, and then click the = button.

THE KDE CALCULATOR

OPENING THE KDE CALCULATOR

1. CLICK on the stylized K.
2. MOVE the mouse to **Utilities**.
   A menu opens.
3. CLICK **Calculator**.
   The KCalc window opens and should look similar to Figure 11.2.

USING THE KDE CALCULATOR

KCalc has the standard title bar at the top that you can use to move it around. The second bar contains a Configure button and a ? button. The ? button is the Help button, which brings up a very good manual.

1. CLICK the **Configure** button.
   You are presented with a dialog window with four tabs. See Figure 11.3.

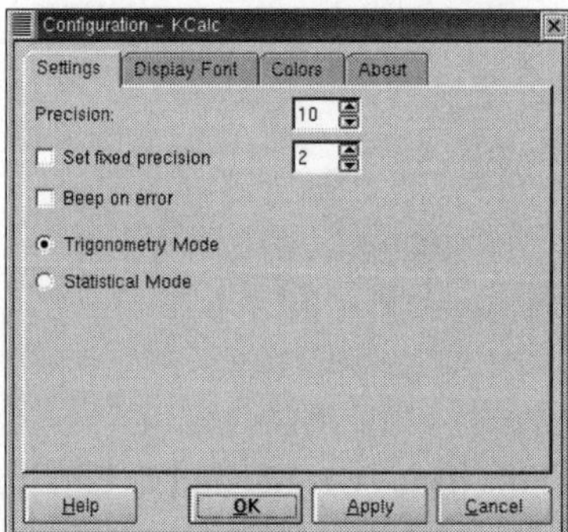

FIGURE 11.3: Configuring KCalc

   The Settings tab is where you can change KCalc into a statistical calculator. It is also here that you can change the number of digits to the right of the decimal point.

2. CLICK the **Display Font** tab.
   The Display Font tab allows you to change the font style and size. For readability, we'll try song ti, bold, and 14 point.

3. SCROLL down the Font list box until you can CLICK **song ti**.
4. CLICK **Bold** and **14** in the Font style and Size list boxes, if they are not already selected.
5. CLICK the **Colors** tab.
   The Colors tab allows you to change the foreground/background colors for the display and the background colors for the major key groupings. Double-click the item you want to change. We will try a light aqua for the display background.
6. DOUBLE-CLICK **Display Background**.
7. CLICK the drop-down arrow in the upper-right corner.
   A menu drops down.
8. CLICK **40 Colors**.
9. CLICK the light aqua box, located on the right side.
10. CLICK **OK**.
11. CLICK **Apply**.
    Now we'll give a light tan color to the function buttons.
12. DOUBLE-CLICK **Function Buttons**.
    "40 Colors" should still be displayed. If not, select it.
13. CLICK the light tan box on the bottom row.
14. CLICK **OK**.
15. CLICK **Apply**.
    Now we'll give a salmon-pink color to the memory buttons.
16. DOUBLE-CLICK **Memory Buttons**.
    "40 Colors" should still be displayed. If not, select it.
17. CLICK the salmon-pink box (top row, fourth in from the right).
18. CLICK **OK**.
19. CLICK **Apply**.
    Now we'll give a light-green color to the number buttons.
20. DOUBLE-CLICK **Number Buttons**.
    "40 Colors" should still be displayed. If not, select it.
21. CLICK the light-green box (middle row, second from left).
22. CLICK **OK**.
23. CLICK **Apply**.
    Now we'll give a light-yellow color to the operation buttons.

24. DOUBLE-CLICK **Operation Buttons**.
    "40 Colors" should still be displayed. If not, select it.
25. CLICK the light-yellow box (in the middle row).
26. CLICK **OK**.
27. CLICK **Apply**.
    If you prefer, you can change all of these back to gray using the same process.
28. CLICK **OK**.
    You applied the color changes.

The calculator behaves as a standard scientific calculator with a few exceptions. You should read the manual about the % button if you do a lot of percentage calculations. You may find some shortcuts in your work because of how it is designed. Converting to a statistical calculator is a matter of a few mouse clicks.

1. CLICK **Configure**.
2. CLICK the **Settings** tab.
3. CLICK **Statistical Mode**.
4. CLICK **OK**.
   The left-most buttons are statistical buttons.

This calculator also does not have a button for the inverse log of base 10 logs. The same technique of raising 10 to the desired power using the x^y button demonstrated for the Gnome Calculator will be used.

1. CLICK **1** and **0** to enter a 10 into the display.
2. CLICK the **x^y** button.
3. CLICK **3**.
   We want to raise 10 to the third power, cubing it.
4. CLICK **=**.
   1000 appears in the display.

Another button missing is the square root button. You have a x^2 button (x squared button). If you take the inverse of x^2, the square root will be calculated.

1. CLICK the **AC** button.
2. CLICK **6** and **2** and **5** to enter 625 into the display.
3. CLICK the **Inv** button.
4. CLICK the **x^2** button.
   25, the square root of 625, is displayed.

The Mod button computes the integer remainder. You may recall in elementary school that when you learned to do division, the teacher required you to do things like write the quotient of a division as "4 R2" where 2 was the integer remainder. Then you learned to do decimals and forgot all about integer remainders. It turns out that finding the integer remainder has a number of useful applications—hence the reason for the Mod button.

What's the integer remainder when 78 is divided by 23?

1. PRESS the **AC** button to clear the screen.
2. CLICK **78** on the number keys.
3. CLICK the **Mod** button.
4. CLICK **23** on the number keys.
5. CLICK =.
   9 is displayed. 9 is the remainder when 78 is divided by 23.

PUTTING A CALCULATOR ON THE DESKTOP

The process is nearly identical for both calculators.

In Gnome:

1. CLOSE the calculator window, if it's not already closed.
2. RIGHT-CLICK on the desktop.
   A menu opens to New and offers a submenu.
3. CLICK **Launcher** under New.
4. TYPE **GCalc** in the Name box.
5. TYPE **Gnome Calculator** in the Comment box.
6. TYPE **/usr/bin/gcalc** in the Command box.
7. CLICK the Type drop-down arrow.
8. CLICK **Application**.
9. CLICK the **No Icon** button.
   A window full of icons is displayed.
10. CLICK the calculator icon (about nine rows down from the top).
11. CLICK **OK**.
12. CLICK **Apply**.
13. CLICK **OK**.
    Now you have a calculator accessible from the desktop.

In KDE:

1. CLOSE the calculator window, if it's not already closed.
2. RIGHT-CLICK on the desktop.
   A menu opens.
3. CLICK **Create New**.
4. CLICK **Link To Application**.
   A dialog box opens.
5. CLICK the icon button in the General tab.
   A window full of icons is displayed.
6. CLICK the calculator icon.
7. REPLACE "Link To Application" in the text box with **KCalc**.
8. CLICK the **Execute** tab.
9. TYPE **/usr/bin/kcalc** in the Command box.
10. CLICK the **Application** tab.
11. TYPE **KCalc** in the Name box.
12. TYPE **KDE Calculator** in the Comment box.
13. CLICK **Application** in the list box on the right.
14. CLICK the double arrows pointing to the left to move "Application" over to the left list box.
15. CLICK **OK**.
    Now you have a calculator accessible from the desktop.

SUMMARY

Linux has two useful desktop calculators, one in Gnome and one in KDE. The KDE calculator is more configurable and has more functions than the Gnome calculator. The Gnome calculator may be more familiar to the casual user.

THE GNUMERIC SPREADSHEET PROGRAM

ÉTUDE 12

Gnumeric performs one task and does it well. It is a spreadsheet program with all of the data-formatting and organizing features you'd expect in a modern spreadsheet program, including multiple paging.

It has a rich set of built-in mathematical functions, many of which are designed for business. If you have an engineering or scientific background, it has an excellent set of functions for imaginary numbers. It has goal-seeking capability and solver capabilities for linear programming. Its built-in help manual is thorough. It has a limited command language programming capability reminiscent of the one available in early Lotus. It includes tools for data analysis. Printing is thoroughly supported, and the built-in manual for printing is thorough and illustrated. Gnumeric can import StarOffice spreadsheets and can save spreadsheets in several formats, including Excel and text.

Gnumeric does not have a built-in graphing or charting capability. Speedy desktop productivity is Gnumeric's strength. For those rare occasions when you need to be a graphic designer or a seasoned slideshow presenter, you can switch over and use StarOffice, mentioned in Appendix A.

This étude assumes that you are familiar with electronic spreadsheet programs.

TOPICS COVERED IN THIS ÉTUDE

- Features of Gnumeric
- Project 1—a frequency of occurrence (Pareto analysis) spreadsheet
- Project 2—an expense report template
- Multiple worksheets

GETTING STARTED WITH GNUMERIC

In Gnome:

1. CLICK on the Gnome footprint.
   A menu opens.
2. MOVE the mouse to **Programs**.
3. MOVE the mouse to **Applications**.
   The Applications menu automatically opens.
4. CLICK **Gnumeric**.

In KDE:

1. CLICK on the stylized K.
2. MOVE the cursor to **GNOME Programs**.
3. MOVE the cursor to **Applications**.
4. CLICK **Gnumeric**.
   When Gnumeric first opens, it looks like Figure 12.1.

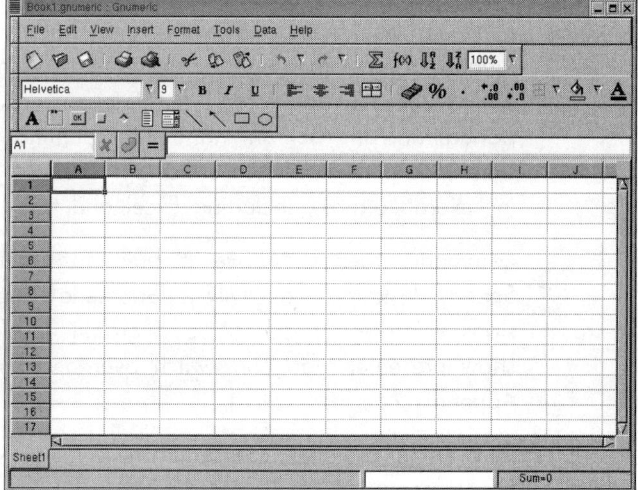

FIGURE 12.1: Gnumeric

FEATURES OF GNUMERIC

The Title Bar

This contains the name of the file and can be used to drag the window around the desktop.

The Menu Bar

This contains items for accessing menus of common operations:

- creating a new spreadsheet
- opening an existing spreadsheet
- saving a spreadsheet
- printing a spreadsheet
- printing a preview of a spreadsheet to the screen
- inserting rows, columns, and sheets
- formatting data
- sorting and filtering data

The Toolbars

The toolbars are located immediately below the menu bar. There are two toolbars. The top toolbar contains commonly used functions grouped by type. The first five icons to the left pertain to file operations. The next three icons pertain to cutting, copying, and pasting. The next two icons (they look like curving arrows) are Undo and Redo. They have drop-down boxes that list the actions you've undone and redone. The next four icons relate to common spreadsheet functions: summing, editing a function, and sorting selected cells into ascending or descending order.

The lower toolbar pertains to formatting text and numbers. The first two icons relate to font style and size. Fonts can be applied to the entire spreadsheet, a range in the spreadsheet, or a single cell. The next three icons relate to bold, italicized, and underlined text. The next four icons relate to justifying: left, right, centered, and centered across a range of cells. The next five icons relate to formatting numbers. The last two icons relate to setting the spreadsheet background color and the font color.

The Drawing Bar

A drawing bar is immediately below the toolbars. You can click on one of these items, then click in the spreadsheet and, while holding the left mouse button down, open an area where the object will be inserted. This could be used for illustration purposes within the spreadsheet, but it has no functional use in the spreadsheet at this time.

The Data Entry Area

The data entry area is the line of text boxes and buttons immediately below the drawing bar. The left-most text box is the current cell indicator. It shows the address of the current cell or shows the range of cells if a range is selected. The X, the Cancel button, deletes inserted data and reverts to any previous data in that cell. This must be pressed before the Confirm button is pressed. The downward-curving arrow is the Confirm button. It sets data in a cell.

The next two items pertain to formulas. The equal sign button is used to begin most formulas. Clicking this item inserts an equal sign into the formula box. The formula box is where a formula can be typed into a cell. This is also where a formula is edited after it has been entered into a cell.

SURVIVAL SKILLS

Here are some quick tips for carrying out simple functions. We will do a few quick exercises.

Editing Cells, Rows, and Columns

1. RIGHT-CLICK in the spreadsheet grid.
   A menu pops up. This is the fastest way to access most editing functions.
2. CLICK somewhere in the grid to close the menu.

Adding and Removing Worksheets

1. RIGHT-CLICK **Sheet1** in the lower-left corner of the spreadsheet.
   A menu pops up.
   This is the fastest way to add a sheet, rename a sheet (give it a name that is more descriptive than sheet1), or make a duplicate of a sheet.
2. CLICK **Add another sheet**.
   The tab for a second sheet appears. Clicking the tabs moves you between the sheets.
3. RIGHT-CLICK the tab **Sheet2**.
   A menu of sheet options pops up.
4. CLICK **Remove this sheet**.
   A dialog box opens asking if you really want to remove this sheet.
5. CLICK **Yes**.

Saving a Spreadsheet

1. CLICK **File**.
2. CLICK **Save As**.

3. TYPE **test** in the text box.
   Our practice file will be named **test**.
4. CLICK **OK**.

Editing Cell Contents

1. CLICK in cell A1.
   We will edit this cell.
2. CLICK in the formula box next to the equal sign button.
   In this text box, you can enter a formula to compute. If there were already a formula in this cell, you could click in the formula box to edit the contents.
   Let's put a formula in this cell to add cells B1 and C1.
3. TYPE =.
4. CLICK in cell B1.
5. TYPE +.
6. CLICK in cell C1.
7. PRESS **Enter**
8. CLICK in cell B1.
   Now that we have our formula set up in A1, let's put some data in cells B1 and C1.
9. TYPE **4**.
10. CLICK in cell C1.
11. TYPE **6**.
12. PRESS **Enter**
    Now "10" is displayed in cell A1.

THE PROJECTS

The following two projects will walk you through some frequently used spreadsheet operations. As you take the various steps of the projects, you will gain experience with different aspects of working with Gnumeric.

PROJECT 1—A FREQUENCY OF OCCURRENCE (PARETO ANALYSIS) SPREADSHEET

This is a good project to start with. It's simple, and it uses a simple but powerful command to yield a high-impact result.

In the late 1800s, the Italian economist Vilfredo Pareto did an analysis of the wealth in Italy. He discovered that 80 percent of the wealth was controlled by 20 percent of the people. This is characteristic of many human systems—20 percent dominates 80 percent. We often hear statements such as 80 percent of the problems are caused by 20 percent of the factors. That is the basis of frequency of occurrence analysis—identifying and then eliminating the few factors that are causing the majority of the problems.

The process is simple. List all of the problems. Count how often each problem occurs over a period of time or in a group of finished items. When enough data have been collected, sort them into descending order based on the number of occurrences. Starting at the top of the list and moving down, compute 80 percent of the sum of all the problem occurrences. Draw a line across the list at that point. Once the problem causes above the line, typically four or five items out of 20 or so, are eliminated, the sources of 80 percent of the number of problems will have been eliminated.

Note: You should notice that this spreadsheet uses the standard format of numbered rows and lettered columns. At the lower-left corner is a tab labeled "Sheet." We'll make use of that later when we create multiple sheets.

Entering the Data

We will enter the data in Figure 12.2 into a spreadsheet.

1. TYPE the top line of text (the title) into cell A1.
   The contents of the cell will expand across the nearby cells. Don't worry about the formatting of the data in Figure 12.2. We'll apply formatting later. For now, just enter the data.
2. TYPE today's date into cell B1.
3. TYPE **Type of Problem** in cell A4.
4. TYPE **Count** in cell D4.
5. ENTER hyphens in cell A5, as shown in Figure 12.2.
6. ENTER the problem types into column A.
   As you enter a problem type, press **Enter** to drop to the next row.
7. ENTER the problem counts into column D.
8. TYPE **Total** in cell A22.

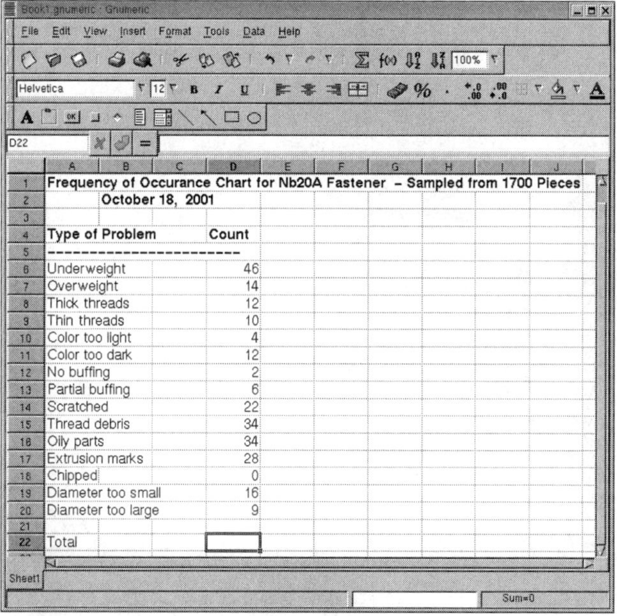

	A	D
1	Frequency of Occurance Chart for Nb20A Fastener - Sampled from 1700 Pieces	
2	October 18, 2001	
3		
4	Type of Problem	Count
5	-----------------------	
6	Underweight	46
7	Overweight	14
8	Thick threads	12
9	Thin threads	10
10	Color too light	4
11	Color too dark	12
12	No buffing	2
13	Partial buffing	6
14	Scratched	22
15	Thread debris	34
16	Oily parts	34
17	Extrusion marks	28
18	Chipped	0
19	Diameter too small	16
20	Diameter too large	9
21		
22	Total	

FIGURE 12.2: Data for the Frequency of Occurrence Spreadsheet

Formatting Text and Numbers

The font is nine-point by default. Twelve-point size would make the text more readable.

1. CLICK in cell A1.
2. DRAG down and to the right to cell D22.
3. RELEASE the mouse button.
   This produces a highlighted area, as shown in Figure 12.3.

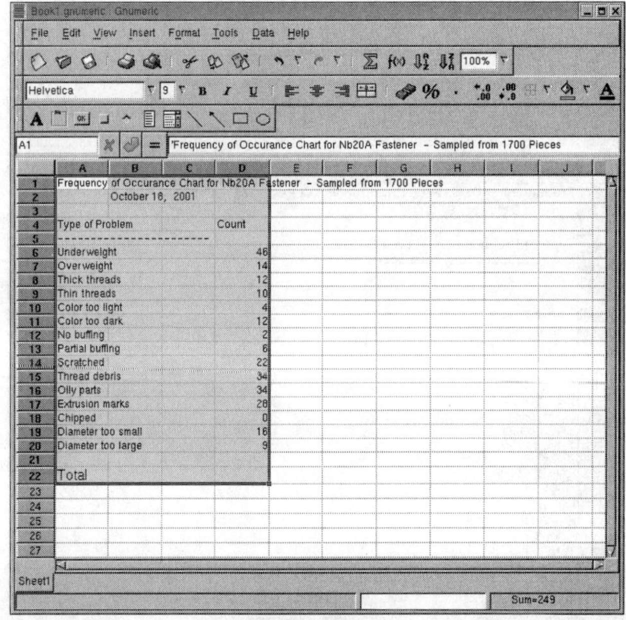

FIGURE 12.3: The Highlighted Formatting Area

4. CLICK the drop-down arrow by the font size (the small text box with a "9" in it) on the toolbar.
   A list box opens.
5. CLICK **12**.
   The font size increases.

   We would also like to make the worksheet title and column headings boldface.
6. CLICK in cell A1.
7. DRAG down and to the right to cell D5.
   This produces a highlighted area.
8. CLICK the **B** on the toolbar (near the font size box you just used).
   The text is now boldfaced.

Saving the Spreadsheet to a Disk

1. CLICK **File**.
2. CLICK **Save As**.
   A dialog box opens.
3. TYPE **proj1** into the Selection text box at the bottom of the window.
   Don't add a file extension. The computer will add one for the spreadsheet.

4. CLICK **OK**.
   The file name in the title bar of the window is is changed to reflect the file name you just entered.

Sorting the Data

Notice that the count is not sorted. We want the most frequently occurring problems at the top of the spreadsheet. We will sort the Count column into descending order. We have to move the labels with the numbers.

1. CLICK in cell A6.
2. DRAG down and to the right to cell D20.
3. RELEASE the mouse button.
   This produces a highlighted area. No titles or column headings are included. See Figure 12.4.

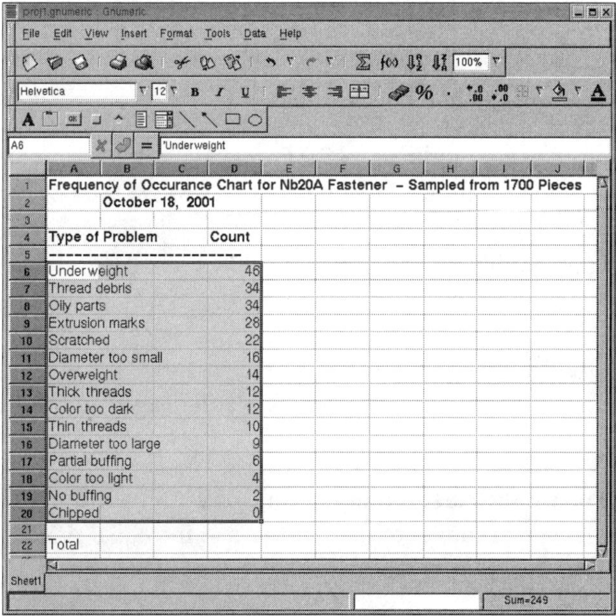

FIGURE 12.4: Sort Range

4. CLICK **Data** on the menu bar.
   A menu drops down.
5. CLICK **Sort**.
   A dialog box opens.
6. CLICK the “Sort by” drop-down arrow.
   We want to sort column D.

7. CLICK **D**.
   The letter D now appears in the Sort by box.

8. CLICK the **Descending** button.
   We want the largest values at the top. Your dialog box should now look like Figure 12.5.

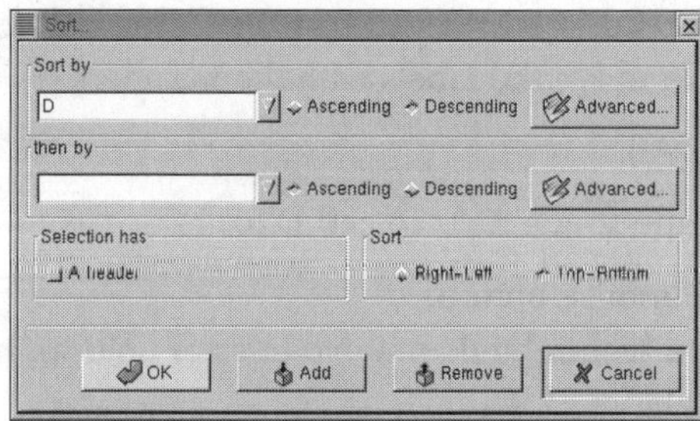

FIGURE 12.5: The Sort Dialog Box

9. CLICK **OK**.
   In an instant, the selected spreadsheet section is sorted.

Entering a Formula and Finding the 80 Percent

We must first sum the count of problem occurrences. We then multiply by 0.8.

You can quickly enter a formula to sum a list of adjacent cells. Formulas begin with a plus sign or an equal sign.

Summing a Column

1. CLICK in cell D22.
   This is where we want the formula to display its results.

2. CLICK the = button.

3. MOVE the cursor to the formula box and click.
   The cursor moves to the right end of the equal sign.

4. TYPE **sum(**.
   We are going to use the sum function to sum the many rows of data in this column.

5. CLICK in cell D6.

6. DRAG down to cell D20.

7. RELEASE the mouse button.
   This produces a selected area with a moving dashed line enclosing it. Your spreadsheet should now look like Figure 12.6.

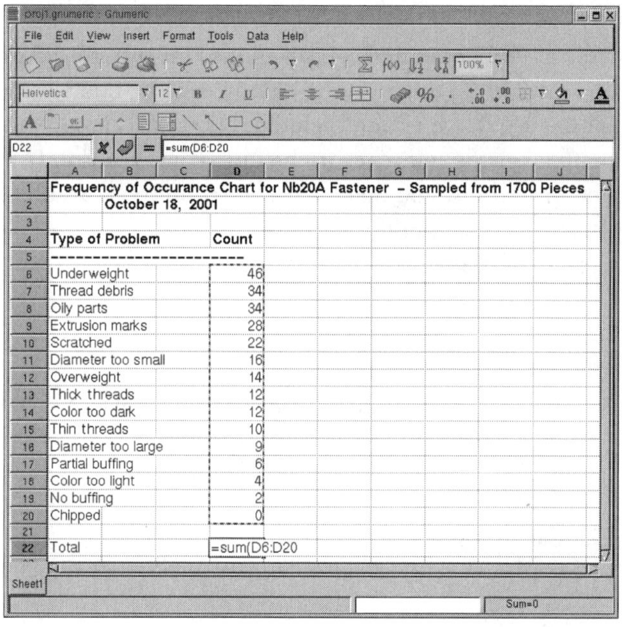

FIGURE 12.6: Sum range and formulas

8. TYPE) at the end of the formula.
9. PRESS **Enter**
   The sum appears in the cell where we entered our formula. If you clicked on cell D22, the formula you entered would be displayed in the formula box.

Computing 80 Percent of the Total (Entering Another Formula)

1. CLICK in cell F22.
2. TYPE **80 % =**.
3. CLICK in cell G22.
4. CLICK the = button.
5. CLICK in cell D22.
   D22 appears in your cell formula and in the formula box.
6. TYPE *** 0.8**.
7. PRESS **Enter**
   The answer appears in that cell.
8. CLICK in cell F22 and drag across to G22 to select the two cells.
9. CHANGE the font size to 12 point.

Identifying the Problems That Cause the 80 Percent

Now we have to sum the count until we reach a count sum of 199 or the first value greater than 199. We can do this with the computer if we make each cell sum from the first value at the top down to and including itself. We can do this by writing a sum formula that makes the reference to the top value an absolute reference. As in other spreadsheet programs, you make a row or column an absolute reference by preceding it with a dollar sign in the formula.

It's easier to do than explain.

1. CLICK in cell F7.
2. CLICK the = button.
3. MOVE the cursor to the formula box and click.
   The cursor is to the right of the equal sign.
4. TYPE **sum**(.
5. CLICK in cell D6.
6. DRAG down to D7.
7. RELEASE the mouse button.
   "D6:D7" appears in the formula box.
8. CLICK in front of the 6 in the formula box.
9. TYPE $.
   The formula now reads **=sum(D$6:D7**.
10. TYPE) at the end of the formula.
11. PRESS **Enter**
    The sum of 80 appears in cell F7.
12. LOOK closely at the black border surrounding the cell.
    Notice that the lower-right corner has a small square.
    This is the autofill handle.
13. CLICK the autofill handle and DRAG to cell F20.
    The cells automatically fill with the sums.
14. CLICK in cell F20.
    The formula in cell F20 is **sum(D$6:D20)**. The dollar sign made the reference to cell D6 absolute. But the reference to cell D7 that we saw in the formula in cell F7 was relative. The formula in cell F20 refers to cell D20, and if you looked at cell F10, you would see that it refers to cell D10.

    Your spreadsheet should now look like Figure 12.7.

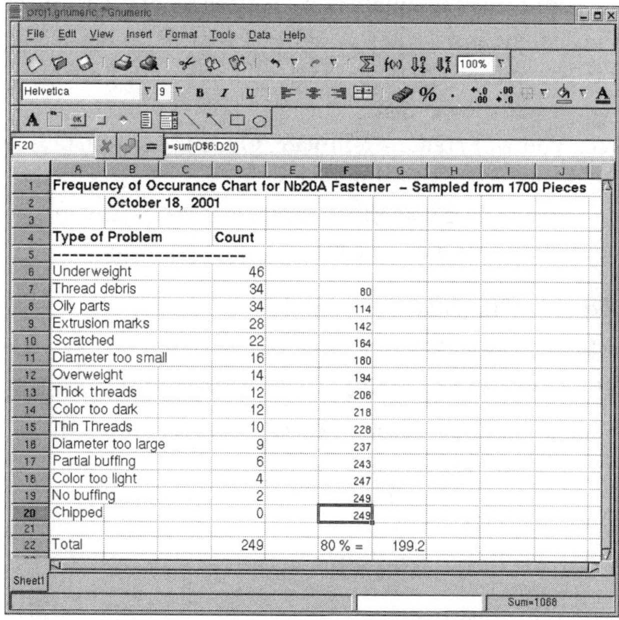

Frequency of Occurance Chart for Nb20A Fastener – Sampled from 1700 Pieces
October 18, 2001

Type of Problem	Count	
Underweight	46	
Thread debris	34	80
Oily parts	34	114
Extrusion marks	28	142
Scratched	22	164
Diameter too small	16	180
Overweight	14	194
Thick threads	12	206
Color too dark	12	218
Thin Threads	10	228
Diameter too large	9	237
Partial buffing	6	243
Color too light	4	247
No buffing	2	249
Chipped	0	249
Total	249	80 % = 199.2

FIGURE 12.7: The top 80 percent computed

We can use the number in column F to see how many of the problems we would have to deal with to solve 80 percent of the problems. We would start working down from the top.

Printing the Spreadsheet

1. CLICK **File.**
2. CLICK **Print preview.**
   This looks good enough for a working document or a report.
3. CLICK the X in the upper-right corner of the preview window.
   The preview window closes.
4. CLICK **File.**
5. CLICK **Print.**
   A dialog box opens.
6. CLICK the button labeled **Printer.**
   If you don't click this, the spreadsheet will be printed to a file.
7. CLICK **Print.**

PROJECT 2—AN EXPENSE REPORT TEMPLATE

Typically, when a company sends you on a trip, you record your expenses and, when you return, you submit an expense report so you can be reimbursed. Years ago, I created a spreadsheet template that matches all of the items on the company expense form I usually have to fill out. When I return, I open the template, fill in some numbers, save it with a new name, fill in the numbers on the company form, and move on to the next task.

In this project, you will create a template. Once the template is saved, you will open the template, fill it in, and print a copy.

This project demonstrates using the autofill feature to fill with common strings, such as days of the week, and demonstrates copying formulas.

Creating an Expense Spreadsheet Template

First, open the program and get your template started.

1. If you don't already have a new spreadsheet open, CLICK the New button on the toolbar to create a new spreadsheet.
2. CLICK cell C4.
3. TYPE **Sunday**.
4. CLICK the autofill handle.
5. DRAG across to cell I4.
   The names of each day of the week appear in sequence. This also works for months and for numbered strings such as Test 1, Test 2, Test 3, and so on.
   Now we'll change the cell widths.
6. CLICK cell A1.
7. DRAG across to cell I1.
   The cells appear highlighted. You've selected them.
8. CLICK **Format** on the menu bar.
   A menu drops down.
9. MOVE the cursor to **Column**.
10. CLICK **Width**.
    A dialog box opens.
11. ENTER **80** in the text box.
12. PRESS **Enter**
    The width of the columns increases to 80 points.
    Now we will enter the remaining labels.
13. COPY the remaining labels from Figure 12.8.
    Ignore the formatting; we'll make those changes later.

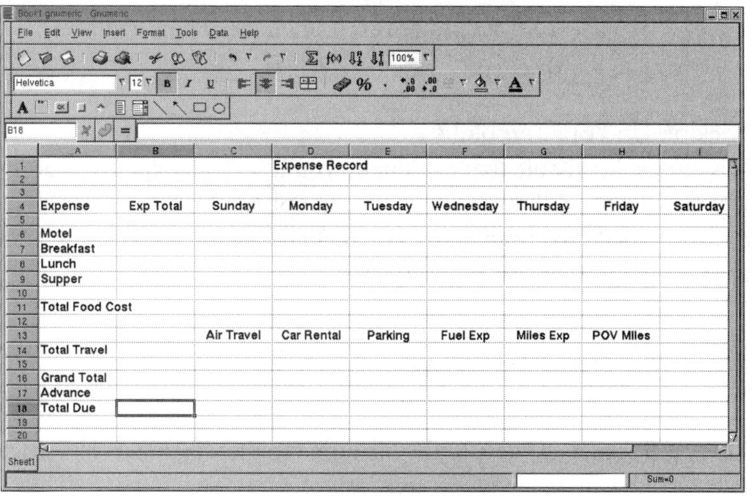

FIGURE 12.8: Expense Template Labels

Changing Font Size and Boldfacing

1. DRAG across from cell A1 to cell I1.
   The cells are highlighted. You've selected them.
2. CLICK **B** (for boldfaced) on the toolbar.
3. CLICK the font size drop-down arrow.
4. CLICK **12**.

Changing Justification

We want the items in column A to be left-justified. Since left-justification is the default, we can leave those columns the way they are. We want the title, the column headings, and the data values centered.

1. CLICK in cell B4.
2. DRAG down to the right to cell I18.
   The cells are highlighted. You've selected them.
3. CLICK the center-justification button on the toolbar. It is in the middle of the formatting toolbar.
   You have now completed entering the labels and formatting for your template.

Saving Your Template

1. CLICK **File**.
2. CLICK **Save As**.
   A dialog box opens.

3. ENTER **ExpenseTemp** in the Selection text box.
4. CLICK **OK**.

Backing Up Your Template

It is almost inevitable that eventually you'll save an expense report without changing the name and thus wipe out your template. But if you have a backup copy of the template, you can then open that and save it with the template name. The template would thus be painlessly restored.

1. CLICK **File**.
2. CLICK **Save As**.
   A dialog box opens.
3. ADD **BAK** to the file name so that it appears as **ExpenseTempBAK** in the Selection text box.
4. CLICK **OK**.

Adding and Using Formulas

It turns out that with a little thought we can also add the formulas to this template. In some templates you can't, such as those where you have to count the cells that actually contain data (as opposed to those that were left blank but don't affect calculations since they have an arithmetic value of zero).

We need formulas that sum across the columns that will total the expenses of the motel, meals, and travel. We also need three formulas that sum down a row. These will compute the total food expense, the grand total of all expenses, and the total due to us beyond our advance. This looks like a lot of work, but by using the sum function and dragging across the range to sum, the work is vastly reduced.

Inserting the Formulas

1. CLICK in cell B6.
2. CLICK the = button.
3. CLICK in the formula box.
4. TYPE **sum(**.
5. CLICK in cell C6.
6. DRAG across to cell I6.
7. TYPE).
8. PRESS **Enter**

Copying that Formula to the Following Three Cells

Since the next three rows are summed the same way, you can copy the summing formula you just entered. This is done using the autofill handle on the lower right corner of the black outline surrounding the selected cell.

1. CLICK in cell B6.
   This cell contains the formula you just entered and is what we want to copy.
2. CLICK the autofill handle in the lower-right corner of the box around the cell.
   The cursor changes to a cross-hair symbol.
3. DRAG down to cell B9.
4. RELEASE the mouse button.
   A relative copy of the formula is made to each of the following cells. The range is selected and is filled with zeros.

Computing the Daily Food Cost

The last set of computations was done across rows. The next set of computations is going to be done across columns.

1. CLICK in cell B11.
2. CLICK the = button.
3. TYPE **sum**(in the formula box.
4. CLICK in cell B7.
5. DRAG down to cell B9.
6. TYPE).
7. PRESS **Enter**

Copying the Meal Total Cost Formula to Each Day

We've just created a formula that sums the total for all breakfasts, lunches, and dinners. We can use this same formula to compute a total cost for each day. We'll use a relative copy of the same formula for Sunday through Saturday.

1. CLICK in cell B11.
   It contains the formula you just entered.
2. CLICK on the autofill handle.
3. DRAG across to cell I11.
4. RELEASE the mouse button.
   A relative copy of the formula is made to each of the following cells.

Computing the Travel Total

This will be another sum across a single row.

1. CLICK in cell B14.
2. CLICK the = button.
3. TYPE **sum(** in the formula box.
4. CLICK in cell C14.
5. DRAG across to cell G14.
6. TYPE).
7. PRESS **Enter**

Computing the Grand Total

The grand total is the sum of three items: the motel total cost, the total of the daily food cost, and the travel total. These have to be summed individually since they are not in adjacent cells.

1. CLICK in cell B16.
2. CLICK the = button.
   The sum function is not used. Don't type "sum."
3. CLICK cell B6 (the motel total expense).
4. TYPE a plus sign (+).
5. CLICK in cell B11 (the food totals).
6. TYPE +.
7. CLICK in cell B14 (the total travel).
8. PRESS **Enter**

Inserting a Formula Using a Constant for Mileage Allowance

The formula for Miles Expense is POV Miles x Mileage Allowance. The mileage allowance is typically in the range of $0.31 per mile. However, this changes as the IRS changes the amount it will allow. We need a place to put the $0.31 so it is visible and is easily changed on the spreadsheet. If it is embedded in a formula, it will most likely be overlooked when it is time to change it.

1. CLICK in cell H16.
2. TYPE **Mil Allowance**.
3. PRESS **Enter**
   Your cursor drops down to cell H17.
4. TYPE **0.31**.

5. PRESS **Enter**
   The formula is Miles Expense = POV Miles x Mileage Allowance. POV Miles is in cell H14, and Mileage Allowance is in cell H17.
6. CLICK in cell G14.
7. CLICK the = button.
8. CLICK in cell H14.
9. TYPE *.
10. CLICK in cell H17.
11. PRESS **Enter**

Computing the Total Due

The total due is the difference between the grand total and the amount of the advance. A simple two-cell subtraction is used.

1. CLICK in cell B18 (Total Due).
2. CLICK the = button.
3. CLICK in cell B16 (Grand Total).
4. TYPE a minus sign (-).
5. CLICK in cell B17 (Advance).
6. PRESS **Enter**

Formatting the Cells for Dollars and Cents

We're going to take advantage of the fact that a dollars and cents format does not have any effect on cells containing labels (it won't put a $ sign on a label such as a column heading).

1. CLICK in cell B6.
2. DRAG to cell I18.
3. RELEASE the mouse button.
4. CLICK the money bundle icon on the toolbar. This is the currency formatting icon.
   All the cells that previously had zeros changed to $ -.
   When you type an amount in a cell, it will automatically be formatted with a dollar sign and two decimal digits.

Removing the Dollars and Cents Formatting from the POV Miles Cells

The cell that contains the POV Miles, cell H14, should not have dollars and cents formatting. We'll reformat that cell to contain a value with zero decimal digits.

1. CLICK in cell H14.

2. CLICK **Format** on the menu bar.
   A menu drops down.
3. CLICK **Cells**.
   A dialog box opens. It should look similar to Figure 12.9.

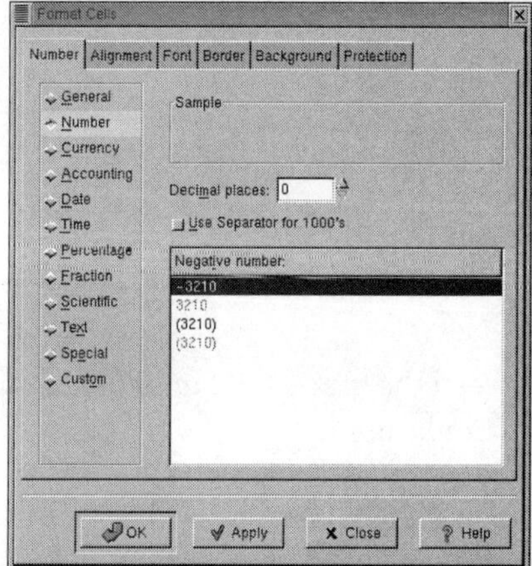

FIGURE 12.9: The Format Cells dialog box

4. CLICK on the **Number** tab.
5. CLICK on the down arrow by "Decimal places" until the number of decimal places is 0.
6. CLICK **Apply**.
7. CLICK **OK**.
   The template is complete. Your spreadsheet should look like Figure 12.10.

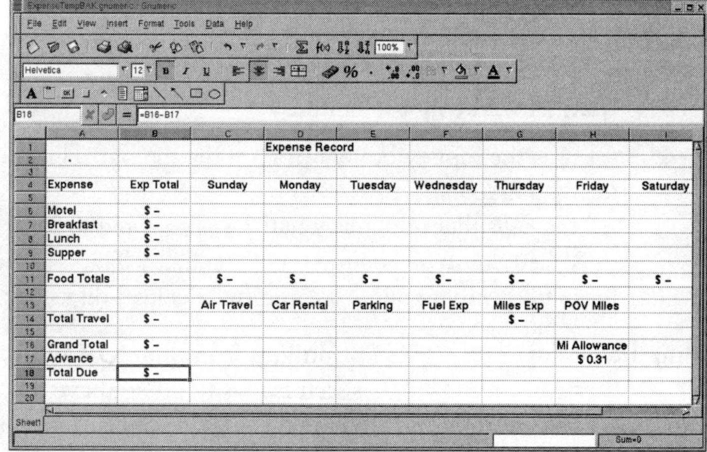

FIGURE 12.10: Completed template

It's time to save the completed template.

8. CLICK **File**.
9. CLICK **Save As**.
10. ENTER **ExpenseTemp** in the Selection text box.
11. CLICK **OK**.
    A dialog box opens and tells you you're about to overwrite your previous copy of this template.
12. CLICK **Yes**.
13. SAVE a backup copy as **ExpenseTempBAK**.

Testing by Entering Data and Inserting Title and Date

Now you need to test your template's validity by entering data and observing the results.

1. OPEN a copy of your template.
2. Immediately SAVE it as **ExpenseTest1**.

Inserting a Title and Date

First we'll insert a title.

1. CLICK in cell D2.
2. TYPE **Fixture Convention**.
   Now we'll insert a date.
3. CLICK in cell D3.
4. CLICK **Insert** on the menu bar.
   A menu drops down.
5. MOVE the cursor to **Special**.
   A submenu opens.
6. CLICK on **Current date**.

Entering the Expense Data

1. ENTER the data shown in Figure 12.11.

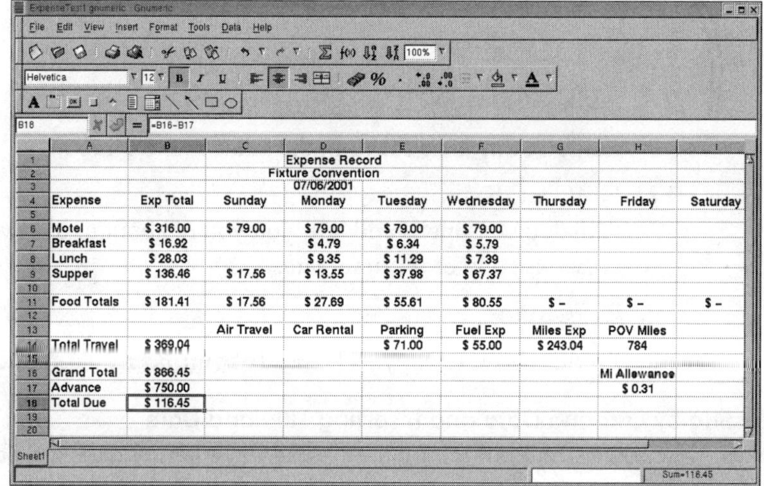

	A	B	C	D	E	F	G	H	I
1				Expense Record					
2				Fixture Convention					
3				07/06/2001					
4	Expense	Exp Total	Sunday	Monday	Tuesday	Wednesday	Thursday	Friday	Saturday
5									
6	Motel	$ 316.00	$ 79.00	$ 79.00	$ 79.00	$ 79.00			
7	Breakfast	$ 16.92		$ 4.79	$ 6.34	$ 5.79			
8	Lunch	$ 28.03		$ 9.35	$ 11.29	$ 7.39			
9	Supper	$ 136.46	$ 17.56	$ 13.55	$ 37.98	$ 67.37			
10									
11	Food Totals	$ 181.41	$ 17.56	$ 27.69	$ 55.61	$ 80.55	$ -	$ -	$ -
12									
13			Air Travel	Car Rental	Parking	Fuel Exp	Miles Exp	POV Miles	
14	Total Travel	$ 369.04			$ 71.00	$ 55.00	$ 243.04	784	
15									
16	Grand Total	$ 866.45						Mi Allowance	
17	Advance	$ 750.00						$ 0.31	
18	Total Due	$ 116.45							

FIGURE 12.11: Expense Data

Do not enter dollar signs. The computer will put them in. Do not enter any data in cells that in Figure 12.11 contain $ -. Those cells contain a formula that will compute the values from the data entered. Make sure that a cell in the template does not contain a formula before you copy a number into it. If a cell contains a formula, wait for it to compute the value itself.

If you have entered the formulas correctly, and if you use the same numbers as in Figure 12.11, your totals should equal the totals in Figure 12.11.

2. SAVE the spreadsheet again.

Making a Landscape Printout

This spreadsheet is best printed if we instruct the computer to turn the sheet of paper sideways and print horizontally across it. This is called a landscape orientation.

1. CLICK **File** on the menu bar.
2. CLICK **Print Setup**.
   The Print setup dialog box opens.
3. CLICK the **Landscape** button in the Orientation area.
4. CLICK the **Print preview** button at the bottom of the dialog box.
   It looks fine.
5. CLOSE the preview window.
6. CLICK on the printer icon on the toolbar.

7. CLICK **Print** in the dialog box.
   Your spreadsheet prints.

MULTIPLE WORKSHEETS

Multiple worksheets can help organize projects. Additional sheets can store additional computations, or they can simply store notes.

The IRS likes to have a list of the names of guests when we claim charges for meals and entertainment as business expenses on our taxes. This information would clutter the first worksheet. It would be better added in a second worksheet.

ADDING A SECOND WORKSHEET AND RENAMING WORKSHEETS

We're assuming that you're coming back to this project after a while. So we will start the program again and open our expense spreadsheet.

1. OPEN Gnumeric.
2. CLICK the open-folder icon on the toolbar.
   A dialog box opens similar to the one shown in Figure 12.12.

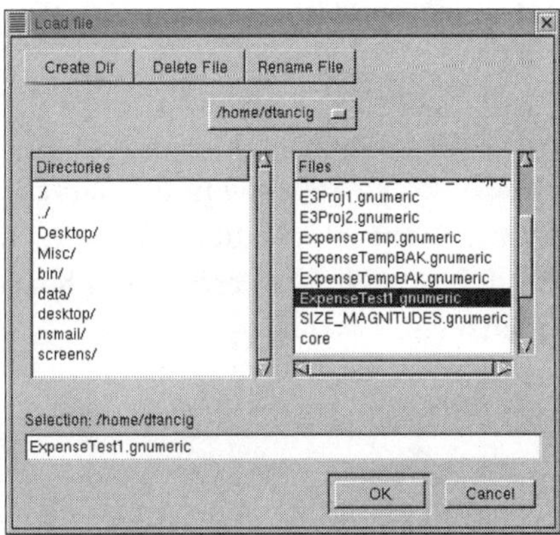

FIGURE 12.12: The Load file dialog box

3. SCROLL until ExpenseTest1 comes into view.
4. CLICK **ExpenseTest1**.
   This file name is now displayed in the Selection box at the bottom of the dialog window.
5. CLICK **OK**.
6. Click the full-screen button in the upper-right corner of the window to increase its size so that all the values are displayed.

ADDING A SECOND WORKSHEET

Look at the lower-left corner of the spreadsheet. You should see a tab labeled Sheet1.

1. RIGHT-CLICK the **Sheet1** tab.
   A menu pops up.
2. CLICK **Add another sheet**.
   A tab marked Sheet2 appears.
3. RIGHT-CLICK the **Sheet2** tab.
   A menu pops up.
4. CLICK **Rename this sheet**.
   A dialog box opens.
5. TYPE **Guest Expenses** in the text box.
6. CLICK **OK**.
7. RIGHT-CLICK the **Sheet1** tab.
8. CLICK **Rename this sheet**.
   A dialog box appears.
9. TYPE **Expense Data** in the text box.
10. CLICK **OK**.
11. CLICK the **Guest Expenses** tab.
    The spreadsheet is ready for you to type in the names of your guests and any other pertinent information. We won't do that in this exercise. We just wanted to see how to create another worksheet within the same spreadsheet.

SUMMARY

Gnumeric is a spreadsheet program with all of the data-formatting and organizing features you'd expect of a modern spreadsheet, including multiple paging. It has a rich set of built-in mathematical functions, many of which are designed for business. It has a thorough built-in help manual that also shows you the basics of using the solver functions with illustrated examples. It can save spreadsheets in Excel 5.0/95 format (and even Excel 2000 can read that format), and Gnumeric can import StarOffice spreadsheets and can save spreadsheets in several formats.

KSNAPSHOT: AN EASY-TO-USE SCREEN CAPTURE PROGRAM

ÉTUDE 13

It is common to need to explain how to do something on a computer. This is difficult if the person you are explaining the procedure to doesn't have a computer to look at. You quickly wish you had a few pictures of the different computer screens to aid your explanation. These pictures are called screen captures, and they are easy to make with KSnapshot.

The KSnapshot window looks like Figure 13.1.

FIGURE 13.1: The KSnapshot window

KSnapshot offers a wide range of screen-capture options. It can capture a specific window rather than the entire desktop. It can also capture only a drop-down menu, if you wish. KSnapshot file save has a feature to easily access the directory where your other graphics are stored. Assigning an image to a directory takes only a few mouse clicks. KSnapshot also has a thorough manual built into the help section.

In this étude, you will walk through the process of making a screen capture, capturing a pop-up menu, saving your images, and opening your image files for viewing in The GIMP, the image manipulator program. In addition, you will use The GIMP to convert your image from one file format to another.

TOPICS COVERED IN THIS ÉTUDE

- The elements of KSnapshot
- Making a screen capture
- Saving a screen capture
- Capturing a pop-up menu
- Changing the image file format

GETTING STARTED

OPENING KSNAPSHOT

In KDE:

1. CLICK on the stylized K.
2. MOVE the mouse to **Graphics**.
   A submenu opens.
3. CLICK **Screen Capture**.

In Gnome:

1. CLICK on the Gnome footprint.
2. MOVE the mouse to **KDE menus**.
   A submenu opens.
3. MOVE the mouse to **Graphics**.
   The Graphics submenu opens.
4. CLICK **Screen Capture**.
   The screen-capture utility appears.

Sometimes, KDE programs are not properly linked to the KDE menus in Gnome. The following is an easy way to make KSnapshot readily available on your desktop.

Most programs that a user runs are located in the /usr/bin directory. We are going to put KSnapshot on the desktop (not the panel).

We'll have to tell the activation program (the launcher) to look in the /usr/bin folder for the KSnapshot program.

Adding KSnapshot to the Gnome Desktop

1. RIGHT-CLICK anywhere on the desktop area (not the panel).
   A menu opens, highlighting New. The New menu is also open.
2. CLICK **Launcher**.
   A dialog box opens.
3. TYPE **KSnapshot** in the Name text box.
4. TYPE **Screen Capture Utility** in the Comment text box.
5. TYPE **/usr/bin/ksnapshot** in the Command text box.
   Note that ksnapshot is all lower case in the Command box.
6. CLICK the drop-down arrow to the right of the Type text box.
   A list of choices appears.
7. CLICK **Application**.
8. CLICK the **No Icon** button.
   After a few moments, a large list of icons you may use is displayed.
9. SCROLL down about 14 rows of icons.
   Gnome-deskguide.png image comes into view. We'll use that.
10. CLICK the **gnome-deskguide.png** icon.
    Its name is highlighted.
11. CLICK **OK**.
    The image now appears on the Icon button. At this point, your dialog window should be filled in as shown in Figure 13.2.

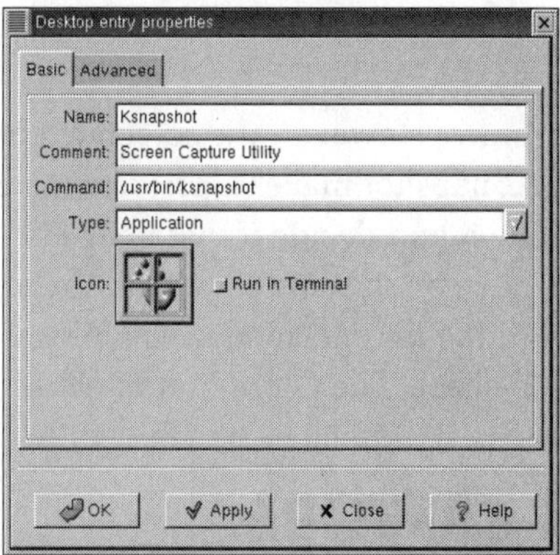

FIGURE 13.2: The completed launcher window

12. CLICK **Apply**.

The icon for KSnapshot appears on your desktop.

13. CLICK **OK**.

14. DOUBLE-CLICK the **KSnapshot** icon.
KSnapshot opens. The KSnapshot screen appears on your screen.

THE ELEMENTS OF KSNAPSHOT

The top bar is the title bar. By clicking on this, you can drag the KSnapshot window to any location so you can look at the window you want to capture.

The capture control panel occupies the upper two-thirds of the KSnapshot window. It contains three items:

- the captured image in a preview window
- the Grab button
- the Save button

The Filename text box is where you can type the name of the image you've captured and want to save. The Open file icon transports you to your file directory where you can select the folder where you want the image stored. You'll type the file name into a text box while you're selecting a folder. You won't often type anything into the Filename box to the left of this button.

Delay dictates the amount of time that elapses between the time you press the Grab button and when KSnapshot makes an image of the screen. For best results, use two or three seconds. This gives you time to position the mouse on the window that you want captured. The delay also gives you time to open a menu and capture only that menu. With delay in use, you do not have to click the image you want to capture. Simply position the cursor and wait until the KSnapshot window reappears with your captured image.

BUTTONS

The Grab button creates a screen capture. However, the screen capture is not automatically saved to a disk. First, KSnapshot makes a preview image of the screen capture. Then you can examine it and decide if that image is what you want to save or if you need to make adjustments and recapture the image.

The Save button saves the image to the file specified in the Filename text box. The Help button accesses a brief help sheet. The Close button closes KSnapshot.

MAKING A SCREEN CAPTURE

The process is to click the Grab button, position the cursor on the window you want captured, and wait until KSnapshot reappears. You don't click the image you want captured.

In this exercise, we're going to make a screen capture of a file manager. To do this, we need to open a file manager window. As you may be aware, Linux has two graphical file managers that correspond to the two desktop environments. One is Gnome Midnight Commander, and the other is the KDE file manager, called Konqueror. If you need help working with either of these file managers, look at Études 3 and 4.

PREPARATION

1. OPEN a file manager window.
2. OPEN KSnapshot.
   Now we'll create a folder for your screen captures in your personal home folder.
3. In KSnapshot, CLICK the open file icon to the right of the Filename text box.
4. CLICK the Home directory icon (the house) in the dialog box.
5. RIGHT-CLICK anywhere in the blank area in the contents window.
   A menu pops up.
6. CLICK **New Directory**.
7. TYPE **Screens**, the name of your new screen capture folder.
8. CLICK **OK**.
   You now have a Screens folder. You are moved to the Screens folder.
9. CLICK in the Location text box.
10. TYPE **testimage1.png**.
11. CLICK **OK**.
    You are returned to the KSnapshot window.
12. CLICK the arrows by "Delay" until the delay is set at three seconds.
13. CLICK the check box labeled "Only grab the window containing the pointer" to put a X in it, if it does not already have an X.
    This is a toggle. Click the box, and the X appears. Click it again, and the X disappears. Click a third time, and the X appears again.

MAKING THE SCREEN CAPTURE

1. CLICK **Grab**.
   The KSnapshot window disappears.
2. Quickly MOVE the pointer to the file manager image (just move the pointer—don't click on anything).

After three seconds, the KSnapshot window reappears. In the preview window is an image of what KSnapshot captured. It should look similar to Figure 13.3.

FIGURE 13.3: A screen capture

This image has not been saved. It is stored in memory. If you don't like the image, you can continue to click Grab as many times as needed until the preview window contains the image you need.

SAVING THE SCREEN CAPTURE

To save the image, click on the Save button. The image will be saved as testimage2.png in your Screens folder.

1. CLICK **Save**.
   Clicking Save incremented the file name to **testimage2.png**. This is done automatically so you don't accidentally overwrite your previously saved image. This click of Save just incremented the file name; it didn't complete the saving process.
2. CLICK **Save** again to save the image.
3. CLICK the **Close** button to close KSnapshot.
   You now have a screen capture of your file manager window.

CAPTURING A POP-UP MENU

When working with many programs and with the desktop, you can right-click to bring up pop-up menus that offer you additional choices. Sometimes you may want a screen capture of one of these menus. But as soon as you click the cursor in the KSnapshot window to bring it into the foreground so you can click the Grab button, the pop-up menu disappears. How do you capture a pop-up menu?

The solution is based on the delay time and the fact that you do not click the cursor in the window you want to capture. You simply position the cursor in the window.

We will use KSnapshot to capture one of its own pop-up menus in this exercise.

1. OPEN two copies of KSnapshot.
2. MOVE the second copy to the left so you can see both windows.
3. In this second KSnapshot window, CLICK the up arrow by "Delay" twice to increase the delay to five seconds.
   We need this extra time because we will have to open all the menus once we click Grab to capture the pop-up menu.
4. CLICK the open file icon.
   Here, we're going to practice bringing up the menu that we want to get a screen capture of.
5. RIGHT-CLICK in the screen that opened.
   A menu pops up.
6. MOVE the cursor to **Sorting**.
   A submenu appears.
7. MOVE the cursor to **By Name**.
   That item in the list becomes a lighter gray. This is what we will get a screen capture of.
8. CLICK the first KSnapshot window.
   This is the one we'll make the screen capture with. Notice that the menus disappeared.
9. CLICK **Grab**.
10. RIGHT-CLICK in the same contents window of the other KSnapshot that you did during practice.
11. MOVE the cursor to **Sorting**.
12. MOVE the cursor to **By Name**.
    Wait until the first KSnapshot reappears with its screen capture. Your KSnapshot window should then look similar to Figure 13.4. If you weren't able to get that menu to pop up in time, go back to the first KSnapshot window and increase the delay time.

FIGURE 13.4: KSnapshot capturing a pop-up menu

If you were able to capture the screen you wanted, you could save the file and then have it available to use. The screen capture itself would look like Figure 13.5.

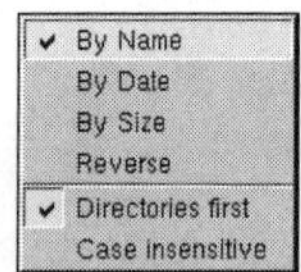

FIGURE 13.5: The captured pop-up menu

CHANGING THE IMAGE FILE FORMAT

Frequently, you will have an image but not in the file format needed by another program or someone else. KSnapshot saves all images as type png. We will import an image into the GIMP program and instruct GIMP to resave it with a different file format. The process is simple and quick.

We are going to use the Gnome image program called The GIMP—yes, that's its actual name. "The GIMP" stands for "The GNU Image Manipulation Program." It's an image manipulation program that rivals commercial products but comes installed with all distributions of Linux.

In this exercise, we will convert testimage1 from .png to .tiff. This is a common conversion. (Use .tiff sparingly; .tiff files are huge and a single image can easily exceed the capacity of a 3½-inch, 1.44-MB floppy disk.)

OPENING THE GIMP

In Gnome:

1. CLICK on the Gnome footprint.
2. CLICK on **Programs**.
3. MOVE the mouse to **Graphics**.

4. CLICK **The GIMP**.
   The GIMP opens. In recent versions of The GIMP, four windows open, all on top of each other. Only one has the title "The GIMP." It looks like Figure 13.6.

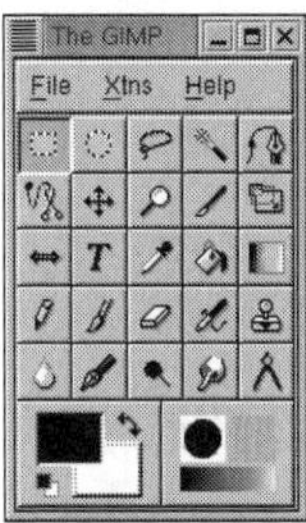

FIGURE 13.6: The GIMP main window

   Move the other windows out of the way until you find one that matches Figure 13.6.

In KDE:

1. CLICK on the stylized K.
2. POINT to **GNOME Programs**.
3. POINT to **Graphics**.
4. CLICK **The GIMP**.
   Sometimes Gnome programs are not properly linked to the GNOME Programs menu in KDE. The following is an easy way to make The GIMP readily available on your desktop if it isn't accessible on the main menu.
   Most programs that a user runs are located in the /usr/bin directory. We are going to put The GIMP on the desktop. We'll have to tell the activation program (the launcher) to look in the /usr/bin folder for the program.

Adding The GIMP to the KDE Desktop

1. RIGHT-CLICK on the desktop.
   A menu pops up.
2. CLICK **Create New**.
   A submenu opens.
3. CLICK **Link To Application**.
   A dialog box opens.
4. CLICK the icon button in the General tab.
   A window full of icons is displayed.

5. CLICK the **gimp** icon.
6. REPLACE "Link To Application" in the text box with **GIMP**.
7. CLICK the **Execute** tab.
8. TYPE **/usr/bin/gimp** in the Command box.
9. CLICK the **Application** tab.
10. TYPE **GIMP** in the Name box.
11. TYPE **Graphics Program** in the Comment box.
12. CLICK **Application** in the list box on the right.
13. CLICK the double arrows pointing to the left to move "Application" over to the left list box.
14. CLICK **OK**.
    Now you have The GIMP accessible from the desktop.
15. CLICK the **GIMP** icon on the desktop.
    The GIMP opens. In recent versions of The GIMP, four windows open, all on top of each other. Only one has the title "The GIMP." It looks like Figure 13.6. Move the other windows out of the way until you find one that matches Figure 13.6.

OPENING YOUR SCREEN CAPTURE IMAGE IN THE GIMP

1. CLICK **File** on The GIMP's menu bar.
2. CLICK **Open**.
   The Load Image dialog box opens.
3. DOUBLE-CLICK **Screens** in the Directories box.
4. CLICK **testimage1.png**.
   The file name appears in the Selection text box at the bottom of the dialog box.
5. CLICK **OK**.
   The image appears.

SAVING YOUR IMAGE IN THE GIMP WITH A DIFFERENT FILE FORMAT

1. RIGHT-CLICK the image that just appeared.
   A menu pops up.
2. MOVE the cursor to **File**.
   A submenu opens.

3. CLICK **Save As**.
   The Save Image dialog box opens.
4. DOUBLE-CLICK **Screens** in the Directories window if you aren't already in the Screens folder.
5. CLICK **testimage1.png** if that doesn't already appear in the Selection text box.
6. CLICK the **By Extension** button.
   A menu pops up, displaying image file types.
7. CLICK **Tiff**.
   The Determine File Type bar is now labeled "Tiff." In the Selection box, the file name extension has been changed to .tiff from .png.
8. CLICK **OK**.
   Another dialog box opens. You are asked if you want to use any file compression methods on the file. "None" is the default. We'll accept None.
9. CLICK **OK**.
   The image file has now been converted and saved as the desired file type.

SUMMARY

Screen captures are easy to make with KSnapshot. It can capture a specific window or the entire desktop. It can even capture only a drop-down menu. KSnapshot has a thorough manual built into the help section.

In this étude, you made screen captures, saved your images, and opened your image files in The GIMP. You also used The GIMP to convert your image from one file format to another. With these two programs, you can meet all of your screen-capture needs.

YABASIC

ÉTUDE 14

For the past 15 years, I've visited a few hundred small businesses throughout the United States and Canada. Until about 1996, about two thirds of the owners would take me aside and show me one or more Basic programs they'd written that solved some unique problem and gave them a market advantage. If you are using Windows 95, 98, or 2000, you won't find Basic. That omission takes away an accessible and easily used tool. Yabasic returns that tool. Since Linux has no commercial driving force, you won't find pressure to discontinue this tool or to brand you or it as being "legacy."

Basic gets a lot of bad press, but it is the people's programming language. That's what it has going for it. It's easy to learn and use and, kept within its limits, can be a very productive tool. Yes, it is interpreted (but so are Perl, Python, and the shell interpreters in Linux). No, it is not structured, and it certainly isn't object-oriented. Those are important features if you're writing commercial software. Most people aren't writing commercial software. They simply want to write 6 to 20 lines of code to quickly check a range of values, compute something related to their business, or to see if they can learn to program and make the computer do what they want it to do.

With Basic, all of the programming and compiling overhead of newer languages is eliminated. Basic is the land of write some code, run it, get quick feedback, and rapidly create a set of custom programs to aid your business, personal life, or recreational pursuits.

Yabasic is easy to download and install. It has an excellent built-in help manual with programming examples and is viewed using your Web browser. With a couple more easy steps, Yabasic programs can be created that run when you type their file name, as though they were compiled, executable programs–but they are not.

TOPICS COVERED IN THIS ÉTUDE

- The built-in help manual
- A programming example
- Making the file executable

GETTING STARTED

DOWNLOADING YABASIC

1. Start your Web browser.
2. TYPE the URL **http://www.yabasic.de**.
3. PRESS **Enter**
4. CLICK **Download**.
5. FOLLOW the instructions to download the program. If you have trouble, download from the alternative Source Forge site presented at the Yabasic Web site. What you want is the latest RPM version. The file is only about 180 kilobytes and downloads quickly.

INSTALLING YABASIC

When I download software, if it is small enough, I download it to a floppy disk. I'm going to assume that's what you have done. If you downloaded it to a subdirectory named, for example, download, modify the following instructions to make that your working directory.

1. LOG IN as root.
2. RIGHT-CLICK the floppy disk icon.
3. CLICK the **Mount** command.

4. CLICK the terminal emulator icon (it looks like a computer monitor).
   The terminal emulator window opens. We will make the floppy our working directory.
5. TYPE **cd /mnt/floppy** Enter
6. TYPE **rpm –i yabasic-2.69-6.i386.rpm.**
   This line will change. You can get guidance on how to install the program from the Web site. The "yabasic" part is the name of the file on your floppy disk or in your download directory. Your terminal emulator window should look similar to Figure 14.1.

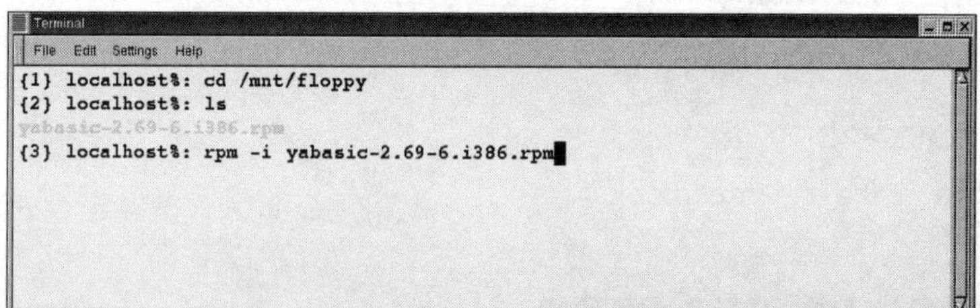

FIGURE 14.1: RPM command for Yabasic

7. PRESS Enter
   Your floppy disk is read. After a few seconds, the command prompt returns in the terminal emulator window.
   Note: The executable file is yabasic. It is in the /usr/bin subdirectory. All you need do is type **yabasic** from the command line to start it. This is available to you as a user. The installation is complete.
8. LOG OUT as root.
9. LOG IN as a user.

THE BUILT-IN HELP MANUAL

Yabasic is not a graphical user interface program but must be run, or invoked, from the command line. This can be frustrating unless you have a document to guide you. The help manual can be viewed using your Web browser.

1. START your Web browser.
   We use Konqueror, but the instructions are the same for any Web browser.
2. TYPE **file://usr/doc/yabasic/yabasic.htm** in the Location box.
3. PRESS Enter
   The Yabasic help manual appears.

4. CLICK **A simple program with input and print** in the middle box labeled "Yabasic by examples."
   The example is displayed. It should look like Figure 14.2.

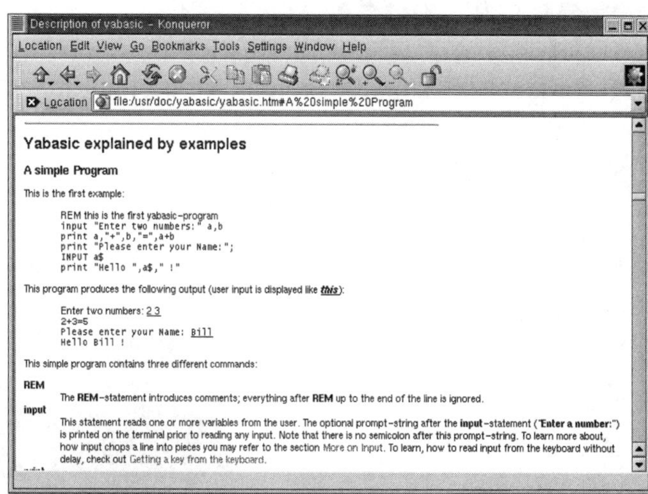

FIGURE 14.2: A built-in help example

5. CLICK the X in the upper-right corner of the Web browser to close the program.

PROGRAMMING USING YABASIC

At least three ways exist to program using Yabasic.

- You can type **yabasic** on the command line. Yabasic will start, and you can then enter your code. When you press **Enter** twice, the program runs the code you entered. The problem is that the code is lost after running; you are just returned to the terminal emulator command line.
- You can type your Yabasic code into a file using a text editor and, on the command line, type **yabasic *file-name***. When you press **Enter**, the code in the file is run. If the editor is in one window, the terminal emulator is in another, and you can use the history key (the up-arrow key) to repeat a command on the command line. This is a rapid way to develop a program.
- You can type your Yabasic code into a file using a text editor and include a line to invoke Yabasic to run the code in the file. You must also make the file executable and be sure the directory with your Yabasic program is on the path. Then all you need to do is type the name of the file on the command line (without **yabasic**). When you press **Enter**, the program runs. This is a useful way to run a program once it has been developed.

This part of the étude will focus on the second method. After the program has been developed, we will set up the third method.

WRITING A YABASIC PROGRAM

We will open a KEdit session and a terminal emulator session. We will begin by walking through the steps with a simple example. Then a more useful program will be tried.

1. START KEdit.
2. CLICK the terminal emulator icon.
3. RESIZE and ARRANGE the windows so they look like Figure 14.3.

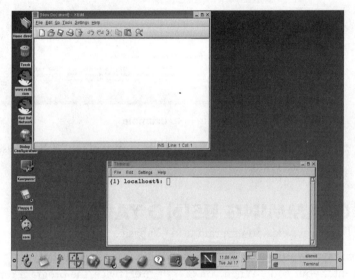

FIGURE 14.3: KEdit and a terminal emulator

4. CLICK the KEdit window.
5. TYPE **print "Hello world"** in the text area.
6. CLICK **File.**
7. CLICK **Save.**
   Since this is the first time this has been saved, you are asked where you want to save it. We need to create a directory named **basic** and then save it there.
8. CLICK the Home directory icon.
9. RIGHT-CLICK in the contents window.
10. CLICK **New Directory** on the menu that pops up.

11. TYPE **basic** in the text box.
12. CLICK **OK**.
    You are automatically placed into the basic directory (folder). In Linux language, this is now your current, or working, directory.
13. TYPE **hellotest.yab** in the Location text box.
    Be sure to include the .yab file name extension. Yabasic looks for this.
14. CLICK **OK**.
15. CLICK your terminal emulator window.
16. TYPE **cd basic** [Enter]
    You need to make **basic** the working directory for the terminal emulator too. (This saves typing.)
17. TYPE **yabasic hellotest.yab** [Enter]
    You should see **Hello world** displayed on your screen. Then the command prompt reappears.

EDITING AND RESAVING YOUR PROGRAM

1. CLICK the KEdit window.
   We're assuming your **hellotest.yab** file is still open in KEdit.
2. PRESS [Enter] to position the cursor on the second line.
3. TYPE **print "This is the second line"**.
4. CLICK **File**.
5. CLICK **Save**.
6. CLICK the terminal emulator window.
7. PRESS the [↑] key.
   The previous Yabasic command line reappears. Linux maintains a list of commands that you can scroll through using the up and down arrow keys.
8. PRESS [Enter]
   Hello world
   This is the second line
   appears on the screen. Then the command prompt appears.

   This is the development process. It is very quick once it is set up. Note the importance of saving the editor file before re-running the program. This is a common mistake new programmers make. They type the code, forget to save it, and then try to run it.

A MORE USEFUL PROGRAM

That exercise demonstrated how you can make some simple commands work. But it didn't produce anything very useful. The following exercise shows some simple commands and demonstrates how to overcome the limitation of Yabasic having only natural log functions.

This program will relate to using a telescope. With telescopes, one of the questions people often ask is how faint a star they can see with it. The brightness of an object in the night sky is stated in terms of its magnitude. A larger number indicates a fainter object. A good approximation to answer this question is given by the equation

$$\text{magnitude} = 6 + 2.51 \text{ x } \log10(\text{obj\_dia}^2/\text{pup\_dia}^2) .$$

The objective diameter (obj_dia) is the diameter of the lens or mirror. The maximum pupil diameter (pup_dia) is taken as 7 millimeters. The 6 is the faintest magnitude the average human eye can see if the pupil is fully opened to 7 millimeters. This number is lowered if the pupil diameter is lowered.

The program will ask a user for the objective diameter in inches and convert this to millimeters. The pupil diameter will be kept constant at 7 millimeters. We will output the magnitude.

A problem arises when you try to use the log function. This equation operates on the basis of taking the base 10 log, not the natural log, of the ratio. Yabasic has only natural log–based functions. They are exp( ) and log( ). Log, as the symbol for a function, has come to mean the base 10 log. The natural log is signified by ln( ), but not in Yabasic.

You may recall from math class that we can find the base 10 log by taking the natural-based log of the number we're taking the log of. This is divided by the natural-based log of the number 10 (or whatever other base we need). It will be coded in Yabasic as:

$$\text{tlog} = \log(\text{ratio})/\log(10)$$

Notice how this is being coded in parts rather than doing the entire equation at once. This aids in troubleshooting.

1. CLICK the KEdit window.
2. CLICK **File**.
3. CLICK **Close**.
4. TYPE the following code in the new document.
   #!/usr/bin/yabasic (this must be typed in the top-most position)

   REM Compute the magnitude limit for a telescope objective
   REM Written by *(your name)*
   REM Date: *(today's date)*

```
input "Enter the objective diameter in inches " diameter
dia_mm = diameter * 25.4
dia_sqr = dia_mm ^ 2
pup_sqr = 49

ratio = dia_sqr / pup_sqr
tlog = log(ratio) / log(10)
mag = 6 + 2.51 * tlog

print "The approximate magnitude limit is ", mag
print
```

5. CLICK **File**.
6. CLICK **Save**.
7. PLACE the new file in the **basic** directory and NAME it **magnitude.yab**.
8. CLICK **OK** to save the file.
9. CLICK the terminal emulator window.
10. TYPE **yabasic magnitude.yab** Enter
    "Enter the objective diameter in inches" appears.
11. TYPE **4.25** Enter
    "The approximate magnitude limit is 11.9644" appears.

CREATING A PROGRAM FILE THAT RUNS AUTOMATICALLY

To run a Basic program on your computer, you must have a Basic interpreter installed. When you type **yabasic *file-name*** on the command line, you are telling the Linux shell to start the Yabasic interpreter and to execute the instructions found in the named file. It would be convenient if we could simply type the name of the file and have the instructions execute without having to type **yabasic**. In Linux, there is a way to add this convenience.

Three steps must be taken to prepare for this automatic action. Two involve the file, and one involves the operating system. All are simple and easy to implement.

Step 1: Encode into the file that the Linux shell is to apply the Yabasic interpreter to the instructions in the file.

If the top-most line in a file begins with #!/ and is followed with the path to the name of an interpreter, then the interpreter will be started and used to execute the instructions in the file. That is why you were instructed to type **#!/usr/bin/yabasic** in the prior program. The precaution is that this must be entered on the top-most line beginning in the left-most position.

Step 2: Make the file executable.

This is done using the chmod command. It is shown below and discussed in Appendix B.

Step 3: Tell the operating system to include the path to your **basic** directory in the directories it searches for executable files.

The PATH instruction will be included in the .bashrc file.

1. CLICK the KEdit window (containing the **magnitude.yab** file). **#!/usr/bin/yabasic** has already been typed into the top-most, left-most position in the file. If the path to the Yabasic program on your computer is not /usr/bin/, you need to replace that part of this line with the path to your Yabasic program.
2. CLICK the terminal emulator window.
3. TYPE **chmod 754 magnitude.yab** [Enter]
   This makes the file executable.
4. TYPE **cd ..** [Enter]
   Now you are moved to your personal home directory, which is where the file you need to edit is located.
5. TYPE **kedit .bashrc** [Enter]
6. CLICK at the bottom of the file in KEdit.
   You're going to add a line to this file, and you want it to be at the very end of the file.
7. TYPE **export PATH=$PATH:~/basic**. (There shouldn't be any spaces in the PATH instruction.)
8. CLICK **File**.
9. CLICK **Save**.
10. CLICK **File**.
11. CLICK **Quit**.
12. CLICK the terminal emulator window.
13. TYPE **source .bashrc** [Enter] on the command line.
14. TYPE **cd basic** [Enter]
    You have changed back to the folder where your **magnitude.yab** file is located.
15. TYPE **magnitude.yab** [Enter]
    The program runs.

Note 1: The **.bashrc** file is a resource file that instructs the system how to set up your personal bash shell environment when it begins.

Note 2: In the line **export PATH=$PATH:~/basic**, **export** tells the bash shell to communicate this path to any shells or subshells it may start.

The PATH assignment could be read, "Assign to PATH the contents of the current PATH ($PATH) and append to it the path of your basic directory (~/basic)." The symbol ~ has the path to your home directory assigned to it at the time you log in.

Note 3: **source** is a command that forces the operating system to reinitialize all of the environment variables within the specified file. (Windows would ask you to reboot.)

SUMMARY

You have learned how to download and install Yabasic. The executable file is automatically copied to the /usr/bin directory. You learned how to use a Web browser to access the built-in help manual. Three ways exist to run Yabasic. Two were demonstrated: one that is suitable for program development, and another that is suitable when the program has been developed. In the latter case, you learned how to make the file executable and how to modify the search path in your system. If you want to pass a Basic program you have written on to a friend, then they, too, must have the Yabasic interpreter installed. The interpreter is small enough that it could be included on disk along with your Basic program.

THE GNUCASH PROGRAM

ÉTUDE 15

Since 1997, when the GnuCash project began (as xacc), it has been working to provide an accounting solution for Linux. GnuCash is a high-quality, stable, simple, and easy-to-use double-entry accounting system. Robert Merkel developed GnuCash. It is maintained and improved through his company gnumatic. The corporate goal is to provide a Linux accounting solution for enterprises of any size. See the references at the end of this étude for their URL.

Even though the accounting system is double-entry, you'll find that both entries are logical and completed in the same window. Why double entry? Because the single-entry checkbook register simply records money in and money out. Until the advent of simple accounting/bookkeeping programs such as Quicken and GnuCash, where the computer could do the tedious posting, adding, and subtracting, most people didn't have the time or training to manage their household with a double-entry system. The significant benefit of double-entry accounting is that it nudges (some people might argue "wrestles you to the ground and forces") you into thinking about organizing your use of your money. It doesn't substitute for your self-discipline, but it does cause you to think about where your money is coming from, where it is going, and what categories you want to keep track of.

This étude will lead you through the steps of setting up a home accounting system. This prepares you for setting up an accounting system for a small business. However, a small business has a lot of considerations that don't occur in a home system, such as payroll and taxes. Once you've set up and used a home accounting system based on GnuCash, if you want to use GnuCash for a small business, you will have the skills to set it up, but you will need more knowledge. The References section at the end of this étude includes a very readable paperback book describing how to set up a small-business, double-entry accounting system. It won't replace your accountant, but it will guide you into setting up a structure your accountant can understand and guide you in adapting to the unique needs of your business.

GnuCash can import Quicken .qif files. Microsoft Excel can export .qif files. Many banks are able to provide you your account information in a .qif file. Obviously, GnuCash has been outfitted with the ability to access the other important sources of financial information. GnuCash also has a large range of reports it can generate: a transaction report that can extract specific information and even a report that you can customize. Also, it can track investments.

GnuCash does not have built-in graphing capability. Allegedly, this can be done in conjunction with gnuplot.

You'll discover GnuCash is an easy-to-use tool—but without clear insight into how a double-entry accounting system is supposed to work, GnuCash won't be used to its fullest capacity. Now I'll let you in on a secret that has been with us since the development of automated tools, going back to the late 1700s. Automated tools, like the lathe (which was the first one), have master-crafting skills built into them. That's why they are useful. For example, with a lathe, anyone hired off the street and given twenty minutes of instruction can cut threads on tens of thousands of screws. Suddenly, it's possible to produce millions of screws, which gives everyone access to the superior holding power of screw-type fasteners.

Your computer and its software are tools for giving utility to information, just as a lathe is a tool for giving utility to physically existing materials. GnuCash has all the master-level accounting knowledge and skills built into it. You don't need to learn about debits, credits, and the reasoning why some accounts are debited and others are credited when they decrease or increase the owners value. All you need is the basic concept of double-entry accounting, knowledge of which account the money is coming from and which account it is going to, how to make the computer create accounts, and how to click on simple reports.

In the design phase, a visual aid called a "chart of accounts" gives most people all the sense of direction they need so they can organize their accounts as they create them. The main GnuCash window actually displays your accounts as a chart of accounts. The accounting software adds the accounting skill to keep your numbers organized in the correct accounts. Instantly, you can see how much you've spent in a category—the critical piece of information you need to stay on a budget. Instantly, you can generate a balance sheet showing you whether your net worth is growing or decreasing.

The first part of this etude takes you on a tour of elementary accounting and shows you how to set up a system for yourself. In the remainder of the etude, we set up a simple accounting system and use it.

TOPICS COVERED IN THIS ÉTUDE

- Simple accounting facts
- Installing GnuCash
- Features of GnuCash
- Creating accounts
- Entering transactions (what do I do with a paycheck, a bill to pay, and so on)
- Reports
- Reconciling your checking account

A SIMPLE ACCOUNTING TUTORIAL

The best way to understand the double-entry accounting concept and why you work with it the way you do is to compare it to single-entry accounting. Single-entry accounting is like trying to run a business with a wad of cash in your pocket. When you receive some income, you layer the bills onto the wad in your pocket. When you pay some expenses, you peel some off. At the end of the month, you don't know where the income came from or how it was spent. If you've got money in your pocket at the end of the month, well, about all we can say is that's good. We could keep a notebook, add income amounts, and subtract amounts taken out. At least at the end of the month, or at any other instant, we'd know our balance. Money suddenly appears and just as suddenly leaves. There isn't enough information to make decisions to control how money is being used.

An improvement is to keep a book with entries about income and expenses. Still, you have to stop, extract, and sum the expenses. But at least we're building in some crude control. Our simple single-entry book is still a problem if we have a larger business with six managers and want them to operate with only the money in their accounts, if we want to budget for expenses and if we want to keep readily available the amount actually spent versus the amount budgeted. We need to organize our money into categories and keep a balance for each category. These categories are called "accounts." You've created accounts if you've ever created a budget.

The next improvement is the step to double-entry accounting/bookkeeping. We create a system where we funnel money between accounts. Each movement of money is called a transaction. For example, we funnel money into a checking account from an income account. Then we'll transfer money from the checking account into various expense accounts—to represent paying those bills. Notice that two accounts are always involved: the account where the money came from and the account where the money went. Now we have control. The only additional ingredient needed is the self-discipline to regularly enter the checks written and to also assign each check entry to its proper category. The computer makes it simple both to enter the amounts and to simply click the two accounts involved.

Let's say that you want to buy another CD and you've budgeted $75 a month for CDs. Bring up your CD account for the month and see how much you've spent. Then you know whether you can buy that CD. Or, perhaps your goal is to save $7,200 a year toward buying a home. That's $600 a month. Some months you can save and some you can't, perhaps because of unexpected emergencies. If you run a balance sheet every month, you'll know how you have to adjust the budgets for future months if you develop a shortfall.

We do have one special account, the equity account. Let's assume that in your household you have a checking account, a savings account, some investments, the value in your home, and the value in your automobiles and household furnishings. For whatever reason, you decide to sell all of these—everything. Assume it's a good month and everything is sold at the end of the month. You have no possessions, but you do have a roll of cash in your pocket. That roll of cash represents the amount of value belonging to you.

Now let's say you decide to start over with a new checking account and deposit that roll of cash into the checking account. That's a transaction. The money came from the owner's pocket and was placed into the checking account. The rule of double-entry accounting is that every transaction involves two parts, a source for the money and a destination for the money. We know the destination in this situation. It's the checking account. What do we call the source? We can't call it income. That would indicate receipt of money for goods and services–and would be taxable. "Owner's Pocket" describes where it came from but not what it represents. The amount of value a person brings to (or has in) a business or home account is called the owner's equity and is deposited to and withdrawn from the equity account.

Two general concepts should be foremost in your mind in working with accounts:

1. A transaction is the movement of money.

2. A transaction always involves two accounts, a source and a destination.

PLANNING YOUR HOME ACCOUNTS

We could open GnuCash at this point, but then we'd have to stop abruptly. What do we enter if we want to build a home accounting system? We'll begin with some general accounts and then take a look at how to organize these into a chart of accounts.

We'll need accounts for equity, income, banking, cash, and expenses. Expenses is a huge account, and most people will want to subdivide it into additional categories. Typical subcategories are Food, Utility, Home & Family, Automotive, Health & Insurance, Family Gifts, and Donations. Even these subcategories might be subdivided. For example, Food could be subdivided into Groceries and Eating Out. Utility might be subdivided into Phone, Internet, Cable, Electric, Gas, and City. Income might be subdivided into Regular and Overtime. Banking might be subdivided into Checking and Savings. Home & Family could be subdivided into a category for each person, and each person could be subdivided into specific accounts such as the amount spent on clothes or CDs.

Perhaps the most important aid in designing these accounts, keeping from feeling overwhelmed, and not "misplacing" money is a chart of accounts. Take a look at Figure 15.1. This is an abbreviated chart of accounts. Notice the numbering scheme. The most general accounts, called top-level accounts, are numbered in separate thousands. The intermediate level is numbered in hundreds. The level subordinate to the intermediate level is numbered in tens. This means that even these lower, third-level accounts can have 10 subordinate accounts. For example, Groceries, Account Number 4110, could be further subdivided into 4111, Food and 4112, Household Supplies. Organize to the level of detail you really need but avoid the temptation to over-fragment. You're more likely to use a simple system with a few accounts. You can expand them later if the need develops. Your system is not cast in concrete. You can reorganize it on the computer as the need arises.

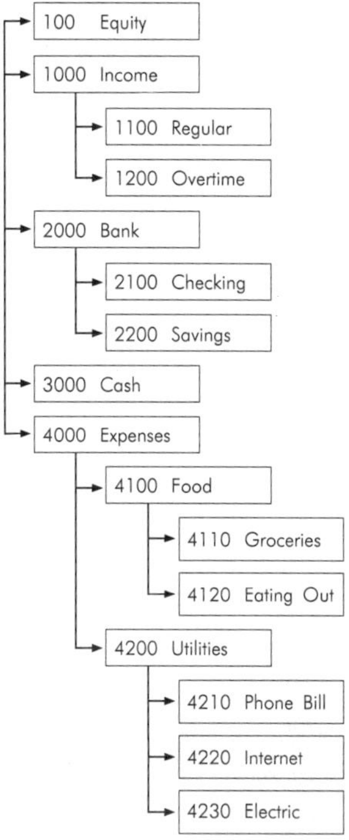

FIGURE 15.1: Organizing your accounting system

To keep the length of the GnuCash tutorial within reason, we'll only work with accounts for equity, income, food and utility expenses, and checking, savings, and cash accounts.

GETTING STARTED WITH GNUCASH

The following instructions assume you are using the Deluxe Workstation distribution of Red Hat 7.1. That distribution comes with two applications-oriented disks. One, the Linux Applications CD, contains the StarOffice 5.2 distribution. The second, the PowerTools CD, contains a few hundred programs. GnuCash and Jpilot (a PalmPilot desktop software) are stored on the PowerTools CD. Jpilot is installed in Étude 16.

GnuCash could be downloaded from the Web and installed. However, two unique libraries are required. It takes a good deal of experience with Linux to track down and install those libraries.

First, GnuCash must be installed onto your hard drive from the CD-ROM and then it must be assigned an icon on the panel or desktop. Other RPM-oriented distributions may also include GnuCash. The instructions for installation will be similar.

INSTALLING GNUCASH FROM THE POWER TOOLS CD

This CD comes with Red Hat 7.1, Workstation distribution. You must log in as root to install GnuCash from the CD-ROM.

1. Open the CD-ROM drive, insert the Power Tools CD-ROM, and close the drive.
   A small window, shown in Figure 15.2, opens.

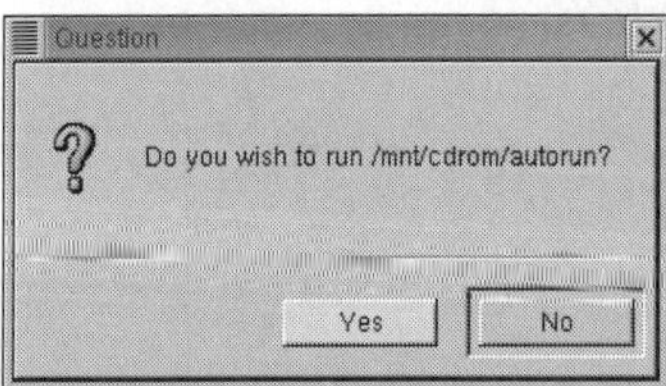

FIGURE 15.2: Autorun question

2. CLICK **Yes**.
   A window shown in Figure 15.3 opens.

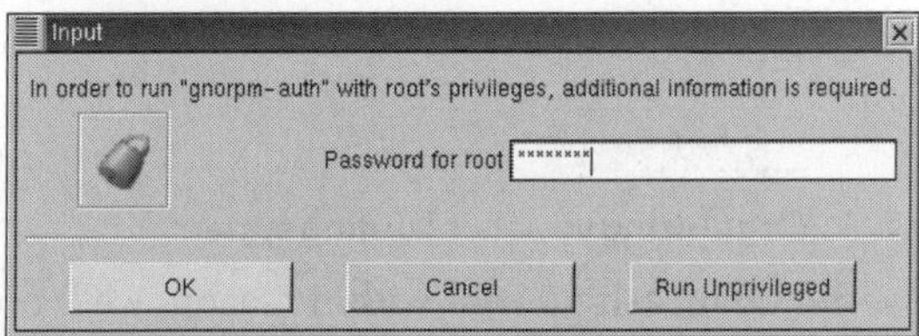

FIGURE 15.3: Root password request

3. TYPE in the root password.
4. CLICK **OK**.
   A window similar to Figure 15.4 opens.

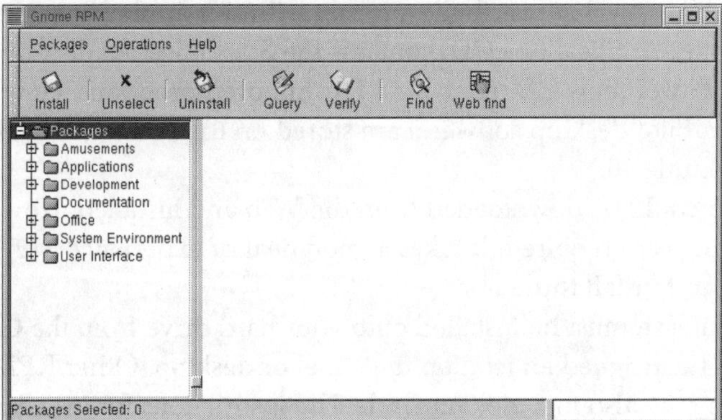

FIGURE 15.4: Gnome RPM

5. CLICK **Install**.
   The CD-ROM LED lights as the CD-ROM is searched. Wait until the CD-ROM LED turns off.
6. CLICK **Applications**.
   The directory tree expands again.
7. CLICK **Productivity**.
   The directory tree expands again.
8. SCROLL to **gnucash**.
9. CLICK the small check box to the right of gnucash 1.4.9-3.
   See Figure 15.5.

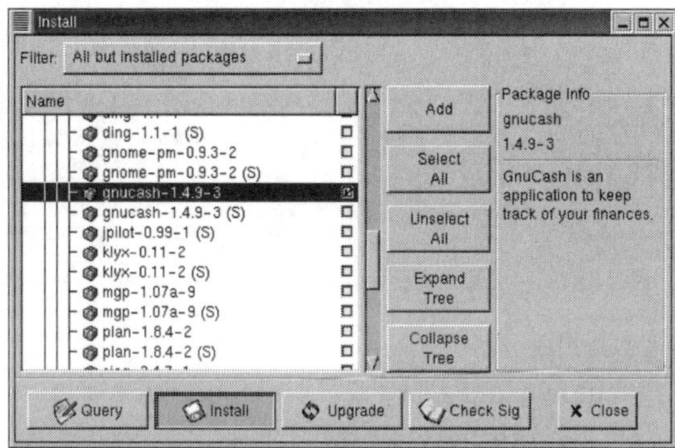

FIGURE 15.5: Select GnuCash

10. CLICK the **Install** button at the bottom of the window.
    After a certain amount of disk spinning and clicking, a dialog window will open that will show you the progress of the installation.

ASSIGNING GNUCASH TO AN ICON ON THE PANEL IN GNOME

The panel is the small box of icons running length-wise across the bottom of your screen. It only takes a single click to launch a program from the panel. This is a program that you'll use regularly, and it will be more convenient to launch it from the panel. This is for the Gnome desktop. If you want to add an icon for GnuCash to the KDE desktop, skip to the next exercise.

1. RIGHT-CLICK on the panel.
   A menu opens.
2. MOVE your cursor to **Panel**.
   A submenu opens.
3. MOVE the cursor to **Add to panel**.

Another submenu opens. At this point, your screen should look similar to Figure 15.6.

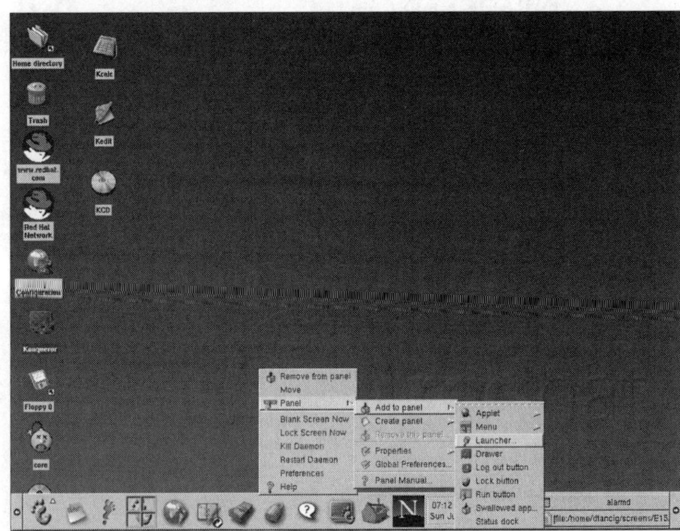

FIGURE 15.6: Panel launcher menus

4. CLICK **Launcher**.
   A dialog window similar to Figure 15.7 opens.

FIGURE 15.7: Create launcher applet

Figure 15.7 shows how it will appear when the following steps are completed.

5. TYPE **GnuCash** in the Name box.
6. TYPE **Accounting Program** in the Comment box.
7. TYPE **/usr/bin/gnucash** in the Command box.
   Note that gnucash is all lower case in the Command box.

8. CLICK the down arrow by "Type" and CLICK **Application** if the box does not already contain "Application."
9. CLICK the **No Icon** button.
   After a few seconds, a window fills with icons that can be selected.
10. SCROLL down until you see the icon that looks like a stack of money.
11. CLICK the icon.
12. CLICK **OK**.
13. CLICK **OK**.
    The icon appears on the panel.

ASSIGNING GNUCASH TO AN ICON ON THE DESKTOP IN KDE

1. RIGHT-CLICK on the desktop.
   A menu opens.
2. CLICK **Create New**.
3. CLICK **Link To Application**.
   A dialog box opens.
4. REPLACE "Link To Application" in the text box with **GnuCash**.
5. CLICK the **Execute** tab.
6. TYPE **/usr/bin/gnucash** in the Command box.
7. CLICK the **Application** tab.
8. TYPE **GnuCash** in the Name box.
9. TYPE **Accounting Program** in the Comment box.
10. CLICK **Application** in the list box on the right.
11. CLICK the double arrows pointing to the left to move "Application" over to the left list box.
12. CLICK **OK**.
    The icon appears on the desktop.

STARTING GNUCASH

1. CLICK the **GnuCash** icon.
   The GnuCash window opens. It appears similar to Figure 15.8.

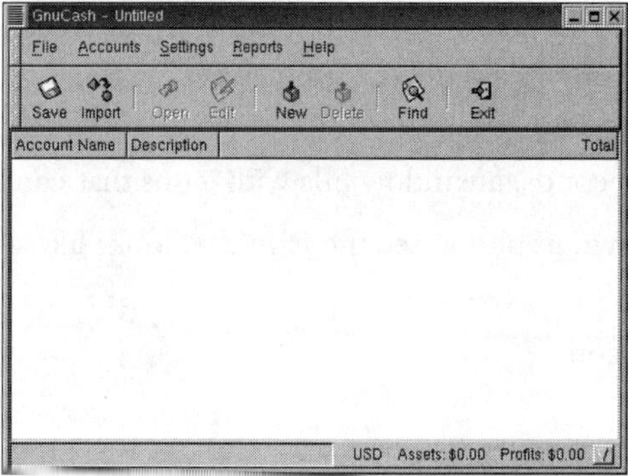

FIGURE 15.8: The GnuCash main window

FEATURES OF GNUCASH

The title bar contains the name of the program and the file in use and can be used to drag the window around the desktop. The menu bar contains items that reveal menus for performing common operations:

File	Create a new file, open, save, save as, import .qif, and exit.
Accounts	Open account, edit account, reconcile, transfer, make a new account, and delete an account.
Settings	Preferences—this lets you set colors and default currency.
Reports	Profit and Loss, Balance Sheet, Stock Portfolio, Account Balance Tracker, Tax, and Transaction Report.
Help	A built-in manual.

The toolbar is located immediately below the menu bar. Clicking one of these buttons immediately launches an action such as saving, importing, creating a new account, opening, editing, finding, or exiting.

The next bar is in the content window and has labels for each column. The labels have no clickable function.

AN ABBREVIATED HOME ACCOUNTING SYSTEM

The following steps will guide you through setting up a home accounting system. The only accounts created will be accounts for equity, income, food, utilities, checking, savings and cash. Food and utility will intentionally be created as "top-level" accounts and then later moved to an expense account, so you can learn how to move accounts to reorganize your system. If you skipped over it, you might find it useful to read "Planning Your Home Accounts," above.

CREATING NEW ACCOUNTS

Equity Account

1. CLICK the **New** button on the toolbar.
2. TYPE **Personal Equity** in the Account Name text box.
3. TYPE **Owner's value** in the Description text box.
4. TYPE **100** in the Account Code text box.
5. CLICK **Equity** in the Account Type box.
6. CLICK **New top level account** in the Parent Account box. Your dialog box should now look like Figure 15.9.

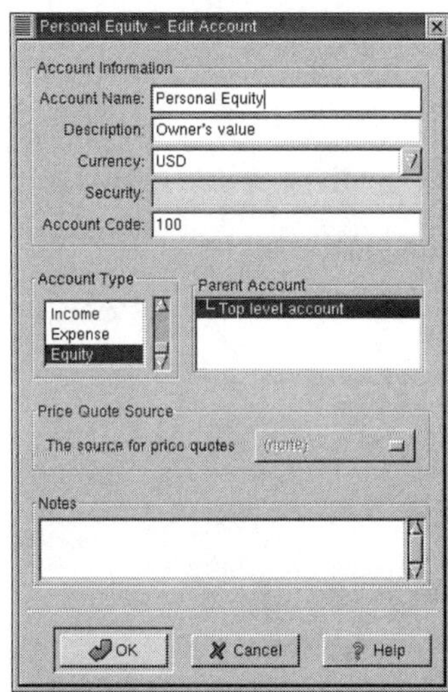

FIGURE 15.9: Setting up an account

7. CLICK **OK**.

Income Account

1. CLICK the **New** button on the toolbar.
2. TYPE **Income** in the Account Name text box.
3. TYPE **Money paid to me** in the Description text box.
4. TYPE **1000** in the Account Code text box.
5. CLICK **New top level account** in the Parent Account box.
6. CLICK **Equity** in the Account Type box.
7. CLICK **OK**.

Food Account

1. CLICK the **New** button on the toolbar.
2. TYPE **Food** in the Account Name text box.
3. TYPE **Money paid for food** in the Description text box.
4. TYPE **2000** in the Account Code text box.
5. CLICK **New top level account** in the Parent Account box.
6. CLICK **Expense** in the Account Type box.
7. CLICK **OK**.

Utility Account

1. CLICK the **New** button on the toolbar.
2. TYPE **Utility** in the Account Name text box.
3. TYPE **Utility Expenses** in the Description text box.
4. TYPE **3000** in the Account Code text box.
5. CLICK **New top level account** in the Parent Account box.
6. CLICK **Expense** in the Account Type box.
7. CLICK **OK**.

Checking Account

1. CLICK the **New** button on the toolbar.
2. TYPE **Checking** in the Account Name text box.
3. TYPE **Money paid by check** in the Description text box.
4. TYPE **4000** in the Account Code text box.
5. CLICK **New top level account** in the Parent Account box.
6. CLICK **Bank** in the Account Type box.
7. CLICK **OK**.

Savings Account

1. CLICK the **New** button on the toolbar.
2. TYPE **Savings** in the Account Name text box.
3. TYPE **Money Saved** in the Description text box.
4. TYPE **5000** in the Account Code text box.
5. CLICK **New top level account** in the Parent Account box.

6. CLICK **Bank** in the Account Type box.
7. CLICK **OK**.

Cash Account

1. CLICK the **New** button on the toolbar.
2. TYPE **Cash** in the Account Name text box.
3. TYPE **Money taken as cash** in the Description text box.
4. TYPE **6000** in the Account Code text box.
5. CLICK **New top level account** in the Parent Account box.
6. CLICK **Cash** in the Account Type box.
7. CLICK **OK**.
   Your GnuCash main window should now appear similar to Figure 15.10.

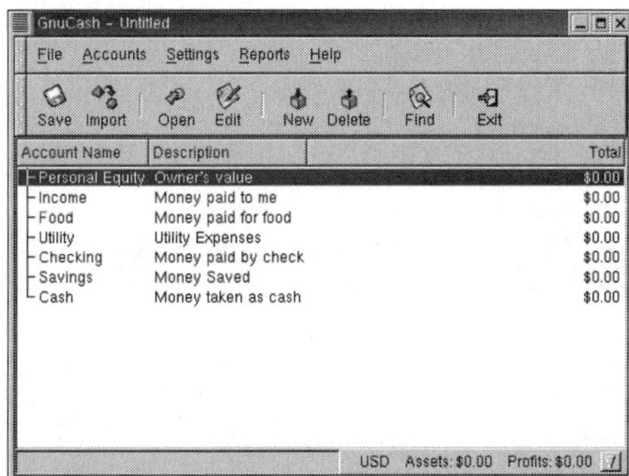

FIGURE 15.10: Newly created accounts

CREATING TRANSACTIONS

Now we will create transactions. When we consider adding transactions, recall that a transaction is the movement of money from one account, the source, to another, the destination.

Receiving Income

Let's say that we were just paid $3,200. This is income, so you would think this goes into the income account. It doesn't. We're going to put this money into the actual checking account and savings accounts and tell the computer it came from the income account. At the end, the income account will have $3,200 reflected as income. In other words, the income account will act as a summary of what we claimed as income as we place the actual money into other accounts.

Don't worry about the fact that we seem to be "taking" money from the income account to put into the checking and savings accounts even though the income account hasn't been given any money. The computer has been programmed to update the income account. It won't give you an error message.

First, we will put $2,200 into the checking account.

1. DOUBLE-CLICK **Checking**.
   A window similar to Figure 15.11 opens.

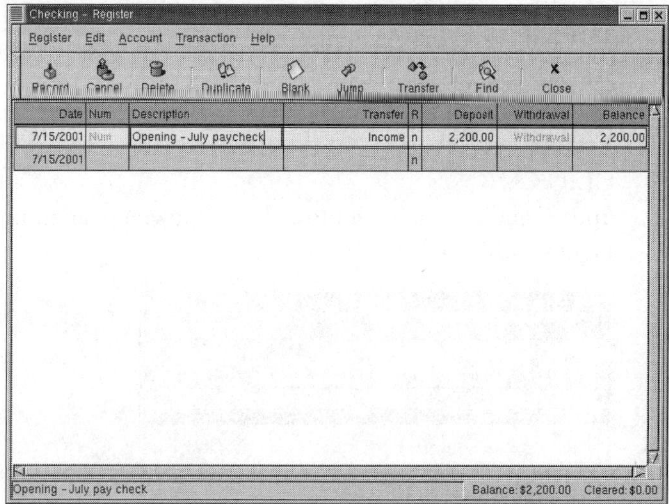

FIGURE 15.11: The checking register

   Figure 15.11 shows the checking register after it has already been filled in with the following information.

2. CLICK in the **Description** box.
3. TYPE **Opening - July paycheck**.
4. CLICK in the **Transfer** box.
   A drop-down arrow appears.
5. CLICK the drop-down arrow.
   A list of all the accounts is shown. You must click where the money is coming from. It is coming from your income account.
6. CLICK **Income**.
7. CLICK in the **Deposit** box.
8. TYPE **2200.00** **Enter**
   The amount is entered, your balance is updated, and a new line is opened and ready for the next transaction.
9. CLICK **Close** on the toolbar.

Transfering Money to a Savings Account

While we're at the bank on payday, we also fill out a deposit slip and deposit $900 to savings. Where did this money come from? From our paycheck—from income.

1. DOUBLE-CLICK **Savings**.
2. CLICK in the **Description** box.
3. TYPE **July savings from pay**.
4. CLICK in the **Transfer** box.
   A drop-down arrow appears.
5. CLICK the drop-down arrow.
   A list of all the accounts is shown. This money is coming from your paycheck—your income.
6. CLICK **Income**.
7. CLICK in the **Deposit** box.
   We will deposit $900 to savings.
8. TYPE **900.00** **Enter**
   The amount is entered, your balance is updated, and a new line is opened and ready for the next transaction.
9. CLICK **Close**.

Transfering Money to Cash

After depositing money to the checking and savings accounts, we have $100 left in cash, which we'll need for those cash payments—to the gas station, for the children's lunch money, and so on. We also need to record this cash. Where did this money come from? From our paycheck—from income.

1. DOUBLE-CLICK **Cash**.
2. CLICK in the **Description** box.
3. TYPE **Cash from paycheck**.
4. CLICK in the **Transfer** box.
   A drop-down arrow appears.
5. CLICK the drop-down arrow.
   A list of all the accounts is shown. This money is coming from your paycheck—your income.
6. CLICK **Income**.
7. CLICK in the **Receive** box.
   We will deposit $100 to cash.

8. TYPE **100.00** Enter

9. CLICK **Close**.
   Your GnuCash main window should look similar to Figure 15.12.

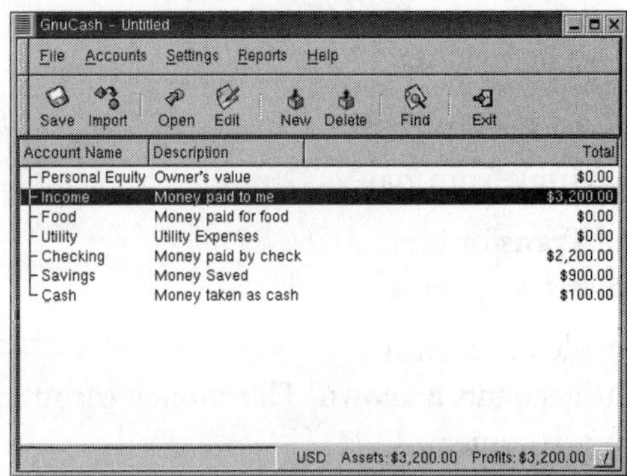

FIGURE 15.12: Income distributed

Notice that the total for income is $3,200.00, which is the sum of the money we deposited to the checking, saving, and cash accounts.

Entering an Expense

Now that we have the paycheck taken care of, it's time to pay some bills. First, we head to the grocery store and pick up two weeks' worth of groceries. We write check number 3670 for $157.62.

There are two ways to do this. Most people would withdraw the money from checking and transfer it to the food expense. You could also go to the food register and enter the amount as an expense and enter the check number, and that check number would show up in the checking account.

We'll use the logical first method of withdrawing from checking.

1. DOUBLE-CLICK **Checking**.
2. CLICK in the **Num** box.
3. TYPE **3670**.
4. CLICK in the **Description** box.
5. TYPE **Groceries for two weeks**.
6. CLICK in the **Transfer** box.
   A drop-down arrow appears.
7. CLICK the drop-down arrow.
8. CLICK **Food**.
9. CLICK in the **Withdrawal** box.
10. TYPE **157.62** Enter

The amount is entered, your balance is updated, and a new line is opened and ready for the next transaction.

11. CLICK **Close**.
12. DOUBLE-CLICK the **Food** account.
    The food account has been updated, including the check number.
13. CLICK **Close**.

Writing More Checks to Pay Other Bills

Now you decide to pay a couple of utility bills that are coming due. The electric bill is $67.20; the gas bill is on a level payment plan of $131 each month; and the city bill for garbage, water, and sewer is $37.45. Check numbers 3671, 3672, and 3673 are used to pay these bills.

1. DOUBLE-CLICK **Checking**.
2. CLICK in the **Num** box.
3. TYPE **3671**.
4. CLICK in the **Description** box.
5. TYPE **July electric bill**.
6. CLICK in the **Transfer** box.
   A drop-down arrow appears.
7. CLICK the drop-down arrow.
8. CLICK **Utility**.
9. CLICK in the **Withdrawal** box.
10. TYPE **67.20** **Enter**
    The amount is entered, your balance is updated, and a new line is opened and ready for the next transaction.
11. CLICK in the **Num** box.
12. TYPE **3672**.
13. CLICK in the **Description** box.
14. TYPE **July gas bill**.
15. CLICK in the **Transfer** box.
16. CLICK the drop-down arrow.
17. CLICK **Utility**.
18. CLICK in the **Withdrawal** box.
19. TYPE **131.00** **Enter**

20. CLICK **Num**.
21. TYPE 3673.
22. CLICK **Description**.
23. TYPE **July city bill**.
24. CLICK **Transfer**.
25. CLICK the drop-down arrow.
26. CLICK **Utility**.
27. CLICK **Withdrawal**.
28. TYPE 37.45 **Enter**
29. CLICK **Close**.
30. DOUBLE-CLICK the **Utility** account.
    The window should look similar to Figure 15.13.

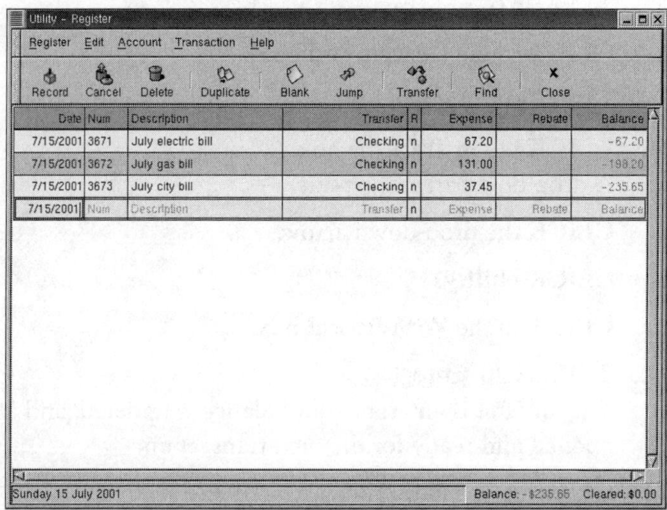

FIGURE 15.13: Utility register

The utility account has been updated with check numbers, descriptions, and individual amounts. The balance column keeps a running total of the utility expenses.

31. CLICK **Close**.

REORGANIZING ACCOUNTS

Your GnuCash main accounts window should now look similar to Figure 15.14.

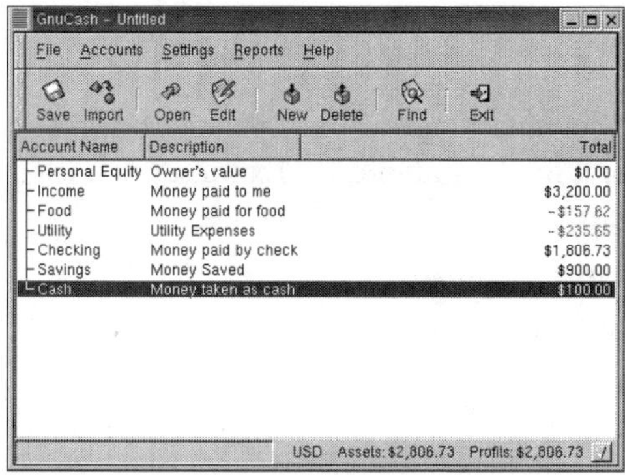

FIGURE 15.14: Completed transactions

A problem is lurking in the way we have developed our accounts. Notice that Food and Utility are both expenses. But if we wanted to total our expenses, we'd have to do so by hand or with a calculator. The same is true if we asked what the total amount was that we deposited in the bank.

This is only the tip of the iceberg. In a normal household accounting system, you'd have expenses for health, automotive and home insurance, car payments, mortagage payments, and personal expenses. That's a lot of adding up to do that the computer can handle. What we need to do is create an Expenses account and a Banking account. We will make major expense categories subordinate to Expenses and the checking and savings accounts subordinate to Banking.

Creating an Expenses Account

1. CLICK **New**.
2. TYPE **Expenses** in the Account Name text box.
3. TYPE **Top Level Expenses Account** in the Description text box.
4. LEAVE the Account Code text box blank.
5. CLICK **New top level account**.
6. CLICK **Expense** in Account Type.
7. CLICK **OK**.

Creating Subordinate Accounts

Food and Utility will now be made subordinate to Expenses.

1. CLICK the **Food** account.
   It is highlighted.
2. CLICK **Edit** on the toolbar.
   A dialog box opens.
3. TYPE **4100** in the Account Code text box.

4. CLICK **Expenses** in the Parent Account box.
5. CLICK **OK.**
   In the main accounts window, Food is now shown as subordinate to Expenses and a total is entered for Expenses that is equal to Food (its only account, so far).
6. CLICK the **Utility** Account.
   It is highlighted.
7. CLICK **Edit** on the toolbar.
   A dialog box opens.
8. TYPE **4200** in the Account Code text box.
9. CLICK **Expenses** in the Parent Account box.
10. CLICK **OK.**
    In the main accounts window, Food and Utility are now shown as subordinate to Expenses, and a total is entered for Expenses that is the sum of Food and Utility.

Create a Banking Account

1. CLICK **New** on the toolbar.
2. TYPE **Banking** for Account Name.
3. TYPE **Bank Accounts** for Description.
4. LEAVE Account Code blank.
5. CLICK **New top level account.**
6. CLICK **Bank** in Account Type.
7. CLICK **OK.**

Create Subordinate Banking Accounts

Checking and Savings will now be made subordinate to Banking.

1. CLICK the **Checking** account.
   It is highlighted.
2. CLICK **Edit** on the toolbar.
3. TYPE **2100** in Account Code.
4. CLICK **Banking** in the Parent Account box.
5. CLICK **OK.**
   In the main accounts window, Checking is now shown as subordinate to Banking, and the total for Banking is equal to Checking (its only account, so far).

6. CLICK the **Savings** account.
   It is highlighted.
7. CLICK **Edit** on the toolbar.
8. TYPE **2200** in Account Code.
9. CLICK **Banking** in the Parent Account box.
10. CLICK **OK**.
    In the main accounts window, Checking and Savings are now shown as subordinate to Banking. A total is shown for Banking that represents the money we have in our checking account plus the money we have in our savings account. That's a useful figure to have immediately available.

    Your GnuCash main accounts window should now look similar to Figure 15.15.

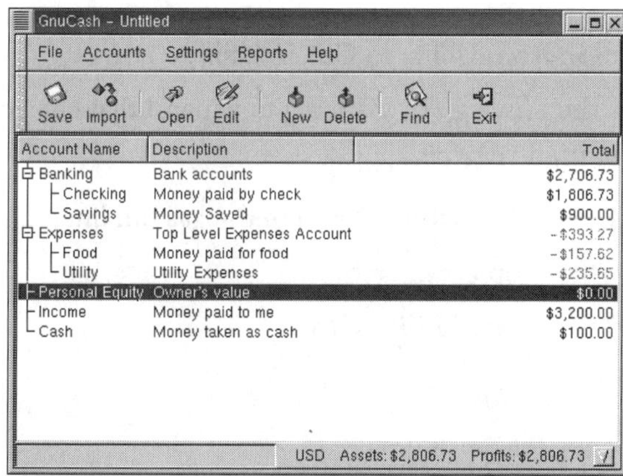

FIGURE 15.15: Subordinate accounts expanded

11. CLICK on the minus signs (-) next to Banking and Expenses.
    The expanded windows collapse. There is less visual clutter, and it's easier to get a summary view of the accounts.

Lower-level Subordinate Accounts

We'll assume that we're going to continue this set of accounts for one year. We want separate accounts for gas, electric, and city utility expenses. For example, we want to create a Gas account that is subordinate to Utility. That's simply a matter of making a new account named Gas and declaring its parent account is Utility. The problem is that in the Checking account, we wrote a check to pay the gas bill but assigned it to Utility. Now, how do we reassign that check to the new Gas account subordinate to Utility? It's just a mouse-click away.

Creating a Gas Account Subordinate to Utility

1. CLICK the plus sign by Expenses to expand that category.
2. CLICK **Utility**.
3. CLICK **New** on the toolbar.
4. TYPE **Gas** for Account Name.
5. TYPE **Gas Bill** for Description.
6. TYPE **4210** for Account Code.
7. CLICK **Utility** for Parent Account.
8. CLICK **Expense** for Account Type.
   Utility and Expense should already be highlighted by the computer, but click them if you need to.
9. CLICK **OK**.

Transfering Transaction from Utility to Gas in Utility

1. CLICK the plus sign by Banking to expand that category.
2. DOUBLE-CLICK **Checking**.
3. CLICK in the **Transfer** column in the gas bill line.
4. CLICK the drop-down arrow.
5. CLICK **Expenses:Utility:Gas**.
6. PRESS **Enter**
7. CLICK **Close**.
8. CLICK the plus sign by Utility to expand that category.
   The Gas account has the amount of the gas payment.
9. DOUBLE-CLICK **Checking**.
10. REPEAT these steps for the electric bill and the city bill.
    Your GnuCash main accounts window should now look similar to Figure 15.16.

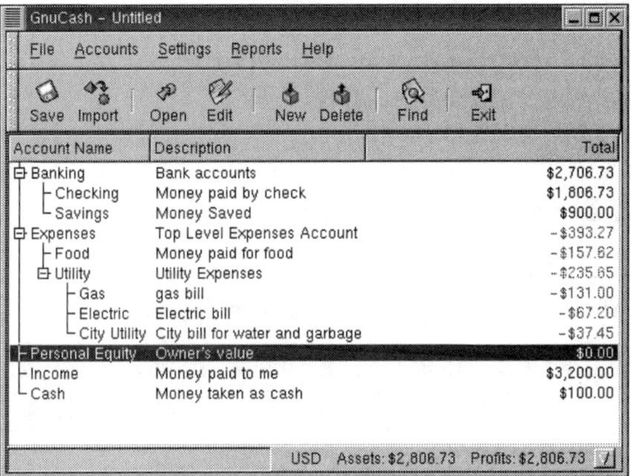

FIGURE 15.16: Completed accounts

What we see is that the computer is displaying our accounts not as simply a list but as a chart of accounts.

REPORTS

If you close all of the expanded account windows by clicking on all the minus signs, you can get a quick visual picture of your money. You had $3,200 in income, you have $2,706.73 in the bank, you've paid $393.27 in expenses, and you have $100 in cash.

A balance sheet will show us what our net balance is.

1. CLICK **Reports** on the menu bar.
2. CLICK **Balance sheet**.
   A report similar to Figure 15.17 is displayed.

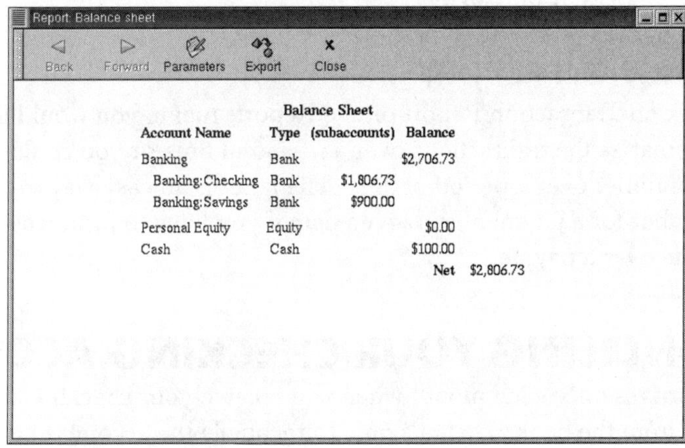

FIGURE 15.17: Balance sheet

The balance sheet basically sums your assets; in this case your checking, savings, and cash; and reports your net worth. A profit and loss report can also be created.

3. CLICK **Close**.
4. CLICK **Reports** on the menu bar.
5. CLICK **Profit and Loss**.
   A report similar to Figure 15.18 is displayed.

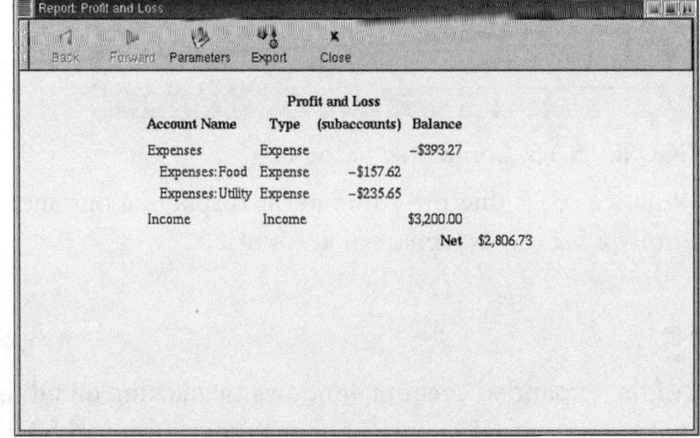

FIGURE 15.18: Profit and loss

A profit and loss statement sums your income, sums your expenses, subtracts expenses from income, and reports the net. Since the balance sheet and profit and loss statement are being done over the same period and both are only based on income, the two net values are the same.

6. CLICK on **Close**.

TRANSACTION REPORT

If you click on Transaction Report on the Reports menu, you would find that you could summarize the transactions over a period of time or you could have it sort by check number over a period of time. The latter is an easy way to find the check number for a payment at a given date if you have to produce the check in a dispute over a payment.

RECONCILING YOUR CHECKING ACCOUNT

The day arrives once each month when you receive your checking account statement from the bank. Then it's time to reconcile the account to be sure your GnuCash entries and the bank entries agree. What you will often find is that you left off a charge the bank made, for example, for the cost of printing another box of checks. This can then be added to your GnuCash account and the two will be reconciled.

1. CLICK the **Checking** account.
2. CLICK **Accounts** on the menu bar.
3. CLICK **Reconcile**.
   The reconcile window opens. Today's date is entered in the Statement Date text box. If you had a real statement, you would enter its date here. You would enter the statement's ending balance in the Ending Balance text box.
4. CLICK **OK**.
   The reconcile window opens and looks similar to Figure 15.19.

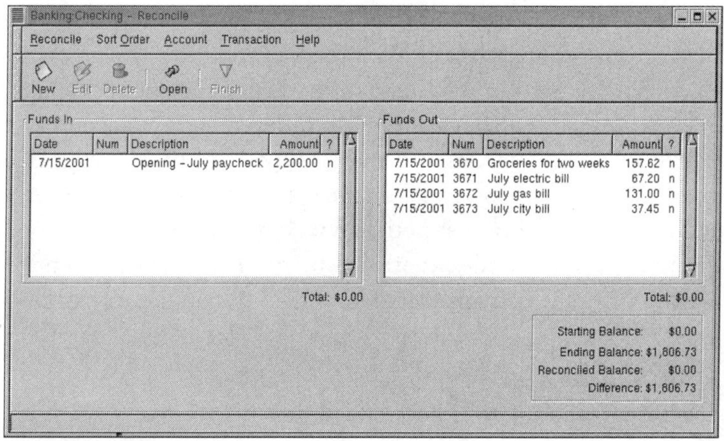

FIGURE 15.19: The Reconcile window

You have two sides, funds in and funds out. You would click the funds-in entries as you saw them on your bank statement.

5. CLICK the funds-in entry.
   The funds-in total at the bottom changes as amounts are checked. In the column labeled with a question mark, the n (for "not reconciled") is changed to a y (for "yes") when an item is checked as being present.
6. CLICK a funds-out entry.
   When you were done reconciling your statement, if everything matched, the difference between the ending balance and the reconciled balance would equal $0.00. This would be the difference between funds in and funds out.
7. CLICK **Finish**.

SAVING YOUR ACCOUNTS

1. CLICK **File**.
2. CLICK **Save As**.
3. TYPE **HomeAccount2001** in the Selection text box.
4. CLICK **OK**.

EXITING GNUCASH

1. CLICK the **Exit** button on the toolbar.

SUMMARY

This étude has only guided you through the basics of using GnuCash. The first step in using GnuCash is to learn the basics of double-entry accounting as presented, above. Next is to design your system of accounts on paper. As you've seen, you can easily reassign accounts to different parent accounts and you can easily reassign payments to new accounts if you decide to reorganize your system. Before committing your personal finances to GnuCash, it would be wise to work through this étude and gain experience with how it responds to your entries. If you desire to import .qif files, there can be problems that you'll have to fix by hand. Read the built-in manual and then read the online reference material.

REFERENCES

GnuCash Project. *GnuCash - Accounting Software for Linux.* 2001. <http://www.gnucash.org>

Merkel, Robert. "Managing Your Money with GnuCash." *Linux Journal* (April 2001): 122–127.

Ragan, Robert. *Step-by-Step Bookkeeping: The Complete Handbook for the Small Business.* Rev. ed. New York: Sterling Publishing Company, 2001.

J-PILOT: A PALMPILOT DESKTOP PROGRAM

ÉTUDE 16

Personal digital assistants (PDAs) are used by approximately five million people. I've used a 3COM Corporation Palm IIIe for about nine months. It has rapidly become one of my key organizing tools. A useful feature is that it can link to a personal computer and synchronize the data stored on the PDA and on the computer.

Linux support for these PDAs used to fall short of the Windows community support for PDAs. That has changed. J-Pilot is a graphical user interface-based Palm-type desktop program similar to the one 3COM Corporation provides for Microsoft Windows. It is currently in release version 0.99 and has proven to be stable and reliable after several months' use.

J-Pilot is available on the PowerTools CD that comes with Red Hat 7.1 Deluxe Workstation. It is also easily downloaded and installed from the J-Pilot Web site. Both options are described. Étude 26 follows up on this étude. Read that if you have any further questions.

TOPICS COVERED IN THIS ÉTUDE

- Getting J-Pilot
- Installing J-Pilot

- Creating a J-Pilot icon
- Using J-Pilot
- Troubleshooting

GETTING J-PILOT

If you have Red Hat 7.1 Deluxe Workstation, J-Pilot can be installed directly. It is almost as easy to download J-Pilot from its Web site and install it. This next section will deal with downloading and installing it. The section after this will deal with installing it from the CD.

GETTING J-PILOT FROM THE WEB

Downloading J-Pilot

J-Pilot has a home page at **http://www.jpilot.org**.

1. OPEN your Web browser.
2. TYPE **www.jpilot.org** into the location bar of your Web browser and press **Enter**
3. CLICK **Download** in the left frame of the J-Pilot Web site.
   You are given the option to download the Red Hat RPM (the Red Hat Package Manager), the Slackware RPM, or the source code in an collected, compressed file called a "tar ball." You used to have access to a release for Debian here too, but it appears to have had some bugs.
4. CLICK on the version you want to download.
   A window opens, telling you what you have requested to download.
5. SAVE this file to a floppy disk.
   Make sure you have a floppy disk inserted in the drive. Using the typical 56Kbs connection available in our semi-rural community, the nearly 500-KByte file downloaded in just under two minutes.

While You Are At the J-Pilot Site

Also at the J-Pilot site are links to useful Web sites. The Links page has links to magazine articles about J-Pilot. The article for *Linux Magazine* contains seven detailed steps to downloading and installing J-Pilot.

If you are not familiar with packages and how to download and install them, *Linux Magazine* has an excellent three-part, online article, "Installing Software Packages." These articles can be found at **http://www.linux-mag.com/depts/newbies.html**. Scroll down to August 2000.

Installing J-Pilot

I'm going to make the assumption that you have the file downloaded on a floppy disk. If you download it to a subdirectory named download, modify the following instructions to make that your current (working) directory. I'm also assuming that you're working in the Gnome environment for these next steps.

1. LOG IN as root.
2. RIGHT-CLICK the floppy disk icon.
3. CLICK the **Mount** option.
4. DOUBLE-CLICK the floppy disk icon.
   The file manager opens.
5. RIGHT-CLICK the J-Pilot RPM file.
   A menu pops up.
6. CLICK **Install.**
   After a few moments, the file is installed. The executable file is stored in /usr/bin as **jpilot**.
7. LOG OUT as root.
8. LOG IN as a user.

Verifying Installation

1. CLICK the terminal emulator icon.
2. TYPE **jpilot** [Enter] on the command line.
   The J-Pilot graphical user interface opens. It should look similar to Figure 16.1.

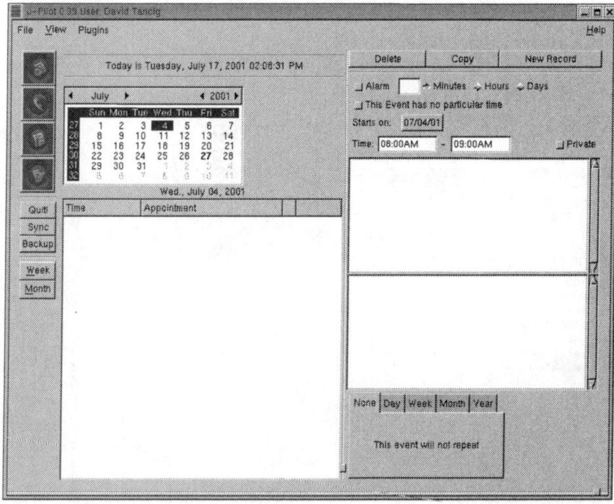

FIGURE 16.1: J-Pilot

Note: If you have a partially blank graphical user interface, click on **View**. Then click on **Datebook**. The view should now look like Figure 16.1.

GETTING J-PILOT FROM THE CD

Installing J-Pilot

1. LOG IN as root.
2. Open the CD-ROM drive, insert the Power Tools CD-ROM, and close the drive.
   A small window, as shown in Figure 16.2, opens.

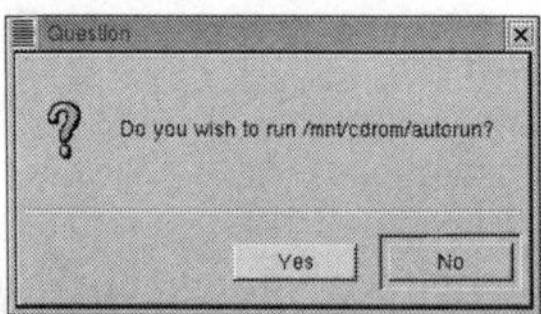

FIGURE 16.2: Autorun question

3. CLICK **Yes**.
   A window, as shown in Figure 16.3, opens.

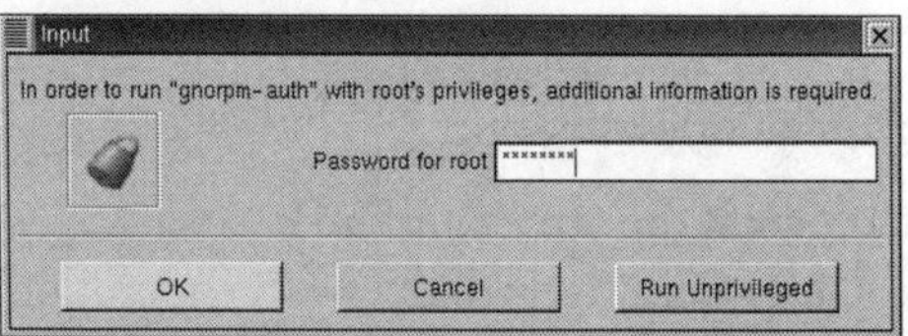

FIGURE 16.3: Root password request

4. TYPE in the root password.
5. CLICK **OK**.
   A window similar to Figure 16.4 opens.

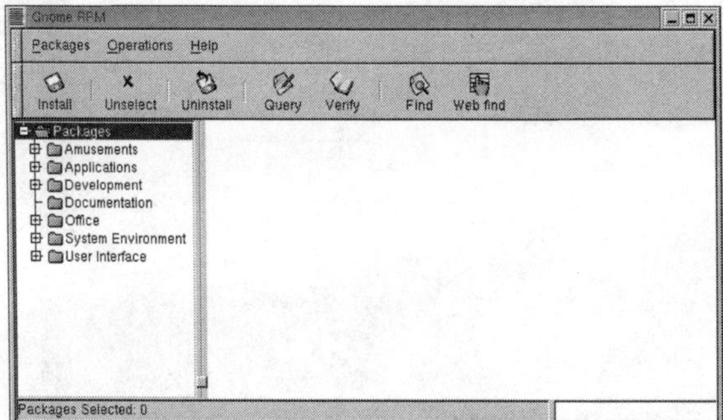

FIGURE 16.4: Gnome RPM

6. CLICK **Install.**
   The CD-ROM LED lights as the CD-ROM is being searched. Wait until the CD-ROM LED turns off.
7. CLICK **Applications.**
   The directory tree expands.
8. CLICK **Productivity.**
   The directory tree expands again.
9. SCROLL to **jpilot.**
10. CLICK the small check box to the right of jpilot.
11. CLICK the **Install** button at the bottom of the window.
    After a certain amount of disk spinning and clicking, a dialog window opens that shows you the progress of the installation.

Verifying Installation

1. CLICK the terminal emulator icon.
2. TYPE **jpilot** Enter on the command line.
   The J-Pilot graphical user interface opens. It should look similar to Figure 16.1.
   Note: If you have a partially blank graphical user interface, click on **View**. Then click on **Datebook**. The view should now look like Figure 16.1.

DESKTOP COMMUNICATION WITH YOUR PALMPILOT

SET-UP

Three steps are involved:

1. Connect your HotSync cradle cable to the COM1 serial port.
2. Create a symbolic link to that serial port.
3. Set the data transfer rate in the home directory resource file.

Connecting the HotSync Cable

1. Connect the serial-connector end of your HotSync cradle to the COM1 serial port on the back of your computer. (In Linux it is called /dev/ttyS0.)

Creating a Symbolic Link to the Serial Port

1. LOG IN as root.

2. CLICK the terminal emulator icon.
3. TYPE **ln –s /dev/ttyS0 /dev/pilot** Enter
   Note: If you are using the COM2 serial port, type the following line instead:
   ln –s /dev/ttyS1 /dev/pilot
   /dev/ttyS1 is COM2.

Setting the Data Transfer Rate

Now we need to open the bash resource file.

1. TYPE **kedit .bashrc** Enter
2. CLICK immediately following the section that sets what are called "aliases" (each line begins with the word "alias").
3. TYPE **PILOTRATE=57600** Enter
   Note: Run all of the text together. Do not put spaces around the equal sign.
4. TYPE **export PILOTRATE** Enter
5. CLICK **File**.
6. CLICK **Save**.
7. In the terminal emulator, TYPE **source .bashrc** Enter
   If, after a moment, the command prompt reappears, it probably worked. If you get a long listing of commands, or if you are told that permission was denied, then shut down and restart the computer. Don't just log out. In either case, you are forcing the computer to reinitialize itself with the new instructions in the bash resource file.

INSTALLING AN ICON FOR THE PROGRAM

In Gnome:

1. RIGHT-CLICK on the panel.
2. MOVE the cursor to **Panel**.
   A submenu opens.
3. MOVE the cursor to **Add to panel**.
   Another submenu opens.
4. CLICK **Launcher**.
   A dialog box opens, as shown in Figure 16.5.

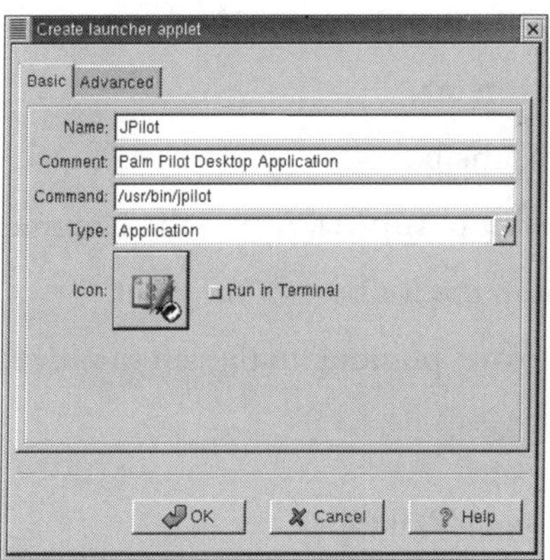

FIGURE 16.5: The launcher dialog box

5. TYPE the following information into the dialog box:
   Name: **J-Pilot**
   Comment: **PalmPilot desktop application**
   Command: **/usr/bin/jpilot**
   Type: **Application**
6. CLICK the **No Icon** button.
   A display of icons opens on your screen. About nine rows down is an icon that looks like an appointment book. It is called **gnome-calendar-conduit.png**.
7. CLICK on the icon.
8. CLICK **OK**.
   You are taken back to your Launcher dialog box.
9. CLICK **OK**.
   The icon appears on your panel.

In KDE:

1. RIGHT-CLICK on the desktop.
   A menu opens.
2. CLICK **Create New**.
3. CLICK **Link To Application**.
   A dialog box opens.
4. CLICK the icon button in the General tab.
   A window full of icons is displayed.
5. CLICK the **plan** icon.
6. REPLACE "Link To Application" in the text box with **J-Pilot**.
7. CLICK the **Execute** tab.

8. TYPE **/usr/bin/jpilot** in the Command box.
9. CLICK the **Application** tab.
10. TYPE **J-Pilot** in the Name box.
11. TYPE **PalmPilot desktop application** in the Comment box.
12. CLICK **Application** in the list box on the right.
13. CLICK the double arrows pointing to the left to move "Application" over to the left list box.
14. CLICK **OK**.
    The icon appears on your desktop.

COMPLETING A HOTSYNC

1. Insert your PalmPilot into its HotSync cradle.
2. CLICK the **J-Pilot** icon.
   The J-Pilot graphical user interface opens. It should look similar to Figure 16.1.
   Note: If you have a partially blank graphical user interface, click on **View**. Then click on **Datebook**. The view should now look like the figure.
3. CLICK the **Backup** button, located on the left side of the screen.
   You see a message in the bottom text box telling you to press the HotSync button on your cradle.
4. PRESS the HotSync button on your HotSync cradle.
   The HotSync takes place.
5. CLICK the phone symbol for addresses.
   It shows the addresses on your PalmPilot. If this occurs, the installation has been successful.

USING J-PILOT

Using J-Pilot is almost like using your PalmPilot. How you use it will depend on how you have your data organized. An electronic organizer by itself does not make you more organized. That comes from how you use it. If you've never studied the problem of personal organization for business, an excellent reference is *The Organized Executive* by Stephanie Winston.

TROUBLESHOOTING

The installation should proceed smoothly and work on the first try. If you repeat the steps and it still doesn't work, work through Étude 26, which is about Palm-link. J-Pilot is built on Palm-link. Étude 26 walks you through identifying which serial port is active and walk you through verifying that Palm-link is working. Once you get that far, J-Pilot should install.

SUMMARY

The best of the PalmPilot desktop organizers is J-Pilot. It puts Linux on the same footing with the Palm desktop software available in Windows. It can be downloaded from the J-Pilot Web site. It can be installed from the Red Hat 7.1 PowerTools CD that comes with the Deluxe Workstation distribution. Installation then involves three steps: connecting the cable, creating a symbolic link to the serial port you are using, and setting the communication rate in the bash resource file. Creating an icon for this application is useful. This program will be used frequently, and then launching the program will take only a single click. Étude 25 continues where this étude leaves off. Read that if you have further questions.

REFERENCE

Winston, Stephanie. *The Organized Executive: The Classic Program for Productivity: New Ways to Manage Time, Paper, People, and the Digital Office.* New York: Warner Books, 2001.

PATHS: NAVIGATING THE DIRECTORY TREE FROM THE COMMAND LINE

ÉTUDE 17

The goal of this étude is to help you visualize paths and use paths to access and save files. Why is this important? In Linux, the directory tree concept is hidden, to some extent, when you use office suite software. Many utility programs also hide the directory tree concept. Although you don't have to write the path when using application software, you at least have to be able to visualize it and click your way through it to the desired folder. This is where learning how to move through the directory tree while using the command line becomes important—it helps reinforce your knowledge of the way files and folders are organized. Also, for some operations, it is faster.

TOPICS COVERED IN THIS ÉTUDE

- Elements of terminal emulators
- The command line
- Using the command line

GETTING STARTED

Regardless of which desktop environment you use, there is only one command line. There are two ways to access the command line. A business user would most likely use what is called a terminal emulator. That is the method focused on here. (The other method is to turn off X Window System and use the shell command line exclusively, an option which is highly unlikely to be adopted by a business user.)

Although there is only one command line, each terminal emulator has slightly different options. Gnome has one terminal emulator: Gnome terminal emulator. KDE has two terminal emulators: Kvt and Konsole. This étude will cover the terminal emulators for both Gnome and KDE.

You have three possible terminal emulators:

- Gnome has one terminal emulator: Gnome terminal emulator.
- KDE has two terminal emulators:
  - Kvt
  - Konsole

Business Desktop Users

If you are a business desktop user and have Gnome installed, select the Gnome terminal emulator. It comes closest to having a professional, commercial look and feel. It lets you control the font size, the font style, and the foreground and background colors. (The foreground color is the color of the type. The background color is the color of the screen behind the type.) The Gnome terminal emulator also has a useful Help menu.

If you are a business desktop user and do not have Gnome installed, select Kvt. You will have control over the font size, the font style, and the foreground and background colors. Furthermore, the File command gives you the option of opening a second, separate terminal emulator window with a single mouse-click. Kvt has a Help command, but when clicked, it says that Help has not been implemented yet (even though this dates to 1997!). Unfortunately, Kvt has been declared obsolete by the KDE project. It is supposedly replaced by Konsole, but Konsole is hardly adequate for someone spending a lot of time working at the command line.

Systems Administration

If you are doing systems administration work, you might prefer to use Konsole because of the options available in the File Options menu. Konsole does not give you adjustable control over foreground and background colors (you can choose from several predetermined color combinations—a few of which are adequate, some of which presumably are sophomoric attempts at humor). You do not have control over the font size in points or the font style. You can choose font size from a list of descriptions. Try "Large." Konsole's Help section discusses only internal technical features and is not a helpful user's guide.

Which Terminal Emulator Starts with KDE?

If you are in KDE, the terminal emulator that starts when you click on the terminal emulator icon depends on which emulator is linked to that icon. You can click on Help and read which terminal emulator you have. If you have Kvt and want Konsole, type "konsole" at the command line and press **Enter**. Konsole will start. If you have Konsole and want Kvt, type "kvt" at the command line and press **Enter**. Kvt will start.

The fact is, you spend so little time at the command line, which emulator you use doesn't really make any difference. The only options that the casual user would see as important are the ones related to font size and weight. You can control font size and weight in both of KDE's terminal emulators.

STARTING THE TERMINAL EMULATOR

In Gnome:

1. CLICK the icon on the panel that looks like a computer monitor with the Gnome footprint in front of it.
   A window with a black background opens.

In KDE:

1. CLICK the icon on the panel that looks like a computer monitor.
   A window with a white background opens.

ELEMENTS OF TERMINAL EMULATORS

Terminal emulators open like typical windows. They have a title bar at the top. You can use the title bar to drag the window wherever you need to on the screen. The menu bar is immediately below the title bar.

The Gnome terminal emulator and Kvt both let you use the File menu to create a second, separate terminal emulator window. This is useful when you want to modify the instructions or data in a file and then run a command from the command line. You can simply move back and forth between the two windows without opening and closing files.

Konsole doesn't have this feature for opening two separate windows. However, you can start a separate session of Konsole either by typing "konsole" at the command line or by clicking on the icon associated with Konsole. (If you type "konsole" from inside the Konsole terminal, the second window will probably be on top of the other. You may not think you have a second window because it's hard to see. Grab the title bar and move one of the windows.)

Your terminal emulator has either a Settings item or an Options item on the menu bar. You can click on Settings on the menu bar to access Preferences. Clicking on Preferences accesses the dialog box that helps you set colors, font styles, and font sizes.

Options also lets you set window preferences. From the Options menu, you can click on choices to set the font and colors.

THE COMMAND LINE

In a terminal emulator window, there is a brief line of text extending out from the left side of the screen. That line of text is the command prompt. The cursor will move as you type your commands.

The command prompt can be customized to show a wide range of information. During the course of the command line études, you'll be shown ways to change the command line prompt.

USING THE COMMAND LINE

There are two things to remember about using the command line.

Rule 1: Linux is case sensitive.

Rule 2: All commands are typed in lowercase letters.

ABSOLUTE PATH OR RELATIVE PATH?

To save a file in the correct location, Linux must be instructed how to get to the desired directory. It needs a set of instructions about which folders it must travel through to reach the file. This set of directories that must be traveled through to reach the desired file or directory is called the "path."

There are two ways to tell Linux the path. You can use the root directory as a starting point and then end at the desired directory. A path that begins with the root directory is called an "absolute path." Also, you can use the current directory as the starting point and then end at the desired directory. A path that begins with a directory other than the root directory is called a "relative path," a path relative to your current position rather than relative to the root (base) directory of the file system.

Before the availability of graphical file managers, proficiency with relative paths could be a real time-saver. However, when most of today's software tools ask you what path to travel to save your files, they mean starting from the root. Consequently, this étude will focus on absolute paths.

THE IMPORTANCE OF THE ENTER KEY

There's another rule that applies when you are using the command line.

Rule 3: After you type a command, press the Enter key.

That is how you signal to the operating system shell that you are done issuing commands and want the operating system to take action.

THE PATH TO THE WORKING DIRECTORY COMMAND

Use this command to determine the path to your working directory, the directory you're currently in. The pwd stands for "path to working directory."

1. TYPE **pwd** Enter
   You might see something such as
   /home/dtancig
   where /home/dtancig is a path. This is the absolute path (the path starting from the root directory) to my personal directory.

WHAT THE PARTS OF A PATH MEAN

- The first / means the root.
- home is the directory off the root.
- The second / is merely a separator and means that what follows is another directory or file.
- dtancig is the name of the directory off of the home directory; this is the directory in which I am currently working. Your file system stores information so it can determine whether an item is a file or directory.

Your path will look different, but chances are good that it will follow the lines of /home/login_name.

THE LIST COMMAND

Now that we're in our personal directory, how can we find out if anything is stored there? By using the list command.

The command to list contents is ls.

1. TYPE **ls** Enter
2. LOOK at your screen.
   A listing of files and folders appears.
   In Linux, files will be in black or white and directories will be in blue. Executable programs will be in red. What you have in front of you is the short-form listing. Only the file and directory names are listed.

COMMAND OPTIONS

Many commands in Linux have options that modify how they operate. Let's try using an option with the List command.

Writing a Command and an Option

- In Linux, a command is always the first item on the command line. This is always followed by a space. (In a few rare instances, the space is optional. But always using it saves trouble.)
- Next, type - (a dash) to tell Linux you are specifying an option for a command.
- After the dash, type the letter that specifies the option(s) you want. You can specify more than one option.

1. TYPE **ls -l** Enter
2. LOOK at your screen.
   Another listing appears, with more information than the previous listing. This is called the long form. The "rwx" items on the left that look like gibberish refer to reading, writing, and execution permissions and to directories and directory access. You'll learn how to interpret this later.

CLEARING THE SCREEN

By this time, your screen has a lot written on it.

1. TYPE **clear** Enter
2. LOOK at your screen.
   The screen is erased, and the command line prompt is written in the upper-left corner of the screen.

LISTING HIDDEN FILES

Another command option for the list command is to include all files, including hidden files.

1. TYPE **ls -a** Enter
2. LOOK at your screen.
   Now you see a much longer file listing. Look at the files that are listed first. Notice that they all begin with a period. Files that have a period as the first character in their name are called "hidden files." "Hidden" implies that there is something secret about them. But there is nothing secret about these files. They are merely hidden from view to remove visual clutter.

Most of these files were created when you were assigned an account and have default settings. In most cases, you'll never change these settings. In a few cases, you might. In any case, these are not files that you want to see when you begin your daily work. They are considered visual clutter so they are removed from view even though they continue to exist in the directory.

We will clear the screen again.

3. TYPE **clear** Enter
4. LOOK at your screen.
   The screen is now clear again.

COMBINING COMMAND OPTIONS

Command line options can be combined. In most cases, you can type only one dash and then the letters representing the options one after the other.

Let's tell the list command to show the long form of all the files, including the hidden files.

1. TYPE **ls -la** Enter
2. LOOK at your screen.
   What you see now is the long form, and the hidden files are displayed.
3. TYPE **clear** Enter
   You cleared the screen.

MAKING A NEW DIRECTORY

Now let's create a new directory named **notes** that will be subordinate to your working directory.

1. TYPE **mkdir notes** Enter
2. LOOK at your screen.
   Not much seemed to happen, but you did create a new directory. We'll change to the new directory in a moment. Notice the command you just typed, "mkdir notes."
   - First, you typed the command.
   - Second, you typed a space.
   - Third, you typed the file or directory name you wanted to act on.

CHANGING TO A DIFFERENT DIRECTORY

The command to change to a different directory is cd.

1. TYPE **pwd** Enter

2. LOOK at your screen.
   This shows you the path to your current directory. Now change to the notes subdirectory (subfolder).
3. TYPE **cd notes** Enter
4. TYPE **pwd** Enter
5. LOOK at your screen.
   In the first listing of pwd, notes is not shown. After changing to the notes subdirectory, pwd lists notes as the last, and also lists it as the working directory.
   Now we need a little more information. We want to see the hidden files.
6. While still in the notes directory, TYPE **ls -a** Enter
7. LOOK at your screen.
   What you see now are the hidden files and directories in the notes folder. Only two items appear, and both are symbols. One symbol is a single period (.). This is the address to the working (current) directory.
   Another symbol is a double period (..). The double period represents the address to the parent directory of the working directory. All directories, except the root directory, have a parent directory. You can think of the parent directory as the folder directly above the current folder in the directory tree.

MOVING TO THE PARENT DIRECTORY

It's time to move in with your parents—uh, I mean move up the directory tree. The command to move up to a parent directory is cd .. (cd space double period).

You are currently in the notes subdirectory. The parent directory to notes is your personal directory. We should end up in our personal directory when we type **cd ..**.

1. TYPE **pwd** Enter
   This establishes where we are. On my screen I have /home/dtancig/notes.
2. TYPE **cd ..** Enter
   Nothing seems to happen.
3. TYPE **pwd** Enter
   You should now be back at your home directory. On my screen I have /home/dtancig.

4. NOTICE that the notes subdirectory is not shown—it is no longer the working directory.
   To summarize, you can move though the directory tree the following ways:
   - To move down the directory tree, name the directory you want to make the new working directory.
   - To move up the directory tree to the parent directory, use the double dot (double period) operator.

MOVING TO THE ROOT DIRECTORY

1. TYPE **cd /** Enter (remember that / denotes the root directory).
2. TYPE **pwd** Enter
   You see only the / for the root directory symbol.
3. TYPE **ls** Enter
4. LOOK at your screen.
   You see a listing of the standard directories found in the root directory, such as boot, dev, home, mnt, and so on.

RETURNING TO YOUR PERSONAL DIRECTORY

There is a special symbol for your personal directory. That symbol is the tilde (~). On most keyboards, this is the left-most key in the top row (with the number keys). It is usually above the backward apostrophe (the accent grave) key.

1. TYPE **cd ~** Enter
2. TYPE **pwd** Enter
   You are now back in your personal directory. Now move back to the notes subdirectory.
3. TYPE **cd notes** Enter
4. TYPE **pwd** Enter
5. LOOK at your screen.
   You are back in the notes directory. This time, let's use the ~ operator to return to the personal directory.
6. TYPE **cd ~** Enter
7. TYPE **pwd** Enter
8. LOOK at your screen.
   You are now back in your personal directory. By typing **cd ~** you can return to your personal directory from any location.

SUMMARY

You learned what a path is and what one looks like. For example, /home/leslie/notes is a path from the root, through the home directory, through the leslie directory, to the notes directory. The last directory listed is the working directory.

Linux can operate with an absolute path and a relative path. An absolute path uses the root symbol (/) as the starting point in the path, while a relative path uses the working directory as the starting point in the path.

You learned several rules about command lines:

- Commands in Linux are always typed in lowercase letters.
- A command is always issued first on the command line.
- A command is always followed by a space.
- Commands can have options. An option is indicated by first typing a dash and then typing the letter for that option.

The following commands were introduced:

Command	Action
pwd	Displays the path to the working directory
clear	Clears the screen
ls	Lists the directory contents
ls -l	Lists the directory contents using the long form
ls -a	Lists the directory contents, including the hidden files
ls -la	Combining options; both long form and hidden files are displayed
cd	Changes the directory
cd ..	Changes the directory to the parent directory
cd *name*	Changes to the directory *name* (*name* must be subordinate to the directory where the command is issued)
cd /	Changes the directory to the root directory
cd ~	Changes the directory to your personal directory
mkdir	Makes a new directory subordinate to the working directory

REFERENCES

Greenlaw, Raymond. *Understanding Practical Unix.* Wilsonville, OR: Franklin, Beedle & Associates, 2001.

Sobell, Mark. *A Practical Guide to Linux.* New York: Addison Wesley, 1997.

COMMAND LINE FILE OPERATIONS

ÉTUDE 18

Operations related to file management and organization should normally be done using a graphical file manager, as discussed in Études 2, 3, and 4. However, there are file-related commands that make sense for the business user to issue from the command line. They don't relate to file organization and management, but they can be used to help you get information from files.

The typical commands that are taught that are related to file organization and management are cp for copy, mv for move, rm for remove, and rmdir for remove directory. These commands will not be covered here. For the average businessperson, these functions are best done using the graphical file manager. However, there are several commands that make sense to use from the command line. They are the cat, head, tail, find, and wc commands.

We are assuming that you have completed Étude 17.

TOPICS COVERED IN THIS ÉTUDE

- The cat command
- The head command
- The tail command

- The find command
- The wc command

THE CAT COMMAND

The cat command is used to show the contents of a file on the screen. The "cat" comes from "concatenation," meaning to join. Used with only one file, the output of that file is joined with a location called standard output, and from there the output is sent to the screen. This command can also be used to join the contents of two files.

MAKING A FILE TO READ

1. START a terminal emulator.
2. TYPE **pwd** Enter
   Make sure you are in your personal directory.
3. On the command line, TYPE **kedit** Enter
4. TYPE in the following in the KEdit window. Type all 12 lines. We'll use this file with three commands in this étude.
   line 1 Enter
   line 2 Enter
   line 3 Enter
   line 4 Enter
   line 5 Enter
   line 6 Enter
   line 7 Enter
   line 8 Enter
   line 9 Enter
   line 10 Enter
   line 11 Enter
   line 12
5. CLICK **File.**
   A menu drops down.
6. CLICK **Save.**
   A dialog box opens.
7. NAME the file **numlist.txt.**
8. CLICK **OK.**
   This creates the file in your personal directory.

9. CLICK on the X in the upper-right corner of the editor window to close the editor.

USING THE CAT FILE COMMAND

To use the cat command, follow the command line rules:

1. Type the command.
2. Type a blank space.
3. Type the name of the file you want the command to operate on.

In our case, the file we want to operate on is the one we just created, numlist.txt.

Caution: Notice that all the letters are in lower case. Linux is case sensitive and will expect that you use this case in referring to this file.

1. TYPE **cat numlist.txt** Enter on the command line.
2. LOOK at your screen.
   The information in the file is displayed.
3. NOTICE that there is a scroll bar to the right, which you can use to scroll up to the information that disappeared off the top of the screen.

This is the most common use of the cat command, to write out the contents of an ASCII text file.

THE HEAD COMMAND

The head command shows the first 10 lines of a file (it can be adjusted to show you more or fewer, but 10 is the default). This can be handy when you have several files—perhaps of memos—and you are looking for one that begins in a particular fashion.

Again, follow the command line rules.

1. TYPE **head numlist.txt** Enter
2. LOOK at your screen.
   Lines 1 through and including 10 are displayed.

THE TAIL COMMAND

The tail command shows the last 10 lines of a file (it can be adjusted to show you more or fewer, but 10 is the default). This can be handy when you have several files—perhaps of memos—and you are looking for one that you were last working on or that has a particular ending you want.

Again, follow the command line rules.

1. TYPE **tail numlist.txt** Enter
2. LOOK at your screen.
   Lines 3 through and including 12 are displayed.
   If lines 4 through 12 were displayed, you most likely included an extra blank line at the end of the file–you pressed the Enter key after typing line 12. Remove the blank line from the numlist.txt file, and the tail command it will work as it should. Normally, an extra blank line is irrelevant.

THE FIND COMMAND

Several pages could be written about using the find command. This will be kept brief. Use the find command to locate files in your directories. Because Linux is case sensitive, this command soon earns its keep.

If you know the name of the file you are looking for, issue the find command by typing the word **find** followed by the name of your file. If find returns the file name, then you know that the file exists in the working directory. If you're really lost, you can type **cd** /. This takes you back to the root (base) directory. Then type **find**. Your entire system will be searched.

WHAT IF YOU DON'T RECALL THE CORRECT NAME?

If you don't remember the exact name of a file or if you don't recall whether you used a particular capitalization, you can use a wildcard to take the place of what you don't remember. The most widely used wildcard is the asterisk. The asterisk replaces any characters to its right until it encounters a period.

Let's say you don't remember whether you named a file numlist.txt or numlines.txt. Not a problem. Let the asterisk replace what you don't remember.

1. At the command line, TYPE **find num*.txt** Enter
2. LOOK at your screen.
   numlist.txt is returned.
   A simpler way to use the asterisk wildcard is to look for all the files of a specific type. To do this, you use the asterisk to replace the file names and specify an extension. However, if you have a lot of files in a directory that have the same extension, you may be overwhelmed.
   To find all files of a specific type within a directory:
3. TYPE **find *.txt** Enter
4. LOOK at your screen.
   You should have a listing of all the files in that directory that have the file extension .txt.

If you didn't remember whether you included an extension, you could use a wildcard to denote the extension.

To find all of the files in a directory that begin with the letters "num":

5. TYPE **find num*** Enter

6. LOOK at your screen.
All files that begin with the letters "num" are listed.

However, you must remember that Linux is case sensitive. You can test that here. Again, follow the command line rules.

First, use the proper capitalization to search for your file.

7. TYPE **find numlist.txt** Enter

8. LOOK at your screen.
The file name should be returned, indicating that the file exists.

Now use the improper capitalization to search for your file.

9. TYPE **find Numlist.txt** Enter

10. LOOK at your screen.
You get an error message that reads
find: Numlist.txt: No such file or directory
This is a standard format for an error message. It lists the command it tried to execute, the name of the file it tried to execute it on, and the cause of the error.

This demonstrates that Linux is case sensitive. To summarize:

- **find num*.txt**—Finds any file that begins with **num** and ends with **.txt** regardless of what is in between.
- **find *.txt**—Finds any file that ends with the extension of **.txt**, regardless of the preceding characters.
- **find num***—Finds any file that begins with **num** regardless of what follows.

THE WC COMMAND

In Europe, "wc" is an abbreviation for "water closet," which is what we in the United States call a bathroom. However, in Linux, "wc" is an abbreviation for "word count." This command has three uses. It can count characters, words, and lines. (A line is anything ended by pressing the Enter key. Don't confuse sentences—which seldom end with a press of the Enter key—and lines.)

Let's test the wc command. Again, follow the command line rules.

1. TYPE **wc numlist.txt** Enter

2. LOOK at your screen.

You see output that looks like this:
12 24 87 numlist.txt
It is telling you that you have 12 lines. That's what we typed. You have 24 words. If you used the format of line 1, line 2, and so on; each line has two words; 2 * 12 is 24. You have a total of 87 characters. Last, wc tells you that this came from the file named numlist.txt.

Let's try the option for words. An option modifies the action of a command. To use an option, type the command, a blank space, and then a dash followed by the letter for the option or options you want to apply to the command.

The wc command has three options.

- the letter l for lines
- the letter w for words
- the letter c for characters

3. TYPE **wc -w numlist.txt** [Enter]
4. LOOK at your screen.
   You see
   24 numlist.txt
   You're welcome to try the other options in the same way. We'll make further use of the wc command in a later étude.

SUMMARY

The following commands were covered in this étude:

Command	Action
cat	Displays the contents of an ASCII file
head	Displays the first 10 lines in a file
tail	Displays the last 10 lines in a file
find	Reports whether a file is present (it can be used with the asterisk wildcard character to substitute for part of a file name)
wc	Reports the number of lines, words, and characters (it can be used with the options l, w, and c)

The command line rules (for a command followed by a single file name) are

1. Type the command.
2. Type a blank space.
3. Type the name of the file you want the command to operate on.

PIPING AND REDIRECTION: THE ASSEMBLY LINE OPERATIONS

ÉTUDE 19

The concept of the assembly line is simple: Perform one specific task at one workstation, then move the project to the next workstation to perform the next task. At the input end is raw material. Each step in the process gives the raw material greater utility. At the output end is a product with the desired characteristics.

The design philosophy of Unix, used in Linux, is that each command, and each utility program, performs a single task. This keeps each program relatively simple, easy to use, and easy to troubleshoot. (The same characteristics are found in the software on Palm organizers—part of what makes them easy to use and popular.)

However, if you can perform only a single task at once, that means you must have some way of stringing together commands so that the output of one command can feed the processed information into the next command. Then you have an assembly line refining information into an output form with the characteristics that you want. This "stringing together" to achieve sequential processing of input is called piping and redirection. The rule is that you redirect between a file and a command and you pipe between two commands.

You might use the cat command to write out the contents of a file, use the grep command (which we'll learn in Étude 20) to search for a particular word or pattern of characters, and finally use the sort utility to sort a specified column into ascending or descending order. All of this is done using the techniques of piping and redirection. In Étude 22, the database extraction of an awk command is piped into the sort command.

We assume you have completed Études 17 and 18.

TOPICS COVERED IN THIS ÉTUDE

- The redirection command
- Appending files
- Piping
- The sort command

THE REDIRECTION COMMAND

Three symbols are used with the redirection command:

> means "sends to"

< means "receives from"

>> means "appends to"

At the command line, you might have a command that looks like

ls > dirfile.txt

This would be read as "ls sends to dirfile.txt." Or, you might have the following:

sort < dirfile.txt

This would be read as "sort receives from dirfile.txt." Notice that each case involves a file and a command.

APPENDING

When you append a file, you write the contents of one file to the end of another file. Here is an example of appending a file using the redirection command:

cat furniture_supplies.txt >> office_supplies.txt

This would be read as "furniture_supplies.txt is appended to office_supplies.txt." In this case, the contents of the furniture_supplies.txt file would be written to the bottom of the office_supplies.txt file.

USING > TO SEND OUTPUT TO A FILE

Note: If the file doesn't already exist, the redirection command creates the file.

1. OPEN a terminal emulator.
2. On the command line, TYPE **ls -la > dirfile.txt** Enter
   The output is not displayed on the screen. It went to the file.

3. TYPE **ls dirfile.txt** Enter
   The ls command reports that the file exists.

4. If you haven't done so, MAKE the terminal emulator screen fill the entire screen. The output of the next command should appear properly formatted if you do so.

5. TYPE **cat dirfile.txt** Enter
   The directory listing is now displayed. This proves that the redirected output of the ls -la command was written to the file named dirfile.txt.

USING <

Now let's assume we want the output of a file to be sorted. In the last situation, we sent information to a file. In this situation, the command needs to receive information from a file. This is simple enough, just turn the redirection command symbol around.

We'll look at the sort command in-depth later in this étude. For now, it is enough to know that if it is not given any options, it will sort a file based on the left-most column in the file. In this instance, we're going to sort dirfile.txt. It will sort the column with the -rwxrw-r-- information.

1. TYPE **sort < dirfile.txt** Enter
   The sorted output is displayed on the screen.

2. TYPE **clear** Enter

COMBINING REDIRECTION SYMBOLS

In some situations, you can combine redirection symbols.

1. TYPE **sort < dirfile.txt > sortfile.txt** Enter

2. NOTICE that no file output is displayed to the screen.
   The shell interpreter works from left to right, working with pairs of commands and files.
   - First, dirfile.txt is sent to the sort command.
   - Second, the output of the sort command is sent to sortfile.txt.

3. TYPE **cat sortfile.txt** Enter if you want to see the result.

APPENDING FILES

Appending a file means adding information to the end of an existing file. The characters you use to append are two greater-than symbols in succession (>>). Append is handy if you need to add a short item to a to-do list, add a name to a list of names, or combine the information in one file with another file.

A QUICK WAY TO CREATE TEXT FILES

Now we need to create two short files to demonstrate appending. We could open an editor, but there is a quicker way to create a couple of short text files. This can be especially useful when you want to test a technique. We're going to use the cat command.

1. CLEAR the screen.
2. At the command prompt, TYPE **cat > fileone.txt** Enter
   The cursor drops to the next line and waits for you to type.
3. TYPE **This is the first line.** Enter
4. PRESS the Ctrl + **z** keys (press and hold down the Ctrl key, then press the **z** key).
   You are returned to the command prompt.
5. TYPE **cat fileone.txt** Enter
   The line of text you just entered is displayed.

APPENDING TWO FILES

You can use the cat command to add information to the end of an existing file. This is called appending. You use the greater-than symbols (>>) to tell the computer to append. However, the rule is that the command line must begin with a command, not a file name. Therefore, we cannot type **file1** >> **file2** by itself on the command line. Both are file names. We must begin with a command. It is typical to start the action using the cat command.

Appending the Output of the Cat Command to a File

1. TYPE **cat** >> **fileone.txt** Enter
   The command prompt again drops to the second line and awaits the input you type.
2. TYPE **This is the second line.** Enter
3. PRESS Ctrl + **z** to end the input mode.
4. TYPE **cat fileone.txt** Enter
   You see the following displayed:
   This is the first line.
   This is the second line.

Creating a Second File Using the Same Technique

1. TYPE **cat > filetwo.txt** Enter
2. TYPE **This is input from file two.** Enter
3. PRESS Ctrl + **z** to end the input mode.

Appending Two Files

1. TYPE **cat filetwo.txt >> fileone.txt** Enter
2. TYPE **cat fileone.txt** Enter
3. LOOK at your screen.
   You see the following displayed:
   This is the first line.
   This is the second line.
   This is input from file two.
   The output of the first file was appended to the output of the second file.

PIPING

Piping is sending information from one command to another. The symbol for piping is the vertical bar (|). It is usually located on the upper-right of the keyboard. Let's send the output of the ls -la * command directly to the sort command. This is an example of where piping would be used since we are sending the output of one command to the input of another command.

1. TYPE **ls –la * | sort** Enter
2. LOOK at your screen.
   The sorted long form of the directory listing, along with hidden files, is displayed on the screen.

Piping will be used with other commands as you work through additional command line études.

THE SORT COMMAND

The sort command is frequently used. It has several important options. When it is used without any options, the sort command sorts on the left-most column of the input. If you want it to sort on a different column, you have to give it a number that represents the number of columns it must skip to get to the column you want it to use. For example, to sort by the second column of the file numlist.txt, you would issue the command (following the command rules)

sort +1 numlist.txt

You've told sort to skip the first column and use the next one, which is the second column.

If you wanted to sort by the fourth column in the file dirfile.txt, you would issue the command

sort +3 dirfile.txt

You've told sort to skip the first three columns and use the next, which is the fourth column.

Sort has several options. Three frequently used options are:

- -i means to ignore the case
- -n is used when you are sorting numbers
- -r means to sort in reverse order—from largest to smallest

These last two choices can be used together as nr.

Let's say we wanted to sort the second column of the numlist.txt file, which has numbers in the second column, and we also wanted to sort them from largest to smallest.

1. TYPE **sort +1 -nr numlist.txt** Enter
2. LOOK at your screen.
   Your screen displays the numbers from largest to smallest.
   In the file dirfile.txt, you have several columns. The fifth column is the number of bytes in each file. To sort by file size, from largest to smallest:
3. TYPE **sort +4 -nr dirfile.txt** Enter
   Now you can easily know which of your files are the largest.

SUMMARY

You have learned that you redirect between a command and a file and you pipe between two commands. You also have learned the redirection and append commands. Redirection is for moving information between a command and a file. The symbols for the redirection command are

- > (sends to)
- < (receives from)
- >> (appends to)

Piping is for moving information between two commands. The symbol for piping is | .

Sort sorts on the left-most column, unless you tell it the number of columns to skip before it begins sorting. This is done with a plus sign. It is of the format **sort +*n file-name***. Sort has the following options:

- -i to ignore case
- -r to create a descending order sort
- -n to sort numbers

The column number to sort by and the letter options can be all used on the same command line; for example, **sort +3 -rn dir.txt** would sort the fourth column (after skipping the first three from the left), sort by numbers, and create an output from largest to smallest.

COMMAND SHORTCUTS AND THE SHELL ENVIRONMENT

ÉTUDE 20

We all like shortcuts, and we all like to customize our work environments to maximize productivity (or to minimize annoyances). When you work on the command line, you are actually working in a shell. The shell interprets your commands and sends them on to the kernel. The tc, bash, and korn shells give the user the option of customizing commands so the user can create shortcuts to lengthy commands. These shortcuts are called "aliases."

Shells also give you the opportunity to change the visual environment and to change the way they work through the use of environment variables. If you spend a lot of time on the command line, this can provide visual relief in addition to speeding up productivity.

You can type in these changes each time you start the shell, or you can add them to either the .profile file or the .rcsh file. Adding these changes to one of these files will automatically install them when you begin a shell session.

TOPICS COVERED IN THIS ÉTUDE

- Shells and commands
- The alias command

- The history list
- Preserving aliases and other options

SHELLS AND COMMANDS

When you open a terminal emulator from within X Window System, you see a few symbols and a cursor. This is the command line. The command line exists within a shell. The shell is a command interpreter that takes the commands entered on the command line, interprets them into a form that can be used by the kernel, and passes them to the kernel. As discussed earlier, the kernel is the part of the operating system that communicates directly with the electronic hardware.

Linux has several shells available to the user. The bash shell (Bourne Again Shell) was developed for Linux but, sadly, drags along the awkward Bourne syntax. Fortunately, it is easy to escape this for the modern and less tedious syntax of the tc shell.

SHELLS? WHAT DIFFERENCE DO THEY MAKE?

You can use any of the major shells, Bourne, c or tc, Korn, or even the bash, to execute basic commands from the command line. The difference comes when you begin trying to perform advanced operations and when you begin using what are called "control structures" to write shell scripts. The c shell and tc shell have control structures that look like those in c and follow similar syntax rules. (The "t" in "tc" shell stands for "Tom's," as in "Tom's c shell.")

When you open a terminal emulator in Linux, it starts up with the bash shell. This can be permanently changed for the entire system in the /etc/bashrc file, or it can be changed in your /home/.bashrc file. This will be covered later in this étude, in the section "Preserving Aliases and Other Options."

TEMPORARILY CHANGING SHELLS

1. OPEN a terminal emulator.
2. At the command line, TYPE **tcsh**.
   This starts the tc shell. (Linux starts the tc shell when the command for the c shell, csh, is issued.) Now we'll exit the tc shell.
3. At the command line, TYPE **exit**.
   You have exited the tc shell.

THE ALIAS COMMAND

The alias command allows you to give an alternative name to a command. The original command will still work. The alias is an additional name. Typically, this is used to give a shortened or easier-to-type name to a command or to a command with options and parameters. The alias commands in both tc shell and bash shell are similar but not identical. Each will be treated separately.

ALIASING IN THE TC SHELL

Adding an Alias

The clear command clears the screen. To use the clear command, type clear and press the Enter key. Typing this is a bit awkward. We will give the clear command the alias cls. This command is easily and quickly typed.

The format of the alias command is

alias *new-command old-command*

1. To switch to the tc shell, TYPE **tcsh** Enter
   You are now in the tc shell.
2. TYPE **alias cls clear** Enter
3. TYPE **cls** Enter
   The screen is now cleared by typing cls.

Removing an Alias

To remove an alias, type the command **unalias *alias-name***. For example, to remove cls as an alias:

1. TYPE **unalias cls** Enter
   cls is no longer an alias for clear.
2. TYPE **cls** Enter
   You are told, "Command not found."

Creating an Alias That Includes Options

An alias can also include command options. For example, change the list command so that when you type ls, it actually performs ls -l.

1. TYPE **alias ls ls -l** Enter
2. TYPE **ls** Enter
   The operating system actually executes the command ls -l.

Creating an Alias That Includes an Argument

An alias can also include an argument such as a file name, or it can include special characters such as those used in piping, appending, or redirection. The command that is being aliased must be enclosed in apostrophes.

For example, create an alias dir that lists all files, directories, and directory contents one level down.

1. TYPE **alias dir 'ls *'** Enter
2. TYPE **dir** Enter

You should see the entire directory, with subdirectories and contents listed.

For another example, create an alias drsort that provides a directory listing sorted in reverse order.

3. TYPE **alias drsort 'ls | sort -r'** Enter
4. TYPE **drsort** Enter
   The directory listing is displayed in reverse order.

ALIASING IN BASH

Aliasing is done the same way in bash, except that an equal sign is added to the command. There is no space on either side of the equal sign.

For example, to create the alias drsort as shown above:

1. TYPE **exit** Enter
   You exited to the bash shell.
2. TYPE **alias drsort='ls | sort -r'** Enter
3. TYPE **drsort** Enter
   The directory is displayed, sorted in reverse order.

THE HISTORY LIST

In the c shell, a new capability was added. The operating system kept track of the commands issued on the command line. These could then be referenced by typing the command history and entering a shorthand code, instead of a lengthy command. That capability still exists, but there is now a much faster way to repeat commands.

A FAST TECHNIQUE FOR REPEATING EVENTS

You can scroll through previous commands by pressing the up-arrow key located immediately to the right of the main keys on the keyboard. Pressing the down-arrow key takes you to the most recently executed commands.

Once the desired command appears, press the Enter key to repeat it.

QUICK EDITING

1. TYPE **ls -la | sort -r** Enter
2. TYPE **clear** Enter
3. TYPE **history** Enter
4. TYPE **clear** Enter
5. PRESS the ↑ key until the **ls -la | sort -r** command is displayed.

6. MOVE the cursor to the "a" part of the ls -la command option.
7. PRESS Delete to remove the "a."
8. PRESS the Enter key.
   The output changed. This is a very quick and productive method for editing commands.

PRESERVING ALIASES AND OPTIONS IN THE RESOURCE FILE

Aliases and other options you set up in a shell are not preserved once you leave that shell. Nor are they available if you open another session with that shell or if you log out and log back in. If you want to keep these aliases, you must take steps to preserve them. Let's see how the shell clears the aliases and commands.

CHECKING TO SEE IF ALIASES ARE PRESERVED IN THE TC SHELL

1. TYPE **tcsh** Enter to change to the tc shell.
2. TYPE **alias cls clear** Enter
3. TYPE **cls** Enter
4. TYPE **exit** Enter
   You return to the bash shell.
5. TYPE **tcsh** Enter to change back into the tc shell.
6. TYPE **cls** Enter
   You get the error message that no such command is found.
   This clearly demonstrates that aliases set up in a shell are not preserved once you leave that shell.

WORKING IN THE TC SHELL

How can you get around this problem if you want to keep aliases and other options available for use?

In the tc shell, your aliases and other items can be preserved by placing them in the .tcshrc file. The period, as the first character in the file name, indicates that this is a hidden file. In the remainder of the file name, "tc" stands for c shell, "sh" stands for shell, and "rc" stands for resource. .tcshrc is the c shell resource file. This creates what is called the tc shell environment. It will be referred to every time any c shell is started.

1. TYPE **kedit .tcshrc** Enter

The KEdit window opens. You may have an empty .tcshrc file, or you may already have some predefined aliases and other environment settings entered.

2. In the KEdit window, TYPE **alias cls clear** Enter
   This allows you to type **cls** to clear the screen.
3. CLICK on **File**.
4. CLICK on **Save**.
5. CLICK on **File**.
6. CLICK on **Quit**.
7. On the command line, TYPE **source .tcshrc** Enter
   This forces the operating system to update the environment variables. This means that the new alias is internalized without having to restart the system.
8. TYPE **cls** Enter
   The screen is cleared.
9. TYPE **exit** Enter
   You return to the bash shell.
10. TYPE **tcsh** Enter
    You return to the tc shell.
11. TYPE **ls -la** Enter
    This gives you some writing on the screen to clear.
12. TYPE **cls** Enter
    The screen clears. Note that you did not have to retype the alias.
13. TYPE **exit** Enter
    You exited the tc shell.

WORKING IN THE BASH SHELL

Theoretically, the bash shell is established in a .profile file. This varies in distributions. It might be done in .profile or it might be done in .bash_profile.

If you are working with Red Hat, the aliases will be stored in the .bashrc file. If you are using the Red Hat distribution, take the following steps:

1. TYPE **kedit .bashrc** Enter
2. In the KEdit window, CLICK the cursor under the heading of "User specific aliases."
3. TYPE **alias cls=clear** Enter
   Notice there are no spaces around the equal sign.

4. CLICK **File**.
5. CLICK **Save**.
6. CLICK **File**.
7. CLICK **Quit**.
8. At the command line, TYPE **source .bashrc** **Enter**
9. TYPE **cls** **Enter**
   The screen is cleared.

SUMMARY

In this étude, we have learned what an alias is and how to create one for both the c shell and the bash shell.

We have also learned how to use the history list and the history command, how to use the arrow keys to scroll through the history list, and how to edit and reuse a command from the history list.

We also learned how to preserve aliases in the resource files for the c and bash shells so that the commands do not have to be retyped each time the shell is started.

GREP:
SEARCHING FOR WORDS, PATTERNS, OR DATA

ÉTUDE 21

The grep command, if used with a thoughtfully designed database, can yield significant database-type results with very little effort. In this étude, grep will be used from the command line. In Étude 24, we embed grep in a script and make grep useful even for users who don't know Linux.

Grep stands for "global regular expression pattern (or print)." We will use grep to search for a database item. We will also use it to search through a group of files and report whether it finds the match to a particular word.

Grep displays each line that contains the item being searched for. A line is a set of characters that is ended by the press of the **Enter** key. Don't confuse a line with a sentence. Word wrap may appear to move us down a line, but the text is not considered a line until **Enter** is pressed. In a document with narrative text, we let words wrap to the next line and only press the **Enter** key at the end of a paragraph. This means that if grep finds a match in a paragraph, it will display the entire paragraph.

We are assuming that you have completed Études 18 and 19.

TOPICS COVERED IN THIS ÉTUDE

- The form for the grep command
- Using grep
- Piping grep output
- Using grep to help with systems administration work

THE GREP COMMAND

The form for the grep command is

grep *options search-pattern file-name*

OPTIONS AND SEARCH PATTERNS

Grep can be used with several different search patterns. The following options are used with the grep search patterns in this étude:

-i Ignores the case

-w Displays only the entire word (not the word embedded as part of another word, such as the word "the" in the word "another")

-v Reverses the sense of the test (excludes the lines that contain the search pattern)

If the search string of characters contains a space, such as the apple name "Golden Delicious," the string must be enclosed in quotation marks. The search pattern may also contain substitution characters, called "wildcards," to take the place of unknown characters.

USING GREP

USING GREP WITH A SINGLE VALUE

1. OPEN a terminal emulator.
2. On the command line, TYPE **grep 11 numlist.txt** Enter
   We are working with numlist.txt, the file we created in Étude 17.
3. LOOK at your screen.
   The screen displays line 11. Grep displayed the contents of the entire line.

USING GREP WITH A STRING

1. On the command line, TYPE **grep "line 12" numlist.txt** Enter
2. LOOK at your screen.

You see line 12 displayed.

By the way, you could have used apostrophes instead of quotation marks, in this instance. Apostrophes remove all special meanings from all special characters. Quotation marks remove most special meanings. One notable exception is they do not remove the special meanings of the dollar sign. This leads into a discussion of what is called "quoting." See the references listed at the end of this étude for more information.

USING GREP WITH A SMALL DATABASE

Creating the Database

1. OPEN KEdit.
2. TYPE the following, using tabs to line up the columns:

Claudia	**August 12**	**1992**	**Jean**	**Sandra** Enter
Jeremy	**August 5**	**1995**	**Georgette**	**Andre, Pierre** Enter
Sharon	**October 27**	**1995**	**Frank**	**Mitsy, Jon** Enter
Judy	**February 10**	**1997**	**Jacque**	**Jean, Jacque Jr.** Enter
Linda	**November 11**	**1988**	**Wm**	**none**

   This database lists employees, their birthdays, their starting years, their spouses, and their families.
3. SAVE the file in your personal home directory with the name **mygroup**.
4. CREATE a new file in your editor.
5. TYPE the following:

Justin	**August 11**	**1953**	**Michelle**	**Ralph, Susan, Peter** Enter
Niles	**March 25**	**1965**	**LoriAnn**	**Francis, Joan, Marty**

6. SAVE the file in your personal home directory with the name **myfamily**.
7. CLOSE both files and the editor.

Searching the Database

The month of August is about to begin. Is there anyone you need to send birthday greetings to?

1. In the terminal emulator, TYPE **grep -i august mygroup** Enter
2. LOOK at your screen.
   You get listings for Jeremy and Claudia.

   In Étude 24, you will learn how to embed the grep command into a script command so that you won't have to use the grep command directly.

You've heard that Judy's husband is ill. What is his name?

3. TYPE **grep -i Judy mygroup** Enter

4. LOOK at your screen.
The line displayed shows that his name is Jacque. Notice that the option -i is used to tell grep to ignore case. This is typical since we usually won't recall whether upper or lower case was used.

Now let's assume we want to see all of the birthdays except those in August.

5. TYPE **grep -vi august mygroup** Enter

6. LOOK at your screen.
All the lines in the file that do not contain August are printed.

It's time for giving out pins to those employees who have been with the company a certain number of years. We'll look for who joined the company in 1995.

7. TYPE **grep 1995 mygroup** Enter

8. LOOK at your screen.
Jeremy and Sharon are listed. Of course, we'd be sure to invite Jeremy's wife, Georgette, and Sharon's husband, Frank, to the ceremony. Did you notice that since our search pattern was for numbers, we didn't need to use the -i option?

November 11 is Veteran's Day, a national holiday. People in our group get their birthday off as a bonus benefit. If their birthday is a national holiday, they get the following workday off. Will we have to cover for anyone following November 11?

Problem: If you type **grep -i November 11 mygroup**, you will get an error because grep will assume that the end of the pattern is signaled by the first space following November. You will get a file error message because it will try to find a file named 11.

Solution: If you have to search for a string with a space, enclose the search string in apostrophes or quotation marks.

9. TYPE **grep -i "November 11" mygroup** Enter

10. LOOK at your screen.
We see that we'll need to make sure the work assignments for Linda are covered for the first workday following November 11 since her birthday is on November 11.

True, you could type "11" or "November," but doing it this way yields the specific results we need while leaving no margin of error—such as sorting through a long list of lines, misreading a line, and preparing for the wrong absence.

USING GREP WITH TWO OR MORE FILES SIMULTANEOUSLY

In another scenario, it's the last day of July. We need a list of birthdays for August. However, we need to check two lists—the list for our workgroup and the list for our family. Grep allows both files to be listed following the search pattern. This is a real time-saver.

1. TYPE **grep -i august mygroup myfamily** Enter
2. LOOK at your screen.
   The output looks like:

mygroup: Claudia	**August 12**	**1992**	**Jean**	**Sandra**
mygroup: Jeremy	**August 5**	**1995**	**Georgette**	**Andre, Pierre**
myfamily: Justin	**August 11**	**1953**	**Michelle**	**Ralph, Susan, Peter**

   What you notice is that the file name is printed first and then the line from the file is printed. Since the mygroup file was specified first, the entire mygroup file is searched, and any lines containing the search pattern are displayed. Next, the entire myfamily file is searched for the search pattern. Any lines in that file containing the search pattern are then displayed. The output lines are not mixed.

PIPING GREP OUTPUT

PIPING OUTPUT TO THE PRINTER

The command to send a file to the printer is lpr. This can be made even more convenient. If you worked through Étude 19, you learned how to use piping and redirection. We'll pipe the output to the printer, and then we can take the list with us as we look for birthday cards. No lists to jot down!

1. TYPE **grep -i august mygroup myfamily | lpr** Enter
2. LOOK at the page printed.
   The output looks the same as above, only now it is printed on a sheet of paper.

PIPING OUTPUT TO THE SORT COMMAND

Even this list can be improved by sorting the birth dates. Notice that the month name is in the second column. We want to sort by the date that is in the third column. If you worked through Étude 19, you learned that we need to tell the sort command to skip over the first two columns. We'll do this with +2. Also, remember that since we want to sort numbers (the dates), we need to use the -n option.

1. TYPE **grep -i august mygroup myfamily | sort +2 -n** Enter

2. LOOK at your screen.

   The output looks like the following:

mygroup: Jeremy August 5 1995 Georgette Andre, Pierre
myfamily: Justin August 11 1953 Michelle Ralph, Susan, Peter
mygroup: Claudia August 12 1992 Jean Sandra

   Now we're getting to some convenient planning information. The first birthday is Jeremy's, in our workgroup. Next comes Justin's birthday in our family. The day after our family celebration, we have Claudia's birthday at work. Better pick up a card for Claudia while we're getting Justin's since we probably won't have time the night before to run out and do it.

PIPING OUTPUT TO THE SORT COMMAND AND TO THE PRINTER

What would be really convenient is if we could get a sorted list sent to the printer. We can do that by piping the output from grep to sort and then piping the output from the sort command to the lpr command.

1. TYPE the following:
   grep -i august mygroup myfamily | sort +2 -n | lpr Enter
2. NOTICE that the same output is now printed to the printer.

USING GREP TO HELP WITH SYSTEMS ADMINISTRATION WORK

You've used grep so far to find information in thoughtfully constructed databases. If you were trying to do some systems administration work, you might want a list of all the directories in a particular subdirectory. In Linux, we can pick this out visually because directories are color-coded blue. But what if we wanted these directory names printed before we began to make changes to a system? You sure wouldn't want to have to jot all that down by hand!

If you read through Étude 17, you learned that using the list command with the option -l outputs the long form of the file listing. The left-most item was the file and directory permissions. You may not have noticed it, but all directories start with the form drwx. They may have other information too, but they have at least that much in common. This gives the user reading, writing, and accessing permission to their own directories. Drwx also makes a unique pattern. We'll use this insight in combination with grep to pick out directories.

What will be unique about this situation is that we won't need a file name. The input for grep will come from the ls -la command.

1. TYPE **ls -la | grep drwx** Enter

2. LOOK at your screen.
The output is all of the directories in the subdirectory. If you wanted a listing of all files and no directories, you could invert the search with the -v option.
3. TYPE **ls -la | grep -v drwx**.
4. LOOK at your screen.
The output is all of the files in the subdirectory. None of the directories are listed.

SUMMARY

In this étude, we focused exclusively on the grep command. The syntax for the grep command is

grep *options search-pattern file-name*

Many options are available with grep. We've looked at only three in this étude:

- -i—ignore the case
- -w—display only words, not embedded patterns
- -v—exclude lines that contain the search pattern (perform an inverted search)

The search pattern can be a set of characters, a word, or a string. If a string with a space in it is used, the string must be enclosed in apostrophes or quotation marks. The search pattern may also contain substitution characters to take the place of unknown characters. Multiple file names may be included on the same line. Grep will search the files in turn. Lines containing the search pattern will be preceded by the file name.

Like any other command, grep's output can be redirected to a file, or it can be piped to another command. This allows for refined processing of grep's output. The file name is not used if the output from another command is being piped into grep.

In Étude 24, you'll learn how to embed grep into a script so that you can use the command without having to remember the options and the command syntax.

If you want to do further database processing from the command line, it would be better to use awk, covered in Étude 22. Grep is like having an old-time, single-cylinder, gasoline engine. You can get a lot of work out of it with some clever thought, but ultimately you get to a point of diminishing returns. Then you need to turn to a more suitable tool.

REFERENCE

Quigley, Ellie. "Steps for Using Quoting Correctly." In *Unix Shells by Example.* 2d ed. Upper Saddle River, NJ: Prentice Hall, 2000.

AWK AS A DATABASE PROGRAM

ÉTUDE 22

We haven't yet introduced a database program, but in business a database program is often second in importance only to a word-processing program. Database choices for the Linux desktop cover the typical broad range: database programs in application software suites, stand-alone database programs, and address book programs.

Among Linux office suites, you will find StarBase in StarOffice and the database program in WordPerfect Office for Linux. The WordPerfect Office database is similar to Microsoft Access. StarOffice is essentially free for individual users. WordPerfect Office for Linux is not free and, as product reviews have stated, runs slowly on top of the WINE emulator. Among the stand-alone databases, you will find DB2, Gabby, MySQL, and mSQL. DB2 is a professional database program and can be downloaded with literature from the Red Hat and IBM Web sites. MySQL and mSQL are superb and are well-supported online and in the Linux literature. However, MySQL has more of a learning curve than the smaller applications. Address book programs are found in Gnome and KDE. Gnome Address is an excellent, seasoned address book program.

Is there an easy-to-learn database program that makes it easy to retrieve information and to enter and delete data? Yes. It is awk, a pattern-matching and manipulation programming language. Awk developers gave awk a decided emphasis as a tool that can work easily with text-file databases. It works with simple text files. In other words, you can start a text editor, enter data in whatever table format suits your situation, and save it. Later, you can easily update your database with your editor. That's convenient.

Is awk easy to use to retrieve information? Yes. You tell it the pattern, word, or string to match or the comparison to make. Then you tell it the action to take when it finds that pattern or string (by default, it displays them to the screen). Every time it finds a line (called a "record") in a database file that matches the condition you specified, it takes the action that you specified. Pattern and action are the two parts of an awk command. The output of awk can be sent to other commands, to a file, or to the screen or printer.

Simple awk commands can be issued from the command line. Once you get used to the commands, they are almost intuitive. Awk commands can be written into a script file to perform repetitive tasks, such as generating reports. Awk gives you the capability to create report headings, precisely place output, and create summary reports. The reports that awk generates can be formatted as explicitly as you need.

If you want to do a simple data extraction, as is often the situation, you can issue the awk command on the command line and have your results before most people can even get their sophisticated database program started up. Awk allows you to extract data using standard commands such as "and" and "or," and you can specify a range that data must fit within. Once extracted, the data can be processed using awk's built-in functions.

Awk is not a relational database program. A relational database program organizes data into tables and establishes relationships between those tables. This reduces a lot of redundancy and errors that creep in because of redundancies, such as the typing of a CD title 15 times, once for each separate song listing. However, by the thoughtful choice of an editor and the way you use it, the likelihood of errors from redundancies is minimized.

Although awk has a broader range of capabilities, this étude focuses on its use as a database language. In Étude 27, awk script files, report headings, and summary reports are explained.

TOPICS COVERED IN THIS ÉTUDE

- Awk rules
- Awk patterns
- Awk actions
- Printing with awk
- Awk patterns and actions used together

- Comparisons using awk
- Finding data over a range using awk
- Computations in awk

A FEW AWK RULES

An awk command can consist of five parts:

awk *option pattern* { *action* } *file-name*

The command awk is always present. The option portion is used only if a command option is chosen. The pattern is usually present. This is either a pattern of characters that will be searched for or a comparison that will be tested. The { *action* } is also usually present. This is the action that you want taken when a pattern match is found. Curly braces always enclose the action so the awk program can distinguish the action portion from the pattern portion. More than a single action can be taken. The file-name portion is always present.

If the pattern is omitted but the action is present, then the action is applied to every line. If the action is omitted but the pattern is present, then every line matching the pattern is sent to what is called "standard output." This usually means that the output is sent to the display. The pattern and action can be typed on the command line. They can also be entered into a file. Awk is then directed to the file that stores the pattern and action.

For the following examples, we are going to need a data file to work with.

1. OPEN KEdit.
2. COPY the following data into a file. The semicolon after each item is needed.
   The typing of the following can look daunting. A lot of the tedium can be removed by 1) typing the first line, 2) copying the first line and then pasting it 10 times, and 3) going back and making the correct entry for each field.
   Apple;Red Delicious;Sml;1.00;23
   Apple;Red Delicious;Med;1.09;28
   Apple;Red Delicious;Large;1.19;13
   Apple;Golden Delicious;Sml;1.00;17
   Apple;Golden Delicious;Med;1.19;19
   Apple;Golden Delicious;Large;1.29;22
   Apple;Gala;Sml;1.09;11
   Apple;Gala;Med;1.11;9
   Apple;Gala;Large;1.39;14
   Apple;Mediterranean;Sml;1.79;5
   Apple;Mediterranean;Large;2.09;7
3. SAVE the file in your home directory with the file name of **fruits**.

SOME DATABASE TERMINOLOGY

Each row is called a *record*. Each column in each row is called a *field*.

The following is one record:

Apple;Red Delicious;Sml;1.00;23

Red Delicious is in the second field.

This file that we created contains 11 records. Each record consists of five fields. The semicolon after each field is called the "field separator." A blank space is the default separator. However, notice that in this database "Red Delicious" and "Golden Delicious" are two words separated by a space. We cannot use a blank space as the field separator because then awk will assume that Red and Golden are one field and Delicious is in a separate field unassociated with Red or Golden. The way to fix this is to use a field separator that is not a blank space. We can do this, but we must remember to tell awk what symbol we are using as a field separator.

Now that we have an database file, we are ready to try some awk commands.

PRINTING WITH AWK

We'll look at a few different ways to print and manipulate output. First, we'll print an entire database file.

1. OPEN a terminal emulator window.
2. TYPE **awk {print} fruits** Enter
   The entire database file is displayed. Why? When there is no pattern, the action is applied to every line in the database.
   Now we'll use a pattern to select a line to display.
3. TYPE **awk -F";" '/Sml/' fruits** Enter
   Four lines, each containing the abbreviation "Sml," for "small," are displayed.
   Notice the use of **-F";"**. -F is called a command option. It is used to inform awk of the symbol our database file uses for a field separator. The ; tells awk that it is the symbol used as the field separator. The quotation marks are required, or the shell command interpreter will try to interpret the semicolon as an end of statement. The quotation marks take away the special meaning of the semicolon, and the semicolon is passed to the awk command.
   Notice the use of apostrophes. The apostrophes are used to enclose the entire pattern and action combination. This prevents the command shell from trying to execute any part of the pattern and action. It is all passed intact, as written, to awk.
   Notice the use of forward slashes. The slashes tell awk that a regular expression (a set of characters) is being provided as the pattern to be matched.

Now we'll apply an action to every line and print the data in each column. We want to precede each line that is displayed with the label of Fruit:.

4. TYPE **awk -F";" '{print "Fruit: ",$1,$2,$3,$4,$5}' fruits** **Enter**
Everything inside the curly braces is called the "action."

The $1, $2, and so on specify which columns of data to print. We have told the print action to print the string "Fruit: ". If we want the print action to print any other columns from the data file, we must tell it explicitly which columns to print. The $ in front of the number stands for "the content of ." The content of field 2, the apple type, is printed. The content of field 4, the cost, is printed.

A Linux guru may tell you that $0 will print the entire line and suggest that $0 can replace $1 through $5. This is true only if you want to see the semicolons in the output. However, the semicolons are stripped off if you specify the individual columns of data. Each line will be printed, preceded by "Fruit:."

Fruit: Apple Red Delicious Sml 1.00 23
Fruit: Apple Red Delicious Med 1.09 28
Fruit: Apple Red Delicious Large 1.19 13
Fruit: Apple Golden Delicious Sml 1.00 17
...

Note: If there is no pattern, the action is applied to every line. If you had used only the action {print "Fruit: "}, then the output would have been

Fruit:
Fruit:
Fruit:
...

The other columns would not have been printed.

Also, note the difference in output between using only the action {print} and the action {print "Fruit: ",$1,$2,$3,$4,$5} fruits. With only the print action, the semicolons are shown. With the columns specified, the semicolon, which is the field separator, is stripped off all data sent to the display.

If you did not get this output, check the following:

- There must be a space between the right apostrophe and the file name of **fruits**.
- If the output seems to stop and freeze, you probably made a typing error. Press the **Ctrl** button, and while holding it down, press the letter **c**. This cancels whatever the computer is trying to do and returns you to the command prompt.

SEARCHING A DATABASE

We will look at a few different ways to search the database. First, we'll search for all Sml (small) apples. We will search for all small apples but will print only the apple type and cost. Apple type is in column 2, and cost is in column 4. (In other words, don't print the entire line of each record. Only print the fields from the record that we specify.)

1. TYPE **awk -F";" '/Sml/ {print $2,$4}' fruits** Enter
   /Sml/ is the pattern. What's between the curly braces is the action. This is an example of the pattern-and-action combination usually found in an awk command.
   The output is
   Red Delicious 1.00
   Golden Delicious 1.00
   Gala 1.09
   Mediterranean 1.79
   The comma between $2 and $4 causes spacing to be inserted between the output items. If the comma is left off, the items will run together.

   Now we'll change the order of the fields when they are displayed.

2. TYPE **awk -F";" '/Sml/ {print $4,$2}' fruits** Enter
   The output is
   1.00 Red Delicious
   1.00 Golden Delicious
   1.09 Gala
   1.79 Mediterranean

   Now we'll insert a dollar sign before the amount.

3. TYPE **awk -F";" '/Sml/ {print "$"$4,$2}' fruits** Enter
   The output is
   $1.00 Red Delicious
   $1.00 Golden Delicious
   $1.09 Gala
   $1.79 Mediterranean

   Quotation marks are placed around the $ that is to be inserted immediately before the content of column 4 is printed. This takes away the special meaning of the $ symbol and instructs the awk print action to print the $ sign and not try to interpret it.

   Now we'll specify the field to be checked for a match. In this example, we don't want awk to search everywhere on the line for a match. We will specify the field to be checked for a match. When we find a match, we want to print the cost and the apple type.

Note: The ~, called the tilde, is the match symbol. It indicates that a match is to be located. **$3 ~ /Med/** could be read as "field 3 matches Med."

4. TYPE **awk -F";" '$3 ~ /Med/ {print $4,$2}' fruits** [Enter]
   The output is
   1.09 Red Delicious
   1.19 Golden Delicious
   1.11 Gala
   Why not just use **'/Med/ {print $4,$2}' fruits**? Because this means find a match anywhere on the line (in the record). This would have also listed both Mediterranean apples (because Mediterranean has the pattern "Med" embedded within it), although neither apple is medium-sized. We solve this problem by telling awk to search for a match only in the field containing the apple sizes.

USING A RELATIONAL OPERATOR

Relational operators give us the ability to specify that we want items that are equal to, less than, greater than, greater than or equal to, and so on.

The relational operators are the same ones you learned in math class:

>	greater than
<	less than
>=	greater than or equal to
<=	less than or equal to
==	equal to
!=	not equal to

In this example, we want to print out all apples costing less than $1.12 per pound. Print the cost, the number of pounds, the size, and the apple type. Precede the cost with a dollar sign. Follow the number of pounds with one blank space and the abbreviation "lb." The cost data is in column 4.

1. TYPE the following:
   awk -F";" '$4 < 1.12 {print "$"$4,$5,"lb",$3,$2}' fruits [Enter]
   Slashes are not used since this is a relational expression—a condition to test. It is not a regular expression—a pattern to match. The slashes are used with regular expressions.
   The output is
   $1.00 23 lb Sml Red Delicious
   $1.09 28 lb Med Red Delicious
   $1.00 17 lb Sml Golden Delicious

$1.09 11 lb Sml Gala
$1.11 9 lb Med Gala

Now we'll display the apples that fit within a cost range. We will use a logical "and" to join two relational expressions. The relational expressions will determine the upper and lower limits of the range.

Before we write the instruction, we need to learn how to use logical operators. The logical operators are "and," "or," and "not." The symbols for them are

&& and

|| or

! not

When an "and" logical operator joins two or more relational expressions, if all the relational expressions are true for the line, then the line matches the conditions and the specified data is printed. When an "or" logical operator joins two or more relational expressions, if any one of the relational expressions is true for a line, then the line matches the conditions and the specified data is printed.

We will print out all apples with costs in the range of $1.05 to $1.15 per pound. We will display the cost, the size, and the apple type. The cost is in column 4. In this situation we need the "and" logical operator. We want the cost to be greater than or equal to 1.05, and we want the cost to be less than or equal to 1.15. This shows how we create a range.

2. TYPE the following:
awk -F";" '$4 >= 1.05 && $4 <= 1.15 {print $4,$3,$2}' fruits
Enter
The output is
1.09 Med Red Delicious
1.09 Sml Gala
1.11 Med Gala

Now we'll use the "and" logical operator to test for conditions in two data columns. In this situation, we are not looking for a range. We simply want the data from lines where the conditions for the two specified columns are true.

We want to print out all apples that are medium-size and that cost less than $1.12 per pound. We want to print the cost, the number of pounds, the size, and the apple type. Put the lb symbol after the number of pounds. Separate the number from the symbol with one blank space.

The cost is in column 4. The number of pounds in stock is in column 5. The type of apple is in column 2.

3. TYPE the following:
awk -F";" '$4 < 1.12 && $3 ~ /Med/ {print "$"$4,$5,"lb",$3,$2}' fruits Enter
The output is
$1.09 28 lb Med Red Delicious
$1.11 9 lb Med Gala

In the above expression, awk was instructed to print output for each record where the cost was less than $1.12 per pound and the size Med was matched. When using "and," both conditions must be true for the action to be applied to the record.

Now we'll use the "or" logical operator. We want to test two or more fields. If any of those fields meets the condition (is true), then we want to print out some data from that record.

Print out all apples that are medium-size apples or are Mediterranean type. Print the cost, the number of pounds, the size, and the apple type. Put the "lb" symbol after the number of pounds. Separate the number from the symbol with one blank space.

4. TYPE the following:
awk -F";" '$2 ~ /Mediterranean/ || $3 ~ /Med/ {print "$"$4,$5,"lb",$3,$2}' fruits Enter
The output is
$1.09 28 lb Med Red Delicious
$1.19 19 lb Med Golden Delicious
$1.11 9 lb Med Gala
$1.79 5 lb Sml Mediterranean
$2.09 7 lb Large Mediterranean

In the above expression, awk was instructed to print output for each record where the size matched medium (Med) in field 3 or where the apple type matched Mediterranean in field 2. When using "or," only one condition must be true for the action to be applied to the record.

COMPUTATIONS

Assume that the purchase cost of apples is 40 percent of their selling cost. Display the investment amount of each type of large apple and the apple type. First, we must match all the large apples. The action part will then multiply the cost per pound by the number of pounds and then multiply this by 0.40. The asterisk is the multiplication sign.

1. TYPE the following:
awk -F";" '$3 ~ /Large/ {print "$"$4*$5*0.40,$2}' fruits Enter

The output is
$6.188 Red Delicious
$11.352 Golden Delicious
$7.784 Gala
$5.852 Mediterranean
We multiplied field 4 (the cost per pound) by field 5 (the number of pounds) and multiplied that result by 0.40. The end result was then printed. Next, the data in field 2 (the apple type) was printed. The output could have been limited to two decimal digits, but that finishing touch is beyond the scope of this étude.

SUMMARY

You've learned to carry out simple data extractions from a database created with a simple text editor. An awk command consists of four parts: awk, command options, the search pattern, and the action to be taken when a match is found to the pattern. You've learned to work with a pattern of characters, relational operators, and logical operators. You've also seen how the action portion can contain simple computations.

We've been limited to simple commands because we have been issuing the awk commands with all their component parts on the command line. By writing awk scripts, we can issue as many awk action commands as needed to process the extracted data. Awk scripts and more advanced awk topics are covered in Étude 22.

An excellent summary of awk structure and commands is contained in *Unix in a Nutshell.* The authoritative reference on awk is *sed & awk.* If you decide that what you really need is a relational database, consider MySQL. The authoritative reference on MySQL is *MySQL & mSQL.* Chapter 2 of that book clearly explains how to design a relational database and how to implement it.

REFERENCES

Dougherty, Dale, and Arnold Robbins. *sed & awk.* 2d ed. Sebastopol, CA: O'Reilly & Associates, 1997.

Robbins, Arnold. *Unix in a Nutshell.* 3d ed. Sebastopol, CA: O'Reilly & Associates, 1999.

Yarger, Randy Jay, George Reese, and Tim King. *MySQL & mSQL.* Sebastopol, CA: O'Reilly & Associates, 1999.

SHELL SCRIPTS ÉTUDE 23

A shell script is used to automate the repetition of operating system commands. A script is a file. It can contain a few commands, or it can be a long list of programming-style commands that perform multiple file operations. You type the script's file name on the command line. When you press the **Enter** key, the computer begins carrying out the instructions contained within the shell script file.

A shell script also allows you create new commands or customize how a command works. This is possible for two reasons: 1) the user can pass information about choices into the script from the command line, and 2) each shell has "control structures." These allow the user to program choices using the if control structure. Control structures are covered in Étude 25.

These shell script instructions are given for the tc shell. Bash shell scripts are similar but require slightly different syntax.

TOPICS COVERED IN THIS ÉTUDE

- General steps for writing a script
- Writing your first script
- Giving a script executable permission

CREATING A SCRIPT

Generally, there are four steps to creating a script that is ready for execution as a command.

1. Open an editor with the file name you've chosen for your script.
2. In the upper-left corner, type which shell the command interpreter is to use to execute your instructions.
3. Enter your script instructions, save the file, and exit the editor.
4. Add executable permission to the file using the chmod command.

Examining each line and learning what it does is a good way to begin learning how to write a shell script program. This script will have the file name sday. The instructions contained in the script file will be the following:

```
#!/bin/tcsh
# Purpose: Greet user and display calendar for the current month.
# Created by your name
# Date: creation date
echo "This is the first script"
echo "Good day $USER"
echo The calendar for the month is
cal
```

DISCUSSION

The first line, **#!/bin/tcsh**, tells the shell command interpreter, regardless of which shell you are currently using, that this script is to be run using the tc shell. If you did not want to use the tc shell, the tcsh part would be replaced with the name of the shell you wanted to run. For example, to run the bash shell, because the script was written using bash shell programming language syntax, you would type **#!/bin/bash**.

#!/bin/tcsh must be typed in the upper-left position in the script. The # must be the very first character typed on the line. (No blank column spaces are allowed.)

The second line demonstrates a comment. A # on any line other than the top-most line tells the shell command interpreter that it should ignore the line. (It is there to improve the readability of the script.)

The fifth line demonstrates how to use the echo command. Echo repeats what follows it on the same line. If you want to preserve the spacing—such as in table headings—then place the string inside quotation marks.

The sixth line displays the user's login name. The user's login name is stored in the USER environment variable in the shell. The $ in front of the variable named USER means to print the variable's contents. Without the $, the echo command would print "USER" instead of the user's login name.

The seventh line demonstrates using the echo command without quotation marks. The eighth line is the cal command. This causes a calendar for the current month to be displayed. (Issuing the instruction **cal 3 1986** would display the calendar for March 1986. If you typed **cal 3 86**, the cal command would assume you meant the year 86 A.D.)

WRITING THE SCRIPT

You can give a script file any name you think is appropriate. I've chosen to use sday for "start day." It's easy to type.

1. OPEN a terminal emulator.
2. TYPE **kedit sday** Enter (to open the KEdit editor and create the file named **sday**).
3. In KEdit, TYPE **#!/bin/tcsh** Enter
   (Remember that this must be typed in the upper-left position.)
4. PRESS Enter again to create a blank line.
5. TYPE the following:
   # Purpose: Greet user and display calendar for the Enter
   # current month Enter
   # Created by (type your name here) Enter
   # Date: (enter today's date here) Enter
6. PRESS Enter again to create a blank line.
7. TYPE the following:
   echo "This is the first script" Enter
   echo "Good day $USER" Enter
   echo The calendar for the month is Enter
   cal
   Your completed script should look similar to Figure 23.1.

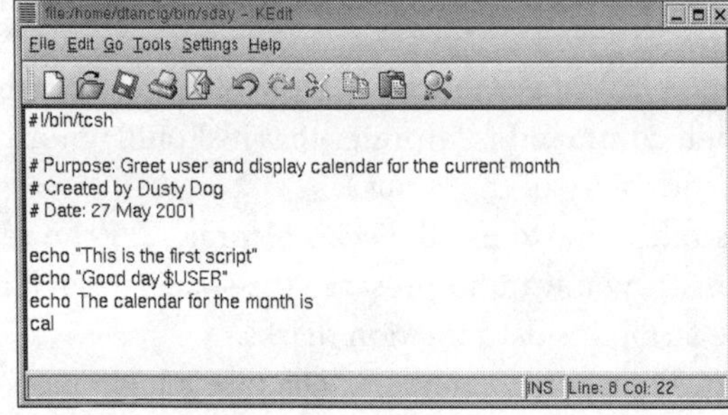

FIGURE 23.1: First script instructions

8. CLICK on **File**.

9. CLICK on **Save**.
10. CLICK on **File**.
11. CLICK on **Quit**.

MAKING THE FILE EXECUTABLE

When you click on Save in KEdit, KEdit saves the file with read and write permission for the user by default. Editors *do not* give ASCII text files executable permission. We must issue explicit commands to make the file executable.

Normally, you only want to give the user executable permission. The command to change permissions is chmod. This is followed by a set of numbers (which are based on the base-eight number system) that tells the chmod command how to set the permissions.

The syntax, or form, for the command is

chmod *permissions file-name*

The permission number 754 will give the user read, write, and executable permission and everyone in the user's group read and execute permission but no write permission (they can read and use the file, but they may not modify it). See Appendix B for more information about the chmod command.

1. In the terminal emulator, TYPE **chmod 754 sday** Enter
2. TYPE **ls -l sday** Enter
   On the left-hand side, you see **-rwxr-xr--**. The x's mean that the user and the workgroup have executable permission. If you typed the script's file name on the command line and pressed Enter, the script would execute the instructions. The script file name would seem to behave like a command.

   Your current directory is probably not on the path of directories to search for executable files. This is done to make your system more secure. It is common practice for users to store their personal executable files, such as scripts, in a directory named "bin," located in their home (also called "personal login" or "local") directory. The path to a script would then be /home/username/bin. The following instructions create such a directory and then add the path to that directory to the search path. If you place all of your scripts in your local bin subdirectory, you will be able to run them regardless of what directory is your current, or working, directory.

   We will create a bin subdirectory and place the sday script in it.
3. TYPE **cd ~** Enter
   This moved you to your personal home directory if you weren't already there.

4. TYPE **mkdir bin** Enter
5. TYPE **mv sday bin/sday** Enter
   This assumes that your sday script is located in your home directory. It moves (mv) the script to your bin subdirectory. If the script is in some other directory, it might be better to open a graphical file manager to move the script from wherever it is to your local bin subdirectory.

   Now we will put the local bin subdirectory on the search path for executable files. We will put a path instruction in the .bashrc file. The export command will make it available to any and all shell sessions. We're assuming that you're in your personal home directory.
6. TYPE **kedit .bashrc** Enter
7. CLICK the cursor at the end of the contents of that file.
8. TYPE **PATH=$PATH:~/bin** Enter
9. TYPE **export PATH**.
10. CLICK **File** and then **Save**.
11. CLICK **File** and then **Quit**.

RUNNING THE SCRIPT

1. In the terminal emulator, TYPE **sday** Enter
   The output looks like Figure 23.2.

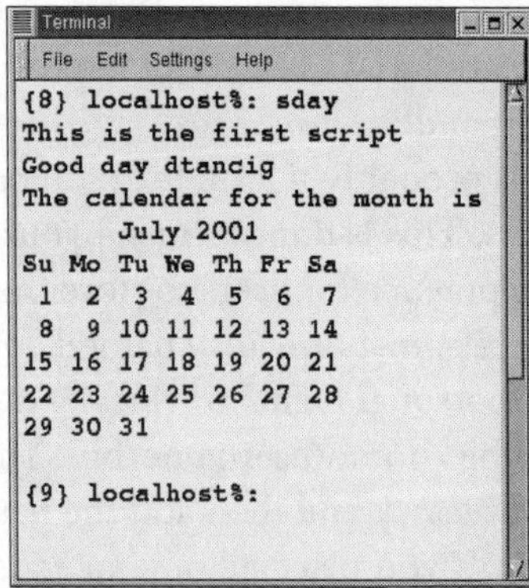

FIGURE 23.2: First script output

EXPANDING THE SCRIPT

A command can access a file from within a script. For example, so far this script causes the computer to greet us and show us the calendar for the month. We can make it more useful by having it tell us the day and date and show us our to-do list.

ADDING A TO-DO LIST

We'll begin by adding a to-do list. However, first we need a file that contains the list of items on our to-do list.

1. In the terminal emulator, TYPE **kedit do_list** Enter
   The KEdit window opens.
2. TYPE the following:
   buy Wed groceries Enter
   call school about freshman orientation Enter
   check clothes for rest of week Enter
   write second part of presentation
3. SAVE the file.
4. CLOSE the editor.
5. In the terminal emulator, TYPE **kedit bin/sday** Enter (to open the KEdit editor and retrieve the file named sday).
6. CHANGE the script to match the following (the text in italics is new):

```
#!/bin/tcsh

# Purpose: Greet user and display calendar for the
# current month
# Created by (your name)
# Date: (creation date)

clear
echo "Good day $USER"
echo ""
echo "Your to-do list is "
echo ""
cat do_list
echo ""
echo The calendar for the month is
cal
```

7. SAVE your file.
8. CLOSE your editor.

The echo "" creates a blank line on your display. The cat do_list line causes the contents of the do_list file to be written to the display. Now run your script.

9. At the command prompt, TYPE **sday** Enter
Your output should look as shown in Figure 23.3.

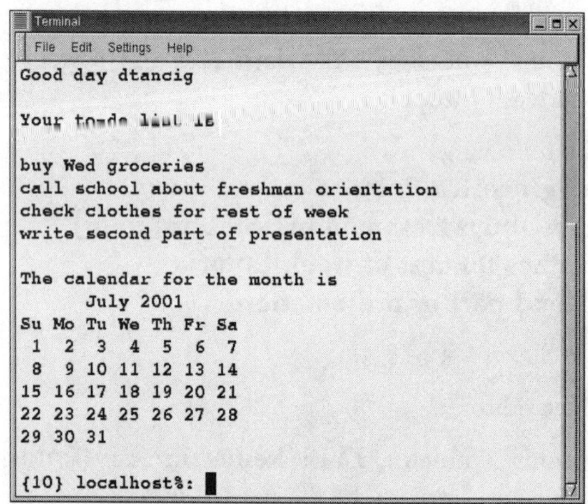

Terminal
File Edit Settings Help
Good day dtancig
buy Wed groceries
call school about freshman orientation
check clothes for rest of week
write second part of presentation
The calendar for the month is
July 2001
Su Mo Tu We Th Fr Sa
1 2 3 4 5 6 7
8 9 10 11 12 13 14
15 16 17 18 19 20 21
22 23 24 25 26 27 28
29 30 31
{10} localhost%:

FIGURE 23.3: Second script output

ADDING THE DATE

First, let's do an experiment and learn about the date command.

1. In the terminal emulator, TYPE **date** Enter
You see the day, the month, the year, and the time information.

    All most people want is the name of the current day, the day's number, and the name of the current month.

    We can force the date command to display only the name of the day, the name of the month, and the number of the day. If you type **man date**, the online manual explains how to format the date the way you want.

    - %A gives the full name of the day of the week
    - %B gives the full name of the month of the year
    - %d gives the number of the day of the month (1–31)

    We will add the following command:

    date +"%A, %B %d"

    Note the quotation marks around the parameters.

    You can try executing this on the command line to see what the effect is.

2. TYPE **kedit bin/sday** Enter

3. ADD the italicized code shown below.

```
#!/bin/tcsh

# Purpose: Greet user and display to-do list, date, and calendar
# Created by (your name)
# Date: (creation date)

clear
echo "Good day $USER"
echo ""
date +"%A, %B %d"
echo ""
echo "Your to-do list is "
echo ""
cat do_list
echo ""
echo The calendar for the month is
cal
```

4. SAVE this file.
5. CLOSE the editor.
6. In the terminal emulator, TYPE **sday** Enter
   The output should now include the date.

EXECUTING A COMMAND FROM WITHIN ANOTHER COMMAND

What we have is fine. But what if we want the output for the date to read, for example,

Today's date is Monday, March 11

We can add the "Today's date is" by using an echo command to echo those three words. The date command can then be used inside the echo command. Take a look at the following:

echo "Today's date is ", 'date +"%A, %B %d" '

Notice that before the word "date" and after the last quotation mark is a special backwards apostrophe. This is called a "grave accent mark." It is the key immediately above the Tab key on many keyboards. When you are running one command and you insert another command in between grave accent marks, as shown above, you instruct the shell to run that command.

1. In the terminal emulator, TYPE **kedit bin/sday** Enter

2. ADD the command shown in italics.

```
#!/bin/tcsh

# Purpose: Greet user and display to-do list, date, and calendar
# Created by (your name)
# Date: (creation date)

clear
echo "Good day $USER"
echo ""
echo "Today's date is "
date +"%A, %B %d"
echo ""
echo "Your to-do list is "
echo ""
cat do_list
echo ""
echo The calendar for the month is
cal
```

3. SAVE the file.
4. CLOSE your editor.
5. TYPE **sday** Enter at the command prompt.
   The output now includes "Today's date is" before the date.

SUMMARY

In this étude you learned the general steps for creating an executable script file and the basic parts of a script file. The script should begin with the name of the shell to run it. This is embedded in the #!/bin/tcsh line. On all other lines, a pound sign in front of the line tells the command interpreter that the line is a comment and is not to be executed. You have also observed that you can use a file from within a script. You have learned some basics about formatting the output of the date command, and you have learned how to embed one command within another. To make a shell script executable, use the chmod command. The chmod command is discussed further in Appendix B.

PASSING INFORMATION INTO YOUR SHELL SCRIPT ÉTUDE 24

Shell scripts are tools in which you invest time to create. You get a much better return on your time investment if you can write one script that can be applied to a range of different but similar situations instead of having to craft a custom script for every variation. It is easy to add this efficiency by writing the script so that the user can type the script name on the command line, then follow the script name with options and arguments that are passed into the script by the operating system shell. You can use this same capability to customize a standard command and make it more user-friendly.

The key to passing information from the shell command line into a shell script is a special data structure called the "argv array." All the Linux shells automatically create this data structure; you don't have to create it. In this étude, you will learn how to pass information to a script from the command line using the argv array.

The shell script instructions in these études are given for the tc shell. Bash shell scripts have a similar structure but use different syntax and have more room for subtle errors. In Étude 23, it was pointed out that the tc shell, which is just as readily available as the bash shell (simply type tcsh on the command line), is every bit as capable as bash. It also has a more familiar, natural syntax that is less tedious and awkward, and therefore less mistake-prone, than the bash syntax. The tc shell also has easier-to-use features when working with numbers.

Not only is the tc shell a better shell for programming, it is also a better shell for learning shell programming. If you work with the bash shell, when you make mistakes, your first focus can be on the syntax rather than wondering if you got the structure correct. Bash was the first free shell for Linux, as well as the default shell, so many scripts have been written using the bash shell. (We won't even go into the irreconcilable c shell vs. Bourne shell dispute, which has grown to the dimensions of a passionate, devotional strife and of which the tc shell vs. Bourne Again shell contention is merely a modern extension.)

In this étude, you will learn how to create a "here" document. A here document is a quick, easy-to-create shell script that has embedded in it the database that is to be searched. It uses the grep command as a simple database search-and-display command. The word "here" means that the database is located here, in this script file.

TOPICS COVERED IN THIS ÉTUDE

- Passing information into a shell script
- Creating a here document
- Using a script file

PASSING INFORMATION INTO A SCRIPT

In Linux, all shells automatically set up a storage mechanism called the argv (argument vector) array. This array stores up to 14 items from the command line. Some implementations might store more. The first item stored is the actual command. This array is set up for you automatically by all shells when you begin a shell session.

An array is a set of adjacent storage locations. In this case they are numbered from 0 through 14 or more. Argv[1] or $1 (both mean the same thing in the tc shell) is the name used to refer to the items from the command line. Argv[0] always stores the command. Remember, the command is always the first item on the command line.

Since the argv array stores all of the items typed on the command line, the first piece of information we need to know is the order in which they are stored in the array from the command line. Knowing this scheme, we can relate argv array storage locations to positions on the command line. The answer is that the items on the command line are stored from left to right, starting with the command. The command is item 0. For example, if you had the command

wc lines text2.txt

"wc" would be stored in the argv array as element number 0. The word "lines" would be stored in the argv array as element number 1. "text2.txt" would be stored in the argv array as element number 2.

To get access to the contents of each element in the array from within the script file, put a $ in front of the array element number. The $ means "the contents of." The $ instructs the computer to use the contents of that named storage location. (The tc shell allows use of either $n or argv[n] to access the contents of an element of the argv array. The bash shell does not allow the use of argv[n]. Bash uses only $n. By using $n throughout this étude, you are learning a technique applicable to both the tc and the bash shells.)

Let's say, for example, that we issued the following command on the command line:

```
Storage position in argv array → 0       1          2
                              count   words   newsfile.txt
                                ↑       ↑          ↑
                             command   first      second
                                      argument   argument
                                ↑       ↑          ↑
                             argv[0]  argv[1]    argv[2]
                              or $0    or $1      or $2
```

If we wrote the command **echo $1** in a script, "words" would be echoed and displayed on the screen.

Let's try an example to gain familiarity with it. We're assuming you have completed Étude 23 and have created a bin folder to hold your scripts.

1. OPEN a terminal emulator.
2. In the terminal emulator, TYPE **kedit bin/script2** Enter
3. In the editor, TYPE **#!/bin/tcsh** Enter as the top-most line in the file.
4. TYPE the following:
   Enter
   # Created by (type in your name) Enter
   # Date: (enter today's date) Enter
   Enter
   echo the value in array element 0 is $0 Enter
   echo the value in array element 1 is $1 Enter
   echo the value in array element 2 is $2 Enter
5. CLICK **File** and then **Save.**
6. CLICK **File** and then **Quit.**
   Now we'll make the file executable.
7. In the terminal emulator, TYPE **chmod 754 bin/script2** Enter

Now we'll run the script.

8. TYPE **script2 first second** **Enter**
   Your output looks similar to
   the value in array element 0 is /home/dtancig/bin/script2
   the value in array element 1 is first
   the value in array element 2 is second

   What you just demonstrated is how to retrieve and use information inside of a script that was typed on the command line by the user. Now we can put this to use.

CREATING A HERE DOCUMENT

The here document uses the grep command and tells the shell that the database to be searched is located "here," in the same file with the script instructions. It then shows the shell where the database is located. Using the argv array, we can pass to the grep command the word we want grep to search for.

For example, let's assume you're keeping a here document with information related to your workgroup. You have given that script the file name of **wkgroup**. You have names in the first column, dates hired in the second column, and birthdays in the third column. This here script file would look as follows:

(*Note:* The line numbers are *not* typed in to the actual file. They are shown here so lines can be accurately and easily referenced in the explanation that follows.)

```
Line 1   #!/bin/tcsh

Line 2   # Purpose: A brief workgroup database
Line 3   # Created by (your name)
Line 4   # Date: (creation date)

Line 5   grep -i "$1" << +
Line 6   Jones, Elliot          June 15, 1990       July 4
Line 7   Markson, Sarah         January 6, 1997     March 25
Line 8   Henderson, Leslie      May 18, 1993        August 5
Line 9   +
```

Line 5, the line with the word "grep" in it, is the grep instruction that will search the database portion of the file line by line and will display each line that contains a match. The -i command option instructs grep to ignore the case. The "$1" tells grep to use the contents of the argv array element number 1 as the pattern to match.

Line 5 ends with << +. The << lets the shell know that the lines to be searched (the database file) follows. These lines are then sent to what is called "standard input"; the processing behaves as though you had redirected the contents of a data file to the grep command.

The first symbol following the << symbols is used by the shell as the beginning and ending markers for the data. In this script, the symbol is a plus sign (+). You may use any symbol so long as it does not appear in the database lines to be searched. Otherwise, the search will stop prematurely.

Lines 6 through 8 contain the data to be searched by grep. Line 9 contains the ending plus sign (+), which tells the shell interpreter that this is the end of the database lines to search. The ending marker must be on a line by itself.

Now we'll create and run the above script file.

1. In the terminal emulator, TYPE **kedit bin/wkgroup** Enter
   A KEdit window opens with the file name of wkgroup.
2. TYPE the following in the editor:
```
#!/bin/tcsh

# Purpose: A brief workgroup database
# Created by (type your name here)
# Date: (enter today's date here)

grep -i "$1" << +
Jones, Elliot          June 15, 1990        July 4
Markson, Sarah         January 6, 1997      March 25
Henderson, Leslie      May 18, 1993         August 5
+
```
3. CLICK **File** and then **Save**.
4. CLICK **File** and then **Quit**.
   Now we'll make the file executable.
5. TYPE **chmod 754 bin/wkgroup** Enter on the command line.
   Now we'll run the wkgroup script.
6. TYPE **wkgroup july** Enter
   You get a display of all the lines with the word "July." We see
   Jones, Elliot June 15, 1990 July 4
   Now before the end of each month, you can type in this command with the name of the following month and immediately know for whom you need to purchase a birthday card and a few flowers or an anniversary pin. (If you have employees with names that are also the names of months, such as April or June, it would be better to use a more selective search tool such as awk, which was first introduced in Étude 22.)

Here's another example. Suppose you want to know the date Leslie Henderson was hired.

7. TYPE **wkgroup Henderson** Enter

   You see

   Henderson, Leslie May 18, 1993 August 5

   This wkgroup script has become much more flexible because you can pass to it, at the time you type the command, the characteristic you want to search for–a name, a month, or even day or year numbers.

SUMMARY

In this étude you have learned how to pass information from the command line into a script file by using the command line variable argument array, the argv array. The parts of the argv array are numbered from 0 through 13 (some argv array implementations allow more than 14 storage locations). The items on the command line, beginning with the command, are stored in this array. When executing instructions from within a script file, you can access the contents of each argv array element by putting a $ in front of the array element number that contains the information you need to use.

A here document contains the grep command, a parameter passed in from the command line, a symbol to indicate that the lines to search are contained "here" in the script (it actually redirects the data lines to standard input), and a symbol that indicates the start and end of the lines to search. This creates a simple database program—quick and easy to use but of limited usefulness because the grep command searches the entire line for a pattern match, not just a specified column such as a name column or date column.

In general, there are four steps to writing a script:

1. Start an editor using as the file name the name you want to give the script.
2. Write #!/bin/*shell-name* (*shell-name* would be tcsh, bash, or ksh, for example). The # must begin in the upper-left position of the file.
3. Write the script instructions, save the file, and exit the editor.
4. Change the file permissions using the chmod command.

REFERENCES

Anderson, Gail, and Paul Anderson. *The Unix C Shell Field Guide.* Upper Saddle River, NJ: Prentice Hall, 1986.

Quigley, Ellie. *Unix Shells by Example.* 2d ed. Upper Saddle River, NJ: Prentice Hall, 2000.

Sobell, Mark. *A Practical Guide to Linux.* New York: Addison Wesley, 1997.

SCRIPTS THAT MAKE CHOICES

ÉTUDE 25

A shell script is a file containing many operating system commands used together to solve a problem or complete a specific task, usually related to some aspect of file operations. In Étude 24, script instructions were introduced that make it possible to pass command options and arguments to the script from the command line. One reason for passing information to a script is to inform the script of choices we want it to select. That means the script needs an instruction that can select choices. Scripts use if structures to select choices. Choices are made depending on how two items compare to each other and on whether an item is determined to be true or false.

In this étude, you will learn to write scripts that use information passed from the command line to choose which instructions to run. The technique of passing information to a script from the command line was the focus of Étude 24. The shell script instructions in this étude are for the tc shell. The bash if structure is similar but uses a notably different syntax.

In this étude we will use the file name of **count** for our script. Once we give executable permission to this file, we will be able to type **count** on the command line, followed by its required arguments. For example, we could type **countwordsfile1.txt** as a command to count the words in the file named **file1.txt**. It is a more memorable word-count command than the cryptic **wc -w**.

We assume that you have worked through Études 23 and 24.

TOPICS COVERED IN THIS ÉTUDE

- The if control structure
- Creating a new command (count) using a script, the wc (word count) command, and the if structure

THE IF CONTROL STRUCTURE

A control structure is a set of special words (called "keywords" or "reserved words," depending on the programming language) used in a specific order and in specific locations that determine which instructions are controlled by that structure. The shell recognizes three control structures and their variations and uses them to control which instructions are executed:

sequential processing	Executes instructions one after the other
selection	Makes a choice about which instruction to execute (the if-else type)
looping	Repeats a set of instructions until an ending condition is met

In this étude, the focus is on using the if control structure to select choices. An if structure is shown and discussed below.

```
if (test condition) then
    {
        instruction_1
        instruction_2
         :
        instruction_n
    }
endif
next instruction following if structure
```

The selection can also begin with the word "switch" if we have several choices to select from. Switch uses a significantly different format and is beyond the scope of this étude.

As you can see by the words "test condition," the if instruction works by testing a condition. The process is:

1. If tests to see if one value or word is greater than, less than, or equal to a second value or word.

2. If the result of the test is true, then the instructions inside the if block are executed.
3. If the result of the test is false, then all the instructions inside the if block are skipped. The next instruction after the if structure is then executed.

This test-condition part of the if structure is called a "relational expression." A relational expression looks like

(*variable1 relational-operator value-or-variable2-that-variable1-is-compared to*)

We have six relational operators. These are the same symbols used in mathematics.

Greater than or equal to	>=
Less than or equal to	<=
Greater than	>
Less than	<
Equal to	==
Not equal to	!=

Here are three examples with different relational expressions:

1. if ($value1 >= 0) then
   :
   endif

2. if ($choice == "words") then
   :
   endif

3. if ($1 == "lines") then
   :
   endif

If the result of testing the relational expression is true, the instructions between the then and the endif are executed. If the result of testing the relational expression is false, the instructions following the if structure are skipped.

In this étude, we'll use a single if structure three times. This isn't as elegant as using if-else, but it works for this example, and it is easier for newcomers to troubleshoot if their script develops problems. This ease of understanding is important because it increases the likelihood you might adapt the technique to one of your unique work situations.

CREATING A NEW COUNT COMMAND

Our goal is to create a new command named count. The count command will count lines, words, or characters, depending on what the user writes on the command line. The user must also state the name of the file to count.

The wc command can do this job. The wc command has the form of

wc option filename

For example, **wc -l text1.txt** will count the lines in the file text1.txt. As stated earlier, the wc command has three options: -w for counting words, -l for counting lines, and -c for counting characters.

Instead of trying to remember abbreviations, we can write a script so that the user can type the script name of **count** on the command line, followed by the description of the item to count: words, lines, or characters. This will be followed by the name of the file (with a space separating the command, the choice, and the file name).

The argv array, discussed in Étude 24, will store the user's choice of words, lines, or characters and the file name. We will use an if statement in conjunction with the argv array to test whether the user passed in words, lines, or characters. When one of the three relational expressions makes a match, the appropriate wc command and option will be issued. The file name stored in the second argv array element will be included in the wc command that is used.

1. OPEN a terminal emulator.
2. TYPE **kedit bin/count** Enter
   A KEdit window opens.
3. TYPE the following:

```
#!/bin/tcsh

# Purpose: Count words, characters, or lines of ASCII
# text files
# Created by (type your name here)
# Date: (enter today's date here)

# Store choice and file name
    set choice = $1
    set filename = $2

if ($choice == "words") then
    wc -w $filename
endif

if ($choice == "characters") then
    wc -c $filename
endif

if ($choice == "lines") then
```

wc -l $filename

endif

4. CLICK **File** and then **Save**.
5. CLICK **File** and then **Quit**.
   Now we'll make the file executable.
6. In the terminal emulator, TYPE **chmod 754 bin/count** Enter

USING THE SCRIPT FILE

To use our newly created script file, we need a file containing ASCII text characters to count. We'll use the script file named **count**. First we'll count words.

1. In the terminal emulator, TYPE **count words bin/count** Enter
   You are instructing the count command to count the words in the file named count in the bin directory. The output is similar to
   61 bin/count
   depending on the number of words you actually have in your count file. 61 is the count of the number of words. "bin/count," which follows the number, is the name of the file in which the wc command counted words.
   Now we'll count characters.
2. In the terminal emulator, TYPE the following:
   count characters bin/count Enter
   You instructed the command to count the characters in the file named count.
   Now we'll count lines.
3. TYPE **count lines bin/count** Enter
   You instructed the command to count the number of lines in the file named count.

SUMMARY

In this étude you have learned how to use the command line information available to a script file through the argv array to make choices using an if structure. An if structure consists of three parts: the keywords if, then, and endif; the relational expression used to make the choice; and the statements to be executed. The statements contained within the if structure will be executed if the result of testing the relational expression is true. Should the result of testing the relational expression be false, the computer will skip over the statements contained within the if structure. We tested conditions against values typed on the command line and stored in the argv array. These values were represented by $1 and $2 in the example.

PILOT-LINK: TESTING THE SERIAL PORTS AND WRITING A PALMPILOT SCRIPT

ÉTUDE 26

Étude 16, "J-Pilot," takes you through the easy steps of installing and using J-Pilot, the Linux desktop software for a PalmPilot. J-Pilot is constructed using Pilot-link, a command-line program that synchronizes and backs up a PalmPilot with storage areas on the computer.

There are three reasons for presenting this étude. If you have difficulty making J-Pilot work, the information presented here gives you a way to backtrack and, in a step-by-step fashion, find out what you need to do to make your hardware work with Pilot-link. Once you verify that your hardware and Pilot-link can communicate, J-Pilot will work with your PalmPilot. Second, if you use a PalmPilot but use the desktop computer only to keep your PalmPilot backed up, a script can be a very fast way to back up or restore your PalmPilot using the desktop computer. Third, études are compositions designed to build skill through practice. Skill is built first by practicing and extending beginning techniques and then by mastering the challenges of more advanced techniques. This étude leads you deeper into the inner workings.

Pilot-link is a suite of tools (utility programs) originally developed by Jeff Dionne and now maintained by Kenneth Albanowski. Pilot-link is automatically installed by all the major Linux distributions. Anyone can reliably set it up by following simple instructions.

To make the command line options easy to use, I wrote a script, included below, that reduces the fairly complex Pilot-link commands to typing just two easy-to-remember words. I used this script on a regular basis for several months until I began using J-Pilot. It is reliable and quick.

TOPICS COVERED IN THIS ÉTUDE:

- Getting set up for Pilot-link
- Verifying that Pilot-link is working with your PDA
- Entering and testing a short version of the Palm script
- Entering and testing the entire Palm script

SETTING UP TO USE PILOT-LINK

Three steps are involved:

1. Identify the serial port that your PDA cradle's serial cable will plug into.
2. Create a symbolic link to that serial port.
3. Set the data transfer rate in the home directory resource file.

IDENTIFYING THE SERIAL PORT

If your computer happens to be set up for dual boot (can start up in either Windows or Linux), start up in Windows. Make sure the Palm desktop software is installed.

1. START the Palm software and verify that you can do a HotSync. This verifies that your serial card is working.
2. Once you know your HotSync is working, LOOK at the back of your computer. Look at the connector where the HotSync serial connector is attached. See if the port is labeled; it would most likely be labeled COM1 or COM2. If the port is labeled, COPY the value onto a note pad. Skip the steps below.
3. If the port is not labeled, after performing a HotSync, CLICK on **HotSync** on the Palm Desktop activities bar.
4. CLICK on **Setup** in the menu that opens up.
5. CLICK on the **Local** tab in the Setup options box that opens up.
6. COPY the value listed in the box labeled Serial Port onto a note pad. This will be COM1, COM2, COM3, or COM4.

If you are unable to carry out these steps, you can reliably guess that the only serial ports available are COM1 and COM2, unless you have personally installed an additional serial card.

Identifying the Active Serial Ports Using Linux

In the Linux world, serial ports are named differently than in the Windows world.

Linux Name	Microsoft Name
/dev/ttyS0	COM1
/dev/ttyS1	COM2
/dev/ttyS2	COM3
/dev/ttyS3	COM4

The /dev means this is the dev subdirectory located off the root directory. The dev subdirectory is where device information is kept. The ttyS*n* is the name associated with a particular address that represents the port. The abbreviation tty harkens back to the Unix days when text terminals were teletype (tty) machines. The S means this is a serial communications port (as compared to a parallel communications port).

What you are about to do is issue the setserial command four times. Each time, you will follow the setserial command with a different serial port designation. In this way, we will test each serial port. From the results, we will know which serial ports are active and useable. Also, you will know if Linux and your serial hardware can communicate.

Note: You may have to have root permission before your system will allow you to use the setserial command.

Using the Setserial Command

First we will test /dev/ttyS0 (COM1).

1. CLICK the terminal emulator icon.
2. TYPE **setserial /dev/ttyS0** Enter
   You probably see something like
   /dev/ttyS0, UART 16550A, Port: 0x03f8, IRQ 4
   This indicates that the port is active.
   If you get a permission-denied error message, this means the command has been reserved for the systems administrator. If this is your personal system and you know the root password, on the command line, take the following steps:
3. TYPE **su** Enter
4. TYPE the root password and press Enter

5. Once the command prompt reappears, PRESS the [↑] key until the setserial command previously issued reappears. Then press [Enter] and note the information for ttyS0 (COM1).
   Now we will test /dev/ttyS1 (COM2).
6. PRESS the [↑] key once.
   The setserial command you just used reappears on the command line.
7. BACKSPACE over the 0 and type **1**.
   The command will now look like **setserial /dev/ttyS1**.
8. PRESS [Enter]
   You probably see similar output for /dev/ttyS1 as you got for /dev/ttyS0.
9. REPEAT steps 6 through 8 for /dev/ttyS2 and /dev/ttyS3.
   Most likely you will see the following:
   /dev/ttyS2, UART: unknown, Port:0x03f8, IRQ 4
   The UART: unknown means that no UART (hardware device) is assigned or connected to that port. This means that /dev/ttyS2 and /dev/ttyS3 are not active.
   Note: If you get "unknown" for the UART for all four serial ports, either you have a serious software incompatibility problem or something is broken. In either case, it must be fixed to the point that one of the serial ports is made active before you will be able to make HotSync work.

CREATING A SYMBOLIC LINK

In this step, you have to create a link between the Linux designation for the serial port that the HotSync cradle will be connected to and the symbol /dev/pilot. /dev/pilot is a general term used in the Pilot-link software. It is up to each individual user to link that to the actual serial port used by their machine. The command to create a symbolic link is

ln -s *specific-name symbolic-name*

The following instructions assume you are using /dev/ttyS0 (COM1). If you are not using S0, substitute the correct number for the serial port you are using.

Note: If permission is denied, then you must have root permission. Issue the su command, type the root password, and then press the up-arrow key twice. The symbolic link command, in step 2 below, will reappear. Press [Enter] to re-execute the command.

1. In the terminal emulator, TYPE **ln –s /dev/ttyS0 /dev/pilot** [Enter]

2. If you used the su command somewhere along the line, TYPE **exit** Enter

SETTING THE SERIAL DATA RATE

We will open the bash resource file.

1. In the terminal emulator, TYPE **kedit .bashrc** Enter
2. CLICK in the text area immediately following the section of the .bashrc file that defines what are called "aliases" (each line begins with the word "alias").
3. TYPE **PILOTRATE=57600** Enter
   Run all of this command together. Do not put spaces around the equal sign.
4. TYPE **export PILOTRATE** Enter
5. CLICK **File** and then **Save**.
6. CLICK **File** and then **Quit**.
7. In the terminal emulator, TYPE **source .bashrc** Enter

The purpose of the source command is to force the operating system to go back and reinitialize the variables in its system from the file named following the source command. Normally, the operating system initializes these system variables only when the user logs in. You've seen the same thing in Windows when you've installed software and Windows has then stated that for the changes to take effect, you must restart the system. Source avoids having to restart the system simply to reinitialize a few variables.

If, after a moment, the command prompt reappears after you issue the source command, the command probably worked. If you get a long listing of commands or if you are told permission was denied, then shut down and restart the computer (don't just log out). In either case, you are forcing the computer to reinitialize itself with the new instructions in the bash resource file.

VERIFYING THAT PILOT-LINK IS WORKING

TRYING THE FIRST PILOT-LINK COMMAND

First, we are going to list databases. Place your PalmPilot into its HotSync cradle.

1. In the terminal emulator, TYPE **pilot-xfer /dev/pilot -l** Enter
   Note: That is a lowercase L, not the number 1.
   A message is displayed on the command line asking you to press the HotSync button.
2. PRESS the HotSync button.

Another message is displayed that says "Connect." After a few moments, the listing is scrolled onto the computer monitor screen.

3. If no connection was made, change the symbolic link from /dev/ttyS0 to /dev/ttyS1.
   It should now work.

BACKING UP YOUR PALMPILOT USING A PILOT-LINK COMMAND

This will store the standard databases (but not special programs) to a file on your PalmPilot. If you should lose the data on your PalmPilot, Pilot-link can restore all of it that had been stored in the file named backup-directory.

1. In the terminal emulator, TYPE **pilot-xfer /dev/pilot –b backup-directory** Enter
   If the file backup-directory does not exist, pilot-xfer creates it for you and then saves each database into this file. Each database name is displayed on the screen as it is backed up.

RESTORING THE DATABASES TO THE PDA

This will restore to your PalmPilot the information stored in backup-directory.

1. TYPE **pilot-xfer /dev/pilot -r backup-directory** Enter
   The database files stored in the file backup-directory are now restored.
   At this point, if you desire to use J-Pilot, it should install and work. If you want to simply use the command line to back up your PalmPilot, you probably noticed that the commands are fairly complicated. The following steps give you the ability to type **palm backup** to do a backup or to type **palm restore** to do a restoration to your PalmPilot. It also has a simple help capability to remind you of how to enter commands. Also, Palm-link has many more utility programs in its suite.

Note: Before creating and trying to run the following script file, please refer to Étude 23 and the section titled "Making the Script Executable." Follow the instructions you find there to create and place this script in a local bin subdirectory and put that bin subdirectory on the path searched for executable files.

If you decide not to do the foregoing and you get an error message similar to **bash: palm: file not found**, make the following test.

1. TYPE **./palm** Enter
   If the script file is accessed, then you need to follow the instructions in the "Making the Script Executable" section of Étude 23.

CREATING THE PALM SCRIPT FILE

If all three of these functions have worked on your PDA, then you are ready to create the script. The functional heart of the script is the three command lines you just wrote.

The name of the script is palm. You will type **palm** on the command line as though it was a command and follow it with the option you want performed. For example, if you wanted a listing of the databases, you would type **palm list**. If you wanted to back up the data on your palm device to your desktop computer, you would type **palm backup**. Finally, if you wanted to restore the databases to the PalmPilot from your desktop computer, you would type **palm restore**. And, if you forget how to use the palm command, you can type either **palm** or **palm help**. Either one will bring up the help menu that explains how to use the script.

ENTERING THE SCRIPT INSTRUCTIONS

Start KEdit and enter the script below. Shell scripts are picky about spacing around certain operators. Type this exactly as you see it. The script is written in c shell programming language. The first instruction, #!/bin/tcsh, instructs the current shell, whatever it might be, to run the script with the c shell command interpreter. This line must be the top-most line and must begin in the left-most position.

1. TYPE in the following script:

```
#!/bin/tcsh

# Palm script uses palm-xfer to perform one of three operations:
#    1. list programs on palm pilot
#    2. back up databases on palm pilot
#    3. restore databases from computer files to palm pilot

# David Tancig
# March 2001

clear
set instruction = $1
if ($instruction == “ || $instruction == “help”) then
   set instruction = “help”
endif

echo “You are doing a ” $instruction
echo “”
```

```
if ($instruction == "help") then
  echo "The palm program will do the following: "
  echo "list databases on your PDA"
  echo "back up databases from PDA to disk files on desktop computer"
  echo "restore databases from your desktop computer to your PDA"
  echo ""
  echo "Type the command palm and follow it with the option you want."
  echo "For example: palm backup"
  echo "This will back up the files on your PDA"

else if ($instruction == "list") then
 pilot-xfer /dev/pilot -l
else if ($instruction == "backup") then
 pilot-xfer /dev/pilot -b backup-directory
else if ($instruction == "restore") then
 pilot-xfer /dev/pilot -r backup-directory
else
 echo "You must type list, backup, restore, or help after the word palm."
 echo "You typed the command --> palm " $instruction

endif
```

If you type these instructions exactly as you see them, they should work correctly. This is the actual script that I run.

2. SAVE the file with the name of **palm** in the bin folder.
   Now you must make the file executable so it can be run.
3. TYPE **chmod 700 bin/palm** Enter
   This changes the permissions on the file so that it is executable for the user.

VERIFYING THAT THE PALM SCRIPT WORKS

The Palm HotSync cable from your HotSync cradle should still be plugged into the serial port on the back of your computer. Your PDA should be placed in its cradle.

Testing the Help Option

1. In the terminal emulator, TYPE **palm** Enter
   You should see the help menu appear.
2. TYPE **clear** Enter
3. TYPE **palm help** Enter

Again, you should see the help menu appear. If all of this occurred, the script works for the help option.

Testing the List Option

1. TYPE **palm list** Enter
   A command should appear in your terminal emulator window telling you to press the HotSync button on your HotSync cradle.
2. PRESS the HotSync button.
   The word "connect" should soon appear. Then a listing will be made, showing you all the files on your PDA. You will then be returned to the command prompt. If all of this occurred, the script works for the list option.

Testing the Backup Option

1. TYPE **palm backup** Enter
   A command should appear in your terminal emulator window telling you to press the HotSync button on your HotSync cradle.
2. PRESS the HotSync button.
   The word "connect" should soon appear. Then a listing will be made showing you the databases on your PDA that are being backed up. You will then be returned to the command prompt. If all of this occurred, the script works for the backup option.

Testing the Restore Option

1. TYPE **palm restore** Enter
   A command should appear in your terminal emulator window, telling you to press the HotSync button on your HotSync cradle.
2. PRESS the HotSync button.
   The word "connect" should soon appear. Then a listing will be made, showing you the databases that are being restored to your PDA. You will then be returned to the command prompt. If all of this occurred, the script works for the restore option.

Pilot-xfer also has a command option of -i to install software to your PalmPilot from the desktop computer. This would be useful if you download programs from the Internet to use on your PalmPilot. The -i option could also be added to the script.

Pilot-link also has a pilot-addresses feature that allows you to create an ASCII text file of the addresses on your PalmPilot. You can add to or edit that ASCII test file and download it to your PalmPilot.

SUMMARY

In this étude, you have successfully connected your PalmPilot to your computer and listed, backed up, and restored data. You have also created a script file that simplifies the commands that must be issued. References have been given case you want to remain on the command line and want to expand the script to the other capabilities available in the Pilot-link suite of PalmPilot utilities.

If you want more information on Pilot-link, a good starting point is to review the built-in, online manual. On the command line, type **man pilot-link**. The built-in manual will list all of the command options along with a brief description of what each does.

One of the best technical references for Pilot-link is the Palm OS Desktop HOWTO. Section 3 discusses the Pilot-link tools. The URL for this reference is listed below.

Another good Pilot-Link reference is an article published in *PalmPower* magazine. On the second page of that article is a comprehensive listing of Pilot-link utility programs. The URL for accessing this article is also listed below.

REFERENCES

Perlow, Jason. "Using Your Palm Device with Linux." *PalmPower Magazine. August 1999.* <http://www.palmpower.com/issues/issue199908/linux001.html>

Silber, David. *Palm OS Desktop HOWTO: Sharing Data Between Palm OS and Linux Systems.* 1999. <http://www.sftw.umac.mo/resource/LDP/HOWTO/PalmOS-HOWTO-3.html>

AWK SCRIPTS AND ADVANCED OPERATIONS

ÉTUDE 27

This is a continuation of Étude 22, "Awk as a Database Program." In Étude 22, you learned basic awk commands and how to use them. However, the command line limited the number of awk instructions we could issue. Also, if we want to repeatedly perform particular database tasks, we have to repeatedly type the same awk commands. Such repetitive typing is a time-consuming annoyance and is also error-prone. What we'd like to do is store the awk commands in a file and command the computer to execute the instructions in that file using a simple, easy-to-remember command. We can do this with a script file, either an awk script file or a shell script containing awk commands.

A number of questions also arise related to the output format when using awk. Awk scripts solve those problems. First, how do we put column headings on the output? Next, how do we command awk to create a summary report? Also, how do we sort the data being output by awk? This étude provides the instructions to accomplish each of these objectives.

TOPICS COVERED IN THIS ÉTUDE:

- Overview of an awk script file
- Pointers on creating a data file

- Passing search topics and data file names into an awk script
- BEGIN pattern to apply headings
- END pattern for summaries
- Sorting output

OVERVIEW OF AN AWK SCRIPT FILE

A couple of ways exist to use script files with the awk command. You can write all the awk instructions into a separate file. Then you type the command awk on the command line, follow it with the -f option, follow that with the name of the file with the awk instructions, and follow that with the name of the data file to be used. This can be a lot to remember if you use the data file only occasionally.

Another method is to create a shell script file and embed the awk commands in it. A shell script is run by simply typing its name on the command line with the names of files and search patterns you want the awk command to use. There are no options to remember. The awk command itself, along with its command options (such as -f), patterns, and actions, is programmed into the shell script file when you write it. Passing parameters into a shell script was described in Études 23 and 24.

THREE PARTS OF AN AWK SCRIPT

An awk script can consist of three parts:

1. BEGIN pattern {action}
   The action following a BEGIN pattern is executed only once, *before* the instructions to be applied to each line in the database are executed. Examples would be the initialization of variables or creating column headings for data that is to be output.
2. database instructions
   This is the set of pattern and action commands that will be applied to every line in the database.
3. END pattern {action}
   These are the instructions that are executed only once, *after* the instructions to be applied to each line in the database are executed. Instructions in the END pattern portion are often used to create a summary report. Column headings for the summary report could be contained in this part, too.

All three parts are not required. A file could have only the BEGIN pattern followed by a single instruction to print the entire data file under those headings. Or, it could contain some database instructions followed by only the END pattern. Last, it could contain only the database instructions and no BEGIN or END pattern.

Remember, an awk command consists of a pattern and an action. Awk recognizes BEGIN and END as special patterns and does not try to match BEGIN or END in the data file. Instead, awk marks it as a set of instructions to be executed before or after the instructions applied to the data file.

SAMPLE DATABASE

This étude uses a different database file from the one used in Étude 21. It is a database file focused on magazine article listings.

The contents of the data file are shown below. The file name for the database file will be **computer_mags**.

```
LinMag  Jul  2000  desktop   56  DesktopPlayer
LinMag  Jul  2000  netware   34  Yes!ItWorksWithNetWare
LinMag  Jul  2000  desktop   72  GettingArtsy&CraftyWithGUI
LinMag  Jul  2000  linux     24  TourLinuxFileSystemPart2
LinMag  Jul  2000  shells    76  AllAboutGroups
LinMag  Jul  2000  hardwre   82  USBDeviceDrivers
LinMag  Jul  2000  hardwre   96  SearchingWebForDeviceDrivers
LinMag  Jul  2000  perl      88  CapturingCGIErrorsAsE-mail
LinMag  Jul  2000  vision    30  LinuxToDesktopStrategy
LinMag  Oct  2000  sec       34  LinuxSystemSecurity
LinMag  Oct  2000  vision    42  FriendlyBigBlue
LinMag  Oct  2000  linux     60  LinuxClusters
LinMag  Oct  2000  pkgs      24  InstallingPackagesPart3
LinMag  Oct  2000  desktop   68  Compiling&InstallingKDE2.0
LinMag  Oct  2000  sec       74  KeepingTrackOfWhatGoesOnPart2
```

TIPS ON DATABASES

The keys to creating a useful database are planning and stating precisely what sorts of output you will want, how you will group your information, and how you will search those categories.

In my database of magazine articles, I include about eight different computer-related magazines. My output needs to state the name of the magazine, publication date, page number, and article title. I can search either by a topic (usually) or for a keyword in the title–such as cdrom or drivers.

What will make or break the success of a database is your choice of topic categories. Categories should start with nouns. Add an adjective at the end if you need to subdivide. You're more likely to remember you have a topic named servers rather than linux_servers. You don't want to be too general, but you don't want to over-fragment. Thumb through several issues of your magazines and consider the topic categories. Make a list and refer to it often as you enter your magazine articles. Be prepared to modify your topic categories as you plan the database. You might even want to create a help menu as part of your script that lists the topics. Such a help menu is demonstrated in the script written in Étude 23.

My "titles" often are a combination of the title and important article content items. Editors often use catchy or humorous titles that don't accurately reveal content.

By default, awk uses either a blank column space or a tab as the default field delimiter. In Étude 21, the semicolon was used as the field delimiter so that blank spaces could be included in data entries. I personally find using a semicolon cumbersome. Instead, I run together the words in titles, starting each word with a capital letter. It works well.

I've created similar databases for use with my woodworking and astronomy magazines. This has given me a powerful data-access tool.

In this exercise, you can enter the data file given above or you can spend some time and create a database file for your unique collection. The following instructions pertain to the data file shown above.

CREATING A DATA FILE

We will create a file named **computer_mags**. This will be the data file.

1. OPEN a terminal emulator.
2. TYPE **kedit computer_mags** Enter
3. In KEdit, TYPE **#!/bin/tcsh** Enter
4. PRESS Enter again.
5. TYPE **# Purpose: Magazine data file** Enter
6. TYPE **# Created by (type your name here)** Enter
7. TYPE **# Date: (enter today's date here)** Enter
8. PRESS Enter
9. TYPE the contents of the data file, as shown on page 279.
10. SAVE the file.
11. CLOSE the editor.

TESTING THE DATA FILE

Before writing the script file, test the data file you just created, since the script file will use this data file too.

1. On the command line, TYPE **awk '/desktop/ {print $1"\t"$2"\t"$3"\t"$5"\t"$6}' computer_mags** Enter
   The output looks like
   LinMag Jul 2000 56 DesktopPlayer
   LinMag Jul 2000 72 GettingArtsy&CraftyWithGUI
   LinMag Oct 2000 68 Compiling&InstallingKDE2.0
   The "\t" inserted tabs between the items.

CREATING THE SCRIPT FILE

The purpose of this script file is to search for the magazine articles in the user-specified category. The script will be given the file name of **findtopic**. Our goal is to create a script where the user types **findtopic** ***topic data-file-name*** on the command line and the computer returns the information.

Note: This script is created one small step at a time. This will simplify troubleshooting if you have problems and will help you see the critical parts that get the job done. We first write a script without any parameters passed in—inflexible but with a solid foundation. Then, we modify the script so we can pass in instructions to awk.

We are assuming that you have already created a bin folder to hold your scripts, as shown in Étude 23.

1. In the terminal emulator, TYPE **kedit bin/findtopic** Enter
2. In the editor, TYPE **#!/bin/tcsh** Enter
3. PRESS Enter
4. TYPE **# Purpose: A script to display all magazine** Enter
5. **# listings for a particular topic** Enter
6. TYPE **# Topics are:** Enter
7. TYPE the following:
   # linux,desktop,util,pkgs,vision,shells,sec(urity),perl Enter
8. TYPE **# clang,python,win2000,netware,hardwre** Enter
9. PRESS Enter
10. TYPE **# Created by (type your name here)** Enter
11. TYPE **# Date: (enter today's date here)** Enter
12. PRESS Enter
13. TYPE **clear** Enter
14. TYPE **echo ""** Enter

15. TYPE **awk '$4 ~ /desktop/ {print $1"\t"$2"\t"$3"\t"$5"\t"$6}' computer_mags** [Enter]
16. TYPE **echo** "" [Enter]
17. SAVE the file.
18. CLOSE the editor.
    Now we will change permissions on the file.
19. In the terminal emulator, TYPE **chmod 754 bin/findtopic** [Enter]
20. At the command prompt, TYPE **findtopic** [Enter]
    Your output should look like the following:

LinMag	**Jul**	**2000**	**56**	**DesktopPlayer**
LinMag	**Jul**	**2000**	**72**	**GettingArtsy&CraftyWithGUI**
LinMag	**Oct**	**2000**	**68**	**Compiling&InstallingKDE2.0**

YOUR SCRIPT DIDN'T RUN?

It is possible you made a typing error either on the command line or among the commands in your script file. If you did, the shell will offer you some slightly cryptic hints about where the error occurred.

If you are using Red Hat, there is a high probability you will get the error message:

bash: findtopic: command not found

Red Hat, and others, attempt to start the user with a secure environment, opting for tight security when they have to make a choice.

If you got that error message, on the command line, type **./findtopic** (run it all together, no spaces). The findtopic script will probably be executed.

If it was executed, the reason it did not execute before was because the PATH environment variable did not have an instruction to search your working directory for executable files. The PATH environment variable contains the list of directories to search for executable files.

It is somewhat traditional in Linux to *not* put the working, or current, directory on the path. For example, if you created a script that you named cat, when you tried to use the actual cat command, it wouldn't execute. Instead, your cat script would execute—or give you an error message about too many arguments. Worse yet, one of the most common commands to issue in a directory is **ls** to list the files and directories. If you named a script ls, the script, not the command would execute. Not too likely you think. The security problem is what if someone hacked into your system and left an ls script that erased all your files? It would be executed the first time you typed ls in that directory, no trace would be left, and you'd be left believing you did something to destroy your files.

The solution will help you organize your scripts and data files.

Most executable programs are kept in a directory named bin. We'll make use of a personal bin subdirectory and put that in the path. These steps are not necessary if you completed Étude 23. We are going to keep all data files, especially those used by scripts, in a local subdirectory named data.

Refer to Étude 23 and the section titled "Making the Script Executable" for instructions on installing the line in step 3, below, into your bash resource file and making it permanently available to all shells and shell sessions.

1. If you do not already have a bin directory, in the terminal emulator, TYPE **mkdir ~/bin** Enter
2. TYPE **mkdir ~/data** Enter
3. If you did not already add bin to your path in Étude 23, TYPE **PATH=$PATH:~/bin** Enter
4. TYPE **mv findtopic ~/findtopic** Enter
5. TYPE **mv computer_mags ~/data** Enter
6. TYPE **kedit bin/findtopic** Enter
7. CHANGE the line that reads

awk '$4 ~ /desktop/ {print $1"\t"$2"\t"$3"\t"$5"\t"$6}' computer_mags

to the following:

awk '$4 ~ /desktop/ {print $1"\t"$2"\t"$3"\t"$5"\t"$6}' ~/data/computer_mags

(You add **~/data/** to the line.)

8. SAVE the file.
9. CLOSE the editor.
10. On the command line, TYPE **findtopic** Enter
    The command executes.

PASSING THE DATA FILE NAME INTO THE SCRIPT

Next, we pass in the file name of the data file to be searched, from the command line. We make use of the argv array. The argv array keeps the command and arguments typed on the command line and stores them for use by the shell—shell scripts in particular. This technique was covered in Étude 23.

1. In the terminal emulator, TYPE **kedit bin/findtopic** Enter
   Your file looks like the following:
   #!/bin/tcsh

   # Purpose: A script to display all magazine

```
# listings for a particular topic
# Topics are:
# linux,desktop,util,pkgs,vision,shells,sec(urity),perl
# clang,python,win2000,netware,hardwre

# Created by (your name)
# Date: (creation date)

clear
echo ""
awk '$4 ~ /desktop/ {print $1"\t"$2"\t"$3"\t"$5"\t"$6}'
~/data/computer_mags
echo ""
```

2. CHANGE the line that reads
   awk '$4 ~ /desktop/ {print $1"\t"$2"\t"$3"\t"$5"\t"$6}' ~/data/computer_mags
   so that ~/data/computer_mags is replaced by $1, as follows:
   awk '$4 ~ /desktop/ {print $1"\t"$2"\t"$3"\t"$5"\t"$6}' $1
   Note: The only change is to replace the reference to the file computer_mags with $1. The $1 at the end of this line represents the first argument on the command line.
3. SAVE the file.
4. CLOSE the editor.
5. On the command line, TYPE the following:
   findtopic data/computer_mags Enter
   Your output should look like the following. If so, you've successfully passed the file name into the script from the command line.

```
LinMag  Jul  2000  56  DesktopPlayer
LinMag  Jul  2000  72  GettingArtsy&CraftyWithGUI
LinMag  Oct  2000  68  Compiling&InstallingKDE2.0
```

PASSING THE TOPIC INTO THE SCRIPT

Now we take the last step.

1. In the terminal emulator, TYPE **kedit bin/findtopic** Enter
2. CHANGE the following line in the script from
   awk '$4 ~ /desktop/ {print $1"\t"$2"\t"$3"\t"$5"\t"$6}' $1
   to
   awk '$4 ~ /'$1'/ {print $1"\t"$2"\t"$3"\t"$5"\t"$6}' $2

Passing the Topic into the Script

Although it may appear as though the $1 is enclosed by apostrophes, that is not how the apostrophes are really working. The **$4 ~ /** is enclosed by apostrophes. The **/ {print $1"\t"$2"\t"$3"\t"$5"\t"$6}** is enclosed by apostrophes. Because these phrases are enclosed by apostrophes, the shell, which is executing the command, does not do anything with the $4, and so on. The special meaning of the $ is suspended by the apostrophes.

However, when the shell encounters the $1 and $2 that are not enclosed by apostrophes, it replaces them with the first and second arguments from the command line, which were stored in element 1 and element 2 of the argv array.

3. After you have made this change, SAVE the file.
4. CLOSE the editor.
   Now the command will be the script name of findtopic. Notice that the $1 represents the topic we want to search for. The $2 represents the name of the file that is to be searched. Therefore, when we use our new script, we'll have to write the command as
   findtopic *topic file-name*
   Desktop is one of our topics, and computer_mags is the name of the data file.
5. TYPE **findtopic desktop data/computer_mags** Enter
   The output should look like

   LinMag Jul 2000 56 DesktopPlayer
   LinMag Jul 2000 72 GettingArtsy&CraftyWithGUI
   LinMag Oct 2000 68 Compiling&InstallingKDE2.0

   This is the same output you obtained before. You can use this to search any of the topics. Let's try another example.
6. TYPE **findtopic hardwre data/computer_mags** Enter (note the spelling of "hardwre"—the letter "a" is omitted).
   The output looks like

   LinMag Jul 2000 82 USBDeviceDrivers
   LinMag Jul 2000 96 SearchingWebForDeviceDrivers

THE BEGIN PATTERN—ADDING COLUMN HEADINGS

Sometimes it can be useful to have headings over each column of output to remind the user what is being displayed. For example, we can modify our current file so the output looks like the following (assuming we've asked to match all of the entries under the desktop topic).

MAG	MON	YEAR	PG	TITLE
====================================				
LinMag	Jul	2000	56	DesktopPlayer
LinMag	Jul	2000	72	GettingArtsy&CraftyWithGUI
LinMag	Oct	2000	68	Compiling&InstallingKDE2.0

To add the column headings, we need to use a BEGIN pattern.

A BEGIN pattern performs one or more tasks, only once, before the rest of the data file is processed. It doesn't try to match a pattern. It simply carries out the startup action.

We're going to take two steps toward incorporating the BEGIN pattern into our script.

A BEGIN pattern is stored in a separate file and added to the list of files the awk command is to process. On the command line, the awk command is told to look for its instructions in a file by using the -f command option. For example,

awk -f cmaghead computer_mags

At this point, we need to create a header file that contains the BEGIN pattern—the file that will contain our column headings.

1. In the terminal emulator, TYPE **kedit bin/cmaghead** [Enter]
2. In KEdit, TYPE **#!/bin/tcsh** [Enter]
3. PRESS [Enter]
4. TYPE the following:
   # Purpose: Create a heading for output from a [Enter]
   # findtopic script [Enter]
5. TYPE **# Created by (type your name here)** [Enter]
6. TYPE **# Date: (type today's date here)** [Enter]
7. PRESS [Enter]
8. TYPE **BEGIN {** [Enter]
   In the following line, put one tab space between the column headings.
9. TYPE the following:
   print"MAG MON YEAR TOPIC PG TITLE" [Enter]
   print"=================================="} [Enter]
   {print}
   This final print causes every line in the data file to be displayed.
10. SAVE the file.
11. CLOSE the editor.

CHANGING PERMISSIONS TO MAKE THE FILE EXECUTABLE

1. In the terminal emulator, TYPE the following:
   chmod 754 bin/cmaghead Enter
   Now it's time to use this file with column headings.
2. On the command line, TYPE the following:
   awk -f bin/cmaghead data/computer_mags Enter
   All of your magazine information is displayed on the screen.
3. CLICK on the scroll bar on the right side of the window.
4. SCROLL up until you see the headings.
   You'll see that the column headings from the BEGIN pattern are lined up over the data columns.

A DETOUR

What we need now is column headings for the output of the findtopic script. We can't use **awk -f bin/cmaghead findtopic *topic file-name*** because the -f option forces awk to consider everything on the command line as a file to be processed—including the topic we want to pass into the findtopic script.

The solution:

1. Inside a shell script, use findtopic as an awk instruction for acting on each line of the data file. Then we can pass in the topic and file name to that awk instruction.
2. Redirect the output (save the output) from that awk instruction to a file named temptopic.
3. Create a file containing the BEGIN pattern.
4. Inside the same shell script, execute a second awk command with the -f option that calls the file with the BEGIN pattern and uses temptopic as its data file.

First, modify cmaghead so that it has column headings for the findtopic script.

1. TYPE **kedit bin/cmaghead** Enter
   We just have to change the column heading line.
2. CHANGE
   print"MAG MON YEAR TOPIC PG TITLE"
   to
   print"MAG MON YEAR PG TITLE"
3. SAVE the file.
4. CLOSE the editor.
   Now we'll open the findtopic script file.

5. TYPE **kedit bin/findtopic** Enter
6. CHANGE your file so that it has two awk commands, as shown below. The italicized lines are the changed lines.

```
#!/bin/tcsh

# Purpose: A script to display all magazine
# listings for a particular topic
# Topics are:
# linux,desktop,util,pkgs,vision,shells,sec(urity),perl
# clang,python,win2000,netware,hardwre

# Created by (your name)
# Date: (creation date)

clear
echo ""
# The next line receives the topic and the file name from the command
# line and then redirects (sends) the output to the file named temp
awk '$4 ~ /'$1'/ {print $1"\t"$2"\t"$3"\t"$5"\t"$6}' $2 > temp
# The next line invokes awk again, but this time reads its instructions
# from cmaghead, which contains the column headings
awk -f bin/cmaghead temp
echo ""
```

7. SAVE the file.
8. CLOSE the editor.
9. At the command line, TYPE the following:
   findtopic desktop data/computer_mags Enter
   The output looks like

```
MAG      MON   YEAR  PG   TITLE
===========================
LinMag   Jul   2000  56   DesktopPlayer
LinMag   Jul   2000  72   GettingArtsy&CraftyWithGUI
LinMag   Oct   2000  68   Compiling&InstallingKDE2.0
```

THE END PATTERN

Like the BEGIN pattern, the END pattern is executed only once—after awk has processed every line in the data file. This is where summary reports can be generated from data that was matched or found while awk was examining each line of the data file.

In this exercise, a simple summary would be to state how many records were found. Awk has a built-in variable that holds the number of the record that is being processed. When awk finishes processing each record in the data file, this variable holds the number of the last record in the file—which is also the number of records in the file.

The name of this variable is NR. We can use NR in the cmaghead file in an END section to state how many records were found that matched the topic we requested.

1. TYPE **kedit bin/cmaghead** [Enter]
   The file should look like the following:

```
#!/bin/tcsh
# Purpose: Create a heading for output from a
# findtopic script
# Created by (your name)
# Date: (creation date)

BEGIN {
print"MAG   MON   YEAR   PG   TITLE"
print"========================================"}
{print}
```

2. After **{print}**, TYPE the following line:
   END {print "Number of entries found was " NR}
   Notice that the END pattern has the same form as the BEGIN pattern: uppercase "END" followed by an action enclosed in curly braces.
3. SAVE the file.
4. CLOSE the editor.
5. On the command line, TYPE the following:
   findtopic desktop data/computer_mags [Enter]
   The output looks as follows.

```
MAG     MON   YEAR   PG   TITLE
==============================
LinMag  Jul   2000   56   DesktopPlayer
LinMag  Jul   2000   72   GettingArtsy&CraftyWithGUI
LinMag  Oct   2000   68   Compiling&InstallingKDE2.0
Number of entries found was 3
```

SORTING

The sort utility is a useful program to use with awk to sort the output data generated by the awk command. Sort has the form of

sort ***-options +number-of-columns-to-skip-before-sort-column data-file-name***

The two most common options are

- -r to reverse the sense of the sort. By default, the sort is in ascending order (smallest to largest).
- -n to instruct sort that it is sorting numbers, not text.

The page numbers are in column four of the output. To have the sort command sort by page number, you must instruct the command to skip the first three columns, counting from the left. It will begin sorting on the next column.

The entire sort command to sort by article page number is

sort +3

We will use the -n option to let the sort command know that we are sorting numbers.

USING SORT IN THE FINDTOPIC SCRIPT FILE

1. In the terminal emulator, TYPE **kedit bin/findtopic** Enter

   The following appears:

```
#!/bin/tcsh

# Purpose: A script to print all magazine
# listings for a particular topic
# Topics are:
# linux,desktop,util,pkgs,vision,shells,sec(urity),perl
# clang,python,win2000,netware,hardwre

# Created by (your name)
# Date: (creation date)

clear
echo ""
# The next line receives a topic and the file name from the command
# line and then redirects (sends) the output to the file named temp
awk '$4 ~ /'$1'/ {print $1"\t"$2"\t"$3"\t"$5"\t"$6}' $2 > temp
# The next line invokes awk again, but this time reads its instructions
# from cmaghead, which contains the column headings
awk -f bin/cmaghead temp
echo ""
```

2. CHANGE the line from

Sorting

```
awk '$4 ~ /'$1'/ {print $1"\t"$2"\t"$3"\t"$5"\t"$6}' $2 > temp
        to
awk '$4 ~ /'$1'/ {print $1"\t"$2"\t"$3"\t"$5"\t"$6}' $2 | sort -n +3 > temp
```

3. SAVE the file.
4. CLOSE the editor.
5. On the command line, TYPE the following:
   findtopic desktop data/computer_mags Enter
   The output is sorted by page number. Why would you want to do this? Each month, many magazines place certain types of articles near certain page numbers. For example, maybe tutorials for beginners always start around page 24 in *Linux Magazine.*

   You might want to go back into findtopic and remove the sort command. Otherwise, findtopic will always sort based on the page number.

GOING FURTHER

If you want to delve further into script writing, a possible next step would be to learn to write a switch structure or an if-else structure. You could create a script that allowed a user to type in the name of the column they want to sort on, and the computer to then translate the instructions to the numeric value the sort command must use to skip columns.

SUMMARY

As you've mastered this script writing related to awk, you've gained a very powerful desktop productivity skill. In this étude, you've learned how to write an awk instruction file and run awk using that file. You've also learned how to add a BEGIN and END pattern to awk instructions so that column headings and a summary report can be generated. You have also learned how to simplify the commands that must be written on the command line for an awk program by writing a shell script file that contains an awk script. Last, you learned some basics of using the sort command with the output of an awk action.

REFERENCES

Dougherty, Dale, and Arnold Robbins. *sed & awk.* 2d ed. Sebastopol, CA: O'Reilly & Associates, 1997.

Robbins, Arnold. "The Awk Scripting Language." In *Unix in a Nutshell.* 3d ed. Sebastopol, CA: O'Reilly & Associates, 1999.

Tansley, David. *Linux & Unix: Shell Programming.* New York: Addison Wesley, 2000.

AFTERWORD

After reviewing this book, many of those familiar with Linux office software may be tempted to say, "Yes, but you forgot . . ." But I probably didn't forget it. Writing this book absorbed an unbelievable amount of time. About 30 percent of that time was spent trying out a lot of promising software in the way it would actually be used in an office, recovering from crashes, and trying again. To be included in this book, software had to meet some general standards.

For the "big three" of word-processing, spreadsheet, and database programs, I expected the programs I included to reliably convert files to a file type compatible with a Microsoft file type or a Quicken file type. Emulators were expected to work with any commercial software.

I have enormous respect for the (probably) millions of accumulated hours devoted to developing, debugging, and documenting all of the software in the Linux domain. However, I have run my own small company, and I have serious management responsibilities in my current work. I'm not about to recommend to another person in a business or a home office a piece of software that either will probably crash and cause them to lose their data or doesn't have a file conversion scheme that gives it a portal to the rest of the world. In business today, people commonly attach Microsoft Word and Excel files to emails and expect the people at the other end to be able to read them. (ASCII file conversion on a word-processing file, which deletes all of the formatting and stylizing, is unacceptable in an office that aims to be productive.)

Koffice is a very strong office suite. I especially like the frame concept in the word processor. This allows the word-processing program to be used for desktop publishing or for simple word processing. The controls for desktop publishing are out of sight if only the word processing is being done. But the word-processing program crashed three times in five minutes when I tried to create a typical document. Neither the word-processing program nor the spreadsheet program convert to a Microsoft file format. The chart program did not import from the spreadsheet. Keep in mind that Koffice is offered as a work in progress, and it is a significant work. It's my guess that it will be at the level of commercial viability within 18 to 36 months. At that point, the world will have a world-class network operating system and a world-class office suite that is distributed, completely installed, with it.

AbiWord is at version 0.7. It is a good word-processing program from the Gnome project. But it isn't at such a level of quality that I'd recommend it to a colleague in an office situation.

Dia is a diagram editor in the Gnome project that has a lot of the functionality of the drawing program in Microsoft Word. It has no documentation, but after an hour or so, I'd figured out most of the features. It's worth working with if you need to create flow charts or electrical schematics, but too often you find yourself backed into a corner with the only way to make a change is to cut and discard an object.

Xinvest is a stock investment program with a lot of strong capabilities but a very minimalist graphical user interface. Pcb is a PC-board layout program. Most business users wouldn't be interested in using it. Likewise, qcad is a computer-aided design program.

In closing, a lot of software was reviewed. The only criteria were that the software was something that would be reliable in an office environment and that it met conversion requirements in situations where those were important. Software has moved radically toward being business-ready in the past year. A year from now, a similar amount of change will have occurred. Two years from now, Linux's future in the office should be secure.

OFFICE PRODUCTIVITY SOFTWARE

APPENDIX A

STAROFFICE

This book has focused on using a wide range of Linux utility programs to increase office and personal productivity. Linux has a free office suite, StarOffice 5.2, that works every bit as well as Microsoft Office. StarOffice is the most widely used office suite in Europe. It was purchased for several million dollars by Sun Microsystems and then basically released to the Linux community.

Is StarOffice business-ready? Absolutely. The entire first draft of this book was written using StarOffice 5.1. Then the files were saved in the Microsoft Office 97 file format, opened in Office 2000 to have their formatting reviewed, and transmitted to the publisher.

For a person setting up a home office or small office, StarOffice 5.2 is the first office productivity suite to install and try. It includes programs for word-processing, creating spreadsheets, charting from spreadsheets, creating presentations, working with databases, editing math formulas, drawing, organizing, scheduling, emailing, and taking part in online discussions.

WORDPERFECT 8 FOR LINUX, PERSONAL EDITION

This is the same world-class WordPerfect you may know from PCs. It runs native on Linux (in other words, it does not run through the WINE emulator as does other office software for Linux from Corel). The Personal Edition can be downloaded free from the Corel Web site.

A word of caution: When you are doing the installation, you will be asked for an installation directory. There is no indication what the program uses for a default. If you are installing as a normal user, use ~/corel. This will place it in a local directory named corel that is off your home directory. In your .bashrc file, go to the bottom and type PATH=$PATH:~/corel. Then, to start the program, you can type xwp on the command line, and your corel directory will be searched for the executable file. You can also install an icon on your panel or desktop so you can just click to run the word processor.

WordPerfect 8 for Linux also does file conversions to Word 97, which can be imported into MS Word 97 and later.

ANYWARE DESKTOP

An evaluation version of this comes on the application software CD included in the Red Hat 7.1 Deluxe Workstation distribution. Anyware Desktop used to be ApplixWare5.0. ApplixWare had very good desktop publishing capability and excellent file conversion to and from Microsoft file types.

DB2

DB2 Magazine, an IBM Corporation publication, ran an extensive article, "Linux: A Contender for the Enterprise Market" (Winter 2000, pages 22–29), that demonstrates that downloading and installing DB2 from IBM and using Red Hat and IBM online documentation is very doable. DB2 offers mainframe-level database capability.

Koffice and AbiWord are discussed in the Afterword.

EMULATORS FOR MICROSOFT SOFTWARE

Another solution is to install Linux, install a VMware emulator, and then run your Microsoft Software using that emulator. This is reliable and can be a good solution, but you give up about one-third of your processing speed—which usually isn't a problem with current processor speeds. A single VMware workstation edition costs about $99. VMware works and is outstandingly reliable. It allows you to emulate Linux and Windows configurations without having multiple machines. In schools and industrial training divisions, it becomes a matter of doing simple software switching between operating systems rather than physically changing operating systems for different classes. MS-DOS and Windows 3.1 software that continues to be productive can also be run using VMware. The version that offers this level of functionality is more expensive. The National Security Agency of the U.S. government recently contracted with VMware to create virtual machines on desktop computers that could securely store classified documents.

WINE is another emulator. But it has failed to run enough of older but still useful programs that I am reluctant to suggest it as an office solution.

CHANGING FILE PERMISSIONS

APPENDIX B

INTRODUCTION

The chmod command is used to change the type of permissions associated with files and directories. The permissions are read, write, and execute. These are abbreviated as r, w, and x. The permission x applied to a directory means the directory is accessible.

When an editor creates a file, it assigns read and write permissions to the file. An editor makes a file executable even if you store executable instructions in the file, such as in a script file. Once chmod is used to change the permissions, those permissions remain in effect until chmod is used again to change the permissions. Retrieving a file into an editor and then resaving it does not change the file permissions.

Two methods exist for changing permissions. One involves using r, w, and x. The other involves using octal-based numbers. The octal-based method is used worldwide and is frequently seen in Linux literature. It is simple to learn and is memorable.

CHMOD SYNTAX

The format for the chmod command is:

chmod *permissions file-name*

The file name is the name of the file the change in permissions is to be applied to.

COMPUTING PERMISSIONS

The chmod command affects permissions for three groups of users: the owner, the workgroup, and everyone else (often referred to as the "world"). If you type **ls -l** on the command line, file permissions are displayed on the left-most side of the display. For a file, you often see

rwxrw-r--

The first three refer to the user, the next three (the rw-) refer to the group, and the last three (r--) refer to the permissions for the rest of the world.

Each is assigned a number:

r = 4

w = 2

x = 1

The numbers within each of the three groups are summed. This yields three sums. These sums represent the permissions for each group.

For example, let's say we want to assign read, write, and execute permission to the user; read and execute permission to the group; and read-only permission to the world. We begin by writing this as:

User	Group	World
rwx	rw-	r--

Next we sum individual group values.

rwx corresponds to 4 + 2 + 1 = 7

The user permissions will be represented by the number 7.

rw- corresponds to 4 + 2 + 0 = 6

Any place a permission is excluded, it is assigned an value of zero. The group permissions will be represented by the number 6.

r-- corresponds to 4 + 0 + 0 = 4

The world permissions will be represented by the number 4. The total permissions for the file is represented by 764.

We can now assign these permissions to the file with the following command. Let's assume the file name is SizeFind.

chmod 764 SizeFind

Assume you wanted to assign read, write, and execute permission to the user; read and execute permission to the group; and no permission to the world. What three numbers would be used with the chmod command? The answer is 750.

INDEX